DO YOU KNOW . . .

- When a pain in the middle of your belly is a case of indigestion . . . or a dangerous ulcer?

- Why chest pain that's worse when a person is lying down requires immediate medical attention?

- What serious infection causes dark spots in the fingernails?

- Why a momentary loss of vision in one eye may be the sign of an oncoming stroke?

- Why a parent should seek expert help if their child has five or more moles?

KNOWLEDGE IS POWER.

GET THE ANSWERS YOU NEED IN . . .

YOUR BODY'S RED LIGHT WARNING SIGNALS

OTHER BOOKS BY THE AUTHORS

Your Body's
RED LIGHT
Warning Signals

MEDICAL TIPS
THAT MAY SAVE YOUR LIFE

Neil Shulman, M.D.,
Jack Birge, M.D.,
and Joon Ahn, M.D.

DELTA TRADE PAPERBACKS

YOUR BODY'S RED LIGHT WARNING SIGNALS, REVISED EDITION
A Delta Book

PUBLISHING HISTORY
Dell mass market edition published April 1999
Delta Trade Paperback revised edition / January 2009

Published by Bantam Dell
A Division of Random House, Inc.
New York, New York

Book design by Catherine Leonardo

ISBN: 978-1-60751-588-3

Printed in the United States of America

Dedicated to the memory of Dad,
Dr. Israel "Sonnie" Shulman,
a great friend who taught me how to live and how to die.
A humble man who knew how to
lead the family and the community
with class.

—Neil Shulman

We salute Robin Voss as coeditor and coauthor of this book. Robin is a dedicated friend and colleague who went beyond the call of duty in making this book happen.

A second salute to Sandra Tarpley for the tireless hours she contributed, and her loyalty to the project. Also, a big hug to Zoe Haugo, who helped make the very complicated task of updating this book a pleasant experience.

ACKNOWLEDGMENTS

Part Four, on pediatrics, was written by Joy Lawn, M.D. We appreciate her dedication to the health of children. We also thank Joe Simon, M.D., for his valuable consultation on the updated version.

Christine Zika, our editor of the first edition, was delightful to work with. She was objective, insightful, and provided invaluable guidance as we worked on that book. We also want to thank our new editor, Beth Rashbaum, and her assistant, Angela Polidoro, for their support and input.

We'd like to thank the hundreds of folks in the health profession and consumers of health care who reviewed this book with a red pen in hand. Thanks, gang!

Peter Abramson, James Adkins, Helmut Albrecht, J. Richard Amerson, Alison O'Neil Andrew, Carol Arnold, Cindy Bachman, Brent Beaird, Justin Bennet, Gregory S. Berns, Christel Biltoft, Allan Bleich, Laurie Boden, Geoffrey Broocker, Charles Brown, Vickie Brown, Larry Bryant, Myrna Bryson, Michael Burke, Joan Burks, James N. Burt, Cassie Cameron, Grant Carlson, Jeff Carney, Dale Carroll, Emily Chang, Larry Chang, Emil Chynn, Steve Clements, Leigh Cole, Marius Commodore, Doyt Conn, Christine Coppinger, Jerard Cranman, Joe Cubells, Farida DaCosta, Sue Daniel, Bill Davis, Prya Dayamani, Harry Delcher, Judith Delgado, Donna Dent, Allen Dollar, John Doran, Carl D'Orsi, Alan Dosik, Arlene Drack, Mike Duffell, Frederik Durden, April Dworetz, Henry Edelhauser, Joyce Essien, Ken Fein, Alan Fixelle, Quinton Foster, Robert Franch, Joe Freschi, Toyomi Fukushima, Tom Gable, Brenda Garza, Bheru Ghandi, Amy Ghiz, Joan Giblin, Hartaj Gill, Tom Gilmore, Mark Gloger, Adam Golden, Russell Gore, Susan Gorman, Troy Gray, Charlene Grim, John Gutheil, Dallas Hall, Yoosun Han, Hunter Hansen, Joe Havlik, Ted Hersh, Jeremy Hess, Joanne Higa, David Holden, Clair Hopkins, Ira Horowitz, Jim Hotz, Lynn Housley, Celene Howard, Wyland Hsiao, Marie Hunter, Bill Hutchinson, Scott Hwang, Scott Isaacs, Shabnam Jain, Debbie Juncos, Maureen Kelley, Elaine Kennedy, Barbara Kenney,

Cathy Kenyon, David Krakow, Alison Lauber, Joanna Lawn, Stephen Lawn, Timothy Lawn, Joyce Lee, Ken Leeper, Erin Lepp, Kylee Lester, David Levine, Richard and Linda Levinson, Robyn Levy, Fred Lewis, Richard Lewis, Jeffrey Linzer, Scott Lopata, Jerre F. Lutz, Marshall Lyon, Cindy Ma, Doug MacKenzie, Suzanne Maddux, Kamal Mansour, Lois Manuel, Luis Marrero, Fray Marshall, Jonathan Masor, Andre Mathews, Douglas Mattox, Natallia Matuzava, Achintya Maulick, Toni Meador, Melissa Meldrum, Greg Melnilcoff, Ken Miller, James Mills, Lori Mills, Stanley Milobsky, Brooks Moore, Mel Moore, Steven C. Morreale, Carla Mosby, Ann Motes, George Murphy, Pat Murrah, Jim Neel, Melissa Neiman, Wilberto Nieves Neira, Jeff Ng, Robert Ord, Fiona O'Reilly, Gonzalo Orejas, Marion Owen, Larry Phillips, Jeffrey Pine, Allan and Susan Platt, Ed Portman, Sue Pressman, Sakib Qureshi, Jim Reed, Stanley Riepe, Linda Robinson, Stephen Rockower, Aaron Rogers, Howard Rowe, Ivor Royston, Grace Rozycki, David B. Rye, Delia Bowman Sattin, Marin Schulman, Ira Schwartz, Richard Seestedt, Kele Sewell, Purna Sharma, Larry Shulman, Stan Shulman, Bob Shuman, Michael Silverman, Dawn Simon, Joe Simon, Reeta Sinha, Cynthia Smith, Bob Sobel, Mia J. Sohn, James Spivey, Sid Stein, Todd Stolp, Henry Storch, Tim Sullivan, Jean R. Sumner, Ty Sumner, Sheela Swaminatha, Joshua Tarkan, Kathryn Taubert, Earle Taylor, Jerry Thomas, Naveen Thomas, Edilson Torres-Gonzalez, Thomas Vandergast, Alvaro Velquez, Glenna Vitch, Jonathan Waltuck, Fadi Wanna, Mark Ward, Ian Weisberg, Barry Werman, Patty Wilson, Neil Winawer, Elliott Winton, Ted Wojno, Eleanor Wood, Jerry Yuan, Maziar Zafari, and Mary Zellinger

and others . . .

Elizabeth Rone, a wonderfully talented artist, made a lot of concepts easier to understand by contributing her artwork.

Many diagrams in this book also come from the book *Let's Play Doctor* (ISBN 0-15-503620-3), available from Rx Humor, 2272 Vistamont Drive, Decatur, GA 30033; tel: (404) 321-0126; fax: (404) 633-9198; website: www.neilshulman.com.

Life is a gift.
Practice damage control.

TABLE OF CONTENTS

INTRODUCTION

MEDICAL TIPS THAT CAN SAVE YOUR LIFE:
LIFE-SAVING SYMPTOMOLOGY

People do not always know when it is urgent for them to see a doctor or to get a child, friend, or loved one to the doctor. They don't know whether to go to the emergency room or to make an appointment with their primary care doctor or a specialist. Aches and pains, lumps and bumps—when are they potentially life-threatening? When is it crucial to get to a doctor within the next few days, hours, or even minutes? Is it safe to drive or is an ambulance needed? Whatever your circumstances, whether you are single, pregnant, a parent, or a child, these are important medical facts you need to know. . . . They can save lives.

Doctors are saddened and frustrated when a patient dies because he or she did not get the appropriate medical attention in time. This book is written as a quick reference guide for you to use when you or your loved ones have a new symptom or a visible body change. Its goal is to save lives by getting you to the right doctor before it is too late.

Whether you have blood in your urine, a stiff neck with a headache and fever, unequal pupils, or red specks in your fingernails, you need to know if these are warning signs of a life-threatening condition. We haved highlighted potential warning signs and symptoms to empower you with information about the most serious illnesses for which you may need to be evaluated. An informed person can advocate for him/herself and for loved ones so that the most serious medical ailments can be ruled out or treated expeditiously. The tips in this book are concise (a few paragraphs to a few pages) and easy to read. Scan through the book and get an overview of its content. Keep the book in an easily accessible spot in your home, and get in the habit of checking its pages whenever something unfamiliar happens with your body, or when a friend or relative complains of an ailment. Whenever possible these symptoms are listed in head-to-toe order in the Table of Red Light Warning Signals, so that you can find them easily. For your added convenience, there is also an alphabetical index at the back of the book.

We've also included sections in this book that highlight emergency life-saving measures to protect hospitalized patients from errors or subsequent illnesses, the basics of emergency first aid (Heimlich maneuver, CPR, and use of an AED), important preventive medical screenings at various stages of life, techniques for self-examinations (for breast and testicular cancers), and medical advice relating to thermometers and elevated temperatures.

Owning this book is almost like having a team of medical experts on your shelf. Make use of it; it may one day save your life or the life of a loved one.

HOW TO USE THIS BOOK

The First Tier of Health

Keeping healthy involves preventive maintenance as well as the ability to identify diseases early, when treatment is most effective. Taking care of your body is analogous to taking care of your car. The preventive measures for an automobile include regular oil changes, the maintenance of fluid levels, and tune-ups. The same goes for your body. Getting adequate exercise; eating a low-fat, high-fiber diet; getting immunized; and sticking to a mentally healthy lifestyle can keep your body humming smoothly. Just as you uncover potential problems with your car by checking the oil and the pressure in your tires, you should have your body checked to detect unsafe levels of blood pressure and cholesterol and early signs of cancer (a routine Pap smear and mammogram, sigmoidoscopic exam, and scan). Appendix C, at the back of the book, provides information on many of the routine screenings you can get to ensure that your body is running properly. In addition, Appendix B provides the instructions for performing a basic level of screening on yourself for certain ailments such as breast cancer and testicular cancer.

The Second Tier of Health

The majority of the material in this book addresses the second tier of maintaining your health: identifying your body's red light warning signals. Responsible drivers keep an eye on their car's dashboard lights so that they will be able to address problems immediately. Repairing a leaking radiator or replacing an alternator can prevent the car from dying on the highway. Likewise, your body flashes signals—symptoms and signs—that can warn you of potential problems. If corrected early, you can remain healthy.

When something that you cannot identify goes wrong with your car, the owner's manual is a smart place to turn for information. This book is an easy-to-access, reader-friendly owner's manual that highlights many of the most common warning signals of your body.

In order to assemble the material in this book, we've mixed our own clinical experience—which adds up to more than 170,000 hours of patient care—with the advice of hundreds of health specialists. It is not possible to include a reference to every important symptom and sign, so you should always consult your doctor whenever you have a concern. However, we do hope that this book will help you articulate your problem to your doctor, particularly since the system of health-care delivery imposes so many limitations on your physician's time.

Head to Toe

We have listed, by body part, many of your red light warning signals, starting from your head and going down to your toes.

If you have a suspicious symptom or find an abnormality on your body, simply look it up in our Table of Red Light Warning Signals by its location on your body. If the problem is not location-specific, refer to Part Two of the book, which covers warning signs associated with your entire body, such as fever or seizures. Part Three deals with pregnancy and post-pregnancy. Although Parts One and Two list signs and symptoms that can also apply to children or teens, Part Four addresses specific pediatric red lights. Like the tips in Part One, these pediatric tips are listed head to toe.

Most people keep the owner's manual for their car in the glove box or another special place where they can find it easily and quickly. Do the same with this book: Keep it in an easy-to-find location. Though we hope you will not need it, it might one day save your life—or the life of your child, a friend, or family member.

The one message we'd like to leave you with is: "Be aware!" Constant vigilance about your health can save you from pain and suffering by helping you avoid exposure to external factors that may make you sick or worsen a preexisting illness. For example, it will help you steer clear of dangers such as toxins released into the water by a leaking waste dump, too much or too little exposure to the sun, the consumption of certain foods and/or impure herbs, and overdoses or insufficiencies of vitamins. Another danger you need to be aware of is the possible side effects of medications. Since some medications may cause you to have an allergic reaction, and others interact dangerously when taken together, you need to be aware of the actions, side effects, and interactions of all of the medications you take. Make sure that you get patient package inserts from the drugstore and discuss your prescription (and nonprescription) medications with your doctor and pharmacist.

Awareness can also help you once you make it to the hospital. Once you're admitted, don't let yourself settle into a backseat role: Help prevent errors. Unfortunately, although patients go to the hospital to get better, errors made by the hospital's health team can sometimes result in serious complications or death. Part Five in this book gives specific advice on how to monitor your care when you are in the hospital.

The best way to prevent errors is to become proactive and monitor what is being done to you or to get a friend or relative to monitor your care and advocate for you. Remember: Even though you are already ill, you can still take measures to protect yourself and prevent your condition from worsening.

We've included an additional section that may come in handy. The two ultimate emergency signs are an inability to breathe and the heart stopping. In case you never took a course in CPR (cardiopulmonary resuscitation) or choking first aid (the Heimlich maneuver), consult Appendix A. You may have taken a course but forgotten the details of these life-saving actions. It's a quick read that may save a life. Read the section to a friend. Who knows? They may end up saving your life . . . a life definitely worth saving!

HOW TO USE THE TABLE
OF RED LIGHT WARNING SIGNALS

This book begins with an extensive Table of Red Light Warning Signals, which also serves as a reference guide. Look up your specific symptoms or signs and then simply turn to the indicated page or tip number.

Notation:

- The signs and symptoms listed in this table sometimes occur alone and sometimes in combination with one another. This varies from person to person.
- It is important to take these red light warning signals seriously, because effective treatments are often available.
- The tips often refer you to a doctor; however, there are many other excellent health professionals—including nurse practitioners, physician assistants, midwives, pharmacists, physical therapists, etc.—who may be able to help you.
- The tips may recommend that you seek care at an emergency room. When deciding whether to call an ambulance (911 in most locations in the United States), consider response time as well as your or another person's ability to safely drive to the hospital. Also consider that an ambulance can often provide on-site treatment and is better suited for transporting people who are sick.
- It is impossible for this book to be all-inclusive, so you should always seek advice from a doctor if you have a concern about a sign or symptom. The human body's reaction to disease varies and there are always exceptions to the usual presentation of an illness.

TABLE OF RED LIGHT WARNING SIGNALS

Head Injury

Psychological Problems

Face—General

EYES
Eyeballs

TABLE OF RED LIGHT WARNING SIGNALS

Eyelids

Vision Abnormalities

Blurred Vision

Nose

Nosebleeds

Mouth

ARMS AND HANDS
Armpits

Arms

Pain

Numbness, Incoordination, Tingling, and Burning Pains

Muscle Weakness, Cramping, and Paralysis

Shortness of Breath

Cough (ing)

Chest Pain or Chest Discomfort

Irregular Heartbeats and Heart Sounds

Rapid Heart Rate

Irregular Heart Rate

Lower Belly Pain

GENITALIA
Male

Female

Groin

BOWEL MOVEMENT
Pain

Form and Frequency

Color

URINE

Appearance

HIPS, BUTTOCKS, LEGS, JOINTS, ANKLES, TOES, AND TOENAILS

Legs

Pain, Tenderness, and Aching

Injury

Numbness, Cramps, Weakness, Paralysis, and Poor Coordination

Discolorations

BACK

Back Pain

PART TWO: General Symptoms and Signs (More Common in Adults): Not Body Part–Specific Conditions

ALLERGIC REACTIONS

ABNORMAL BLOOD PRESSURE, BLOOD TESTS, AND BLEEDING FROM A CUT

SEIZURES

TEMPERATURE CHANGE

WEAKNESS

PART THREE: Pregnancy and Postpregnancy

INTRODUCTION: PREVENTIVE MEASURES TO INCREASE THE CHANCES OF DELIVERING A HEALTHY BABY

Pregnant

PART FOUR: Pediatrics: Body Part–Specific Conditions **(Although more common in adults, Parts One, Two, and Three all list red light warning signals that can occur in children.)**

HEAD
Headache

PSYCHOLOGICAL PROBLEMS

EYES

URINE

BOWEL MOVEMENT

GENITALIA

LEGS

FEET, TOES, AND NAILS

SKIN AND HAIR

WEIGHT LOSS

PART FIVE: Prevention of Errors in the Hospital

HOSPITAL POLICY

SANITIZATION

MISTAKEN IDENTITY AND COMMUNICATION ERRORS

MEDICATION

Appendixes

PART ONE

Body Part–Specific Health Problems

(More Common in Adults)

Listed from Head to Toe

PART ONE

HEAD

Headache

TIP 1

A sudden, agonizing, "thunderclap" headache, more severe than any you have ever experienced, could mean you are bleeding in the brain. This is an emergency.

Most headaches are caused by factors such as stress, sinus infection, seasonal allergies, dehydration, caffeine withdrawal, eye strain, lack of sleep, low blood sugar, or migraines. These types of headaches are usually self-limited and will often go away with rest and/or over-the-counter medication. But if you ever get a sudden, severe headache that you consider the worst headache of your life or that feels different from any headache you have previously experienced, you may have a hemorrhage in your brain. In many cases this occurs after physical exertion. Again, this is a medical emergency.

A *subarachnoid hemorrhage* is the medical term for bleeding around the brain that pools in the subarachnoid space—the space between the skull and the brain. Your skull, which is like a tight-fitting helmet that protects your brain, does not allow room for the blood that accumulates during this kind of hemorrhage. This results in increased pressure on your brain. If the subarachnoid hemorrhage is significant, the blood will continue to accumulate in the skull, which causes spasms of blood vessels, increased fluid in the brain, and increased pressure within the brain. Because the brain has the consistency of Jell-O, this can result in serious damage.

Though more commonly caused by head trauma, a subarachnoid hemorrhage may also result from an aneurysm in the brain. Aneurysms—weakened areas on the walls of arteries—may be congenital (present at birth) or may appear later in life. Their rupture is sometimes the result of cocaine or amphetamine abuse. The symptoms of a hemorrhage in the brain include severe headache, vomiting, dizziness, seizures, blackouts, sleepiness, slurred speech, double vision, unequal pupil size, and/or mental confusion. Often only the severe headache is present, which may sometimes improve briefly, only to be followed by coma.

If you experience the worst headache of your life, or a "thunderclap" headache (one that has maximal intensity at onset), call 911 or get someone to take you to an emergency room immediately. Do not take any aspirin for pain relief—since aspirin blocks the ability of the platelets to form a clot, you may end up bleeding more. If you call 911 or go to the emergency room, you need to make sure they know you are having "the worst headache of your life." This way they will know that you need to be seen by a doctor right away. In addition, if a friend or family member complains of a new, severe headache and then becomes sleepy or difficult to awaken, it may also be a hemorrhage in the brain and a medical emergency.

Early diagnosis is important because if left untreated, at least one in five people dies from this condition. Medication and/or surgery (which can include stopping the bleeding, preventing the rebleeding, and/or decreasing the pressure within the brain by draining fluid and blood from the skull) increases the chances for survival.

TIP 2

Brain tumors usually cause headaches that get progressively worse. These headaches will sometimes worsen in the middle of the night. Other signs, such as seizures, weakness, or loss of sensation in a part of the body, can also occur.

One of the main characteristics of a brain tumor is growth. Your headaches will worsen as the tumor grows, so if you have been having the same type of headache for more than two years, you probably do *not* have a malignant brain tumor. If your headache seems to be worsening over time, look for other symptoms, such as weakness, visual changes, or loss of sensation in a part of the body. It's important to catch these symptoms quickly: Malignant brain tumors usually enlarge to a deadly size within weeks or months (though this can take as long as two years).

The brain sits in a clear fluid that also surrounds the spinal nerves, which descend from the brain down the back. In a healthy person with a normal sleeping schedule (asleep at night and awake during the day), spinal fluid pressure is usually highest in the brain and spinal canal in the middle of the night. Headaches caused by a brain tumor, which increases this pressure, will usually worsen at that time.

If you experience a headache that becomes progressively worse and/or seizures, or if your headaches are not responding to treatment, you need to get medical evaluation as soon as possible.

TIP 3

> A headache accompanied by a stiff neck and fever is an indicator of a serious infection called meningitis.

Meningitis is an often deadly infection of the lining of the brain, also called the *meninges,* and the spinal cord. While meningitis is not common, it can be contagious. Infants, young children, and the elderly are particularly susceptible.

Meningitis often starts like the flu, with high fever, body aches, an oversensitivity to light, and a headache. The telltale sign of meningitis, however, is a stiff neck. If your neck is stiff or if you find that you have difficulty touching your chin to your chest, particularly if you also have a fever and a headache, seek medical evaluation. Meningitis must be diagnosed early, because it is a rapidly advancing disease. Particularly with bacterial meningitis, death can occur as early as thirty-six to forty-eight hours from the onset of symptoms, so any delay in seeking treatment can result in a fatality.

Be aware that elderly patients and babies may not exhibit a stiff neck. Many elderly patients with meningitis will only have a headache and a fever. They may also seem confused and/or tired. Babies suffering from meningitis will not be able to communicate about their symptoms and may only show nonspecific signs of illness. However, young babies may have a bulge in the soft spot on their skull. (See Tip 232 for advice on how to detect meningitis in babies.)

Meningitis is often treatable with antibiotics. If you are exposed to someone diagnosed with meningitis, seek medical advice about preventive measures.

TIP 4

> If you have the symptoms of nausea (possibly with vomiting), headache, and fatigue, consider that you may have carbon monoxide poisoning, especially if you feel worse indoors and someone you live with is experiencing similar symptoms. Other possible symptoms include bright red gums and lips, cherry red skin, weakness, mental confusion, dilated pupils, and/or chest pain (particularly if you are elderly). It is crucial to evacuate the house or the car and seek medical treatment.

Poisoning from carbon monoxide inhalation is a leading cause of accidental death, despite public awareness of its dangers. It can occur very subtly because the gas is odorless and colorless, and there is no way of knowing that it is present until illness occurs. It does not take a lot of exposure to make you very sick—children will usually be affected first, but carbon monoxide poisoning can kill both adults and children quickly. Note: If you have pets, they will also become sick from excess exposure to the gas.

The best way you can protect yourself against carbon monoxide poisoning is to be aware. Have a heat and air company test the air inside your home for carbon monoxide, and test the heating system for proper exhaust once a year. Do not use kerosene heaters, charcoal grills, or camp stoves without proper ventilation, and make sure not to leave your car running in an enclosed area. If you have any of the symptoms of carbon monoxide poisoning while in your car, get the exhaust system checked and make sure there are no holes in the floorboard. If you have a boat with a motor, have the engine and exhaust system checked regularly. This is important, because dangerous levels of carbon monoxide can accumulate on a boat even when it's docked at a pier, by a stone wall, or alongside another boat. Also, make sure that no one ever swims near the boat while the motor is running. Inexpensive carbon monoxide monitors, which are sold at most hardware or department stores, will sound an alarm when levels of carbon monoxide get too high. Consider installing one on each level of your home or boat.

If you suspect that you are being exposed to high levels of CO, you can have your blood tested by a doctor for the presence of carboxyhemoglobin, which can confirm a diagnosis of carbon monoxide poisoning. Note: This test may be inaccurate if you are a smoker, as levels of carboxyhemoglobin can be altered by exposure to tobacco smoke. Also, the level of carboxyhemoglobin will be lower if you have been away from the carbon monoxide for a lengthy period of time.

If you develop any of the red light warning signals of carbon monoxide poisoning, get out of the enclosed area and into fresh air immediately. Go to an emergency room for evaluation and treatment.

TIP 5

> If you have tenderness over your temples and/or blurred vision when you have a headache, you may have a serious condition called temporal arteritis.

Temporal arteritis is a disease (usually occurring in senior citizens) that irritates and inflames the walls of your temporal arteries, which run along the side of your head. This disease may cause headaches and scalp pain (often noticed when combing one's hair), tenderness around the temples, visual disturbances, and sometimes cramping of the jaw muscles while chewing. If the inflammation of the arteries becomes severe enough, blockage of the arteries (a stroke) may occur. If the artery to one of your eyes is blocked, you may also experience blurry vision or even total vision loss.

A stroke can be prevented if this condition is diagnosed and treated early. A few simple blood tests, including an erythrocyte sedimentation rate (ESR), C-reactive protein (CRP), and complete blood count (CBC), may help your doctor make this diagnosis. To be one hundred percent accurate, he or she may order a one- to two-inch biopsy of the temporal artery. While long-term treatment may be necessary to control the ailment, immediate treatment may prevent complications. The cause of the disease is unknown.

Dizziness

TIP 6

It is possible for dizziness to suddenly become so severe as to render you nonfunctional and cause you to fall or—if you are driving—crash your vehicle. Nausea and vomiting may also occur.

Dizziness may take the form of light-headedness (see Tip 7), or it may make you feel like you are spinning on a carousel (vertigo). The balance system consists of multiple factors: To feel balanced, your inner-ear apparatus and cerebellum (the small area of the brain in the back of the skull responsible for coordination) need to be normally functioning (see Figure 1). A breakdown in any of these systems can make you feel dizzy, particularly when you change your body position. Inner-ear

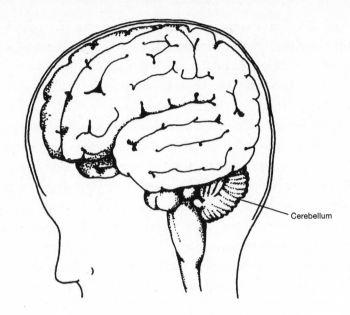

Figure 1. The Brain.

disease can be sporadic, with a sudden and quite severe onset. It may cause vertigo, accompanied by nausea and vomiting. A strained neck may also sometimes cause vertigo.

If you are experiencing vertigo, you are at a higher risk for falls. Falls can lead to serious injuries, such as hip fractures, and if the attack occurs when you are driving, you could have a serious auto accident. Do not drive, and avoid climbing stairs alone until your problem has been stabilized by medical treatment. If you experience vertigo (with or without nausea and vomiting), you need medical evaluation as soon as possible.

TIP 7

Passing out or nearly passing out, with the feeling of light-headedness when you sit up or try to stand, is often the result of a drop in blood pressure (orthostatic hypotension). The potentially life-threatening causes of this condition include internal hemorrhage, serious heart irregularities, and severe dehydration. These symptoms can also occur as side effects of certain medications.

A constant and uninterrupted flow of blood is required by all of your body's organs. The brain is the first organ to fail without nutrition and oxygen from the blood, so even a slight change in blood flow to the brain will produce symptoms such as dizziness or fainting.

When you sit up from lying down or when you stand from a sitting position, your blood vessels and heart automatically adjust by narrowing the vessels below the heart and widening the vessels above the heart that supply the brain, assuring that there will be adequate blood pressure and blood flow to the brain. If there is not enough blood or fluid in your circulation because of bleeding or dehydration, these automatic adjustments will *not* provide adequate blood pressure and blood flow to the brain, and you will feel dizzy or faint.

It is important to know, however, that there are a number of other potential causes for these symptoms—some as serious as heart irregularities, and others as innocuous as eating a large meal or using the bathroom (these latter examples are more common with frail older adults). Another important potential cause is medication—some medications, including water pills (diuretics), certain blood pressure pills, some drugs for psychiatric disorders, and medications for shrinking an enlarged prostate gland, can affect the blood vessels and heart such that they will not adjust properly to provide adequate blood pressure and blood flow to the brain. If you are experiencing this type of dizziness, and are on medication, talk to your doctor and make sure that your symptoms are not a side effect. If they are, your doctor may adjust or change your medication.

Seek immediate medical evaluation when you begin to get

dizzy or faint. If internal hemorrhage, dehydration, or heart irregularities are causing your symptoms, emergency therapy could save your life. If the cause is less serious, and it relates to diet, eating small meals more frequently may help. Regardless, it is important to resolve this situation; dizziness is particularly dangerous in senior citizens, who are more subject to serious injuries when they fall.

TIP 8

> There are unusual presentations of a heart attack, such as a painless heart attack. Awareness can save your life. You may experience any or a combination of the following: a very weak feeling, sudden dizziness, a feeling that your heart is pounding, shortness of breath, and/or a heavy sweat. You may have a feeling of impending doom. Nausea and vomiting often accompany these symptoms.

A heart attack can occur without chest pain, pressure in the chest, or a feeling of indigestion (see Tip 92). A painless heart attack can be just as deadly, but much more difficult to diagnose.

If you experience the above symptoms, you may be having a heart attack, especially if you have other cardiovascular risk factors, including high blood pressure, high cholesterol, diabetes, obesity, a smoking habit, or a family history of early death from a heart attack. Heart attacks without chest discomfort are more often seen among diabetics, women, and senior citizens.

Whether or not you exhibit the classical symptoms of a heart attack, a doctor can usually make the correct diagnosis with an EKG and "dye" (intravenous contrast) studies, examining the small blood vessels that nourish your heart. Blood tests for chemical changes in the heart muscle, special types of X-rays, and scans of the heart are also helpful. Early diagnosis of a heart attack is crucial since it's possible that life-threatening complications can be treated. In certain instances immediate therapy can prevent permanent heart damage.

TIP 9

> Some signs of low blood sugar (hypoglycemia) are weakness, a rapid heartbeat, dizziness, confusion, profuse sweating, "acting weird," blackouts, seizures, and unconsciousness. An extreme drop in blood sugar can occur in diabetics, which can be fatal if left untreated. Drinking fruit juice and putting sugar under the tongue can provide immediate relief for these symptoms, but emergency medical evaluation and treatment may also be necessary.

Hypoglycemia means you have a low blood sugar level, numerically, in the forties or lower. At these levels you will often become weak, jitter, shake, sweat profusely, develop a rapid heart rate, sometimes act "weird" (this behavior is occasionally misdiagnosed as a manic episode of mental illness or as intoxication), become dizzy or faint, and/or have seizures followed by unconsciousness. The symptoms of hypoglycemia usually occur first thing in the morning or anytime when several hours have elapsed since your last meal. If left untreated, it can be fatal.

Keep in mind that diabetes medication can actually drive the blood sugar so low that it causes these problems. Hypoglycemia usually occurs when diabetics take too much insulin or too many oral agents for their diabetes, or when they do not consume adequate amounts of appropriate foods.

Fluctuations in blood sugar levels in diabetics can cause blurred vision due to high amounts of sugar pulling water from the lenses of the eyes. The hypoglycemic symptom of shakiness between meals (called reactive hypoglycemia) is also common in non-diabetics, particularly after consuming sugar-rich meals. Though hypoglycemia is more serious in diabetics, its symptoms can generally be improved in both of these cases by eating small, high protein, low carbohydrate meals more frequently.

A rare cause of very low sugar levels in non-diabetics is a small hormone-producing tumor (insulinoma) in the pancreas, which overproduces insulin. Excess insulin then passes into the bloodstream, causing hypoglycemia. Most of these tumors are noncancerous and a complete cure can often be obtained by removing the tumor.

If you are on beta-blockers, the medications used to treat hypertension and glaucoma, keep in mind that they will occasionally blunt the warning signs that your sugars are getting too low. Some of the common beta-blockers are metoprolol, carvedilol, propranolol, atenolol, and timolol. If you are taking one of these medications, the only symptom of hypoglycemia you may experience is confusion or weakness.

Note: Hypoglycemia is different from hyperglycemia, which refers to high blood sugar as opposed to low blood sugar. However, some of the symptoms are similar. The doctor can distinguish between the two by simply testing the blood for sugar levels. The typical symptoms of hyperglycemia are nausea and vomiting, increased thirst and urination, decreased appetite, and fatigue. It often occurs when a diabetic inappropriately stops their diet, medication, or exercise regimen. Both hypoglycemia and hyperglycemia can ultimately be life-threatening if left untreated.

Head Injury

TIP 10

How do you know how serious a head injury is? One that causes nausea, vomiting, dizziness, drowsiness, mental confusion, or any loss of consciousness requires immediate medical evaluation. Always examine the injured person for paralysis or weakness in any part of the body, unequal pupil dilation, slurred speech, personality changes, convulsions, restlessness, clumsiness, severe headache, neck pain and/or a stiff neck (*do not* move the neck to test the degree of stiffness), and/or any sensory impairment (blurred vision, hearing loss, etc.). These symptoms denote a medical emergency. If any of these symptoms occur within minutes, hours, or days after a head injury, it is a medical emergency.

Before discussing the specific symptoms you should watch out for after you or someone else has experienced a head injury, you need to be aware of the following things that you should *never* do after a head injury:

- *Do not* move the injured person unless it's absolutely necessary.
- *Do not* let the injured person move, get up, or walk around; wait for EMS to arrive.
- *Do not* wash a deep or heavily bleeding head wound.
- *Do not* remove any object that is sticking out of a wound.
- *Do not* shake the person if they seem dazed.
- *Do not* remove a helmet if a head injury is suspected (unless it is necessary because they need CPR).
- *Do not* drink alcoholic beverages or take a sedative or

strong pain medication for at least forty-eight hours after a head injury.

- *Do not* take aspirin after a head injury, as it can increase
the risk of bleeding. Over-the-counter pain medicine
such as acetaminophen (e.g., Tylenol) may be used for a
mild headache if you do not have liver disease or drink
alcohol excessively.

Now, turning to the symptoms—the following categories
of symptoms are all definite warning signs that the injured
person needs *immediate* emergency medical evaluation.

- Any moderate to severe bleeding from the head or face,
swelling at the site of the injury, or facial bruising requires emergency treatment. Call 911 and stop the
bleeding by wrapping gauze or a clean cloth snugly
around the head to cover the wounded area. If blood
soaks through, do not remove the cloth, but place another cloth over the first one. Since there may be a skull
fracture, *do not* apply direct pressure to the bleeding site
unless the bleeding is so severe that the person may die
from blood loss. Direct pressure may damage the brain.
Do not remove any debris from the wound. Apply ice
packs to any swollen areas.
- Someone who develops symptoms such as nausea,
drowsiness, slurred speech, mental confusion, or loss of
consciousness even for a short period of time following
a head injury needs immediate medical evaluation and
close observation. Note: Any loss of consciousness after
a blow to the head indicates a concussion, which is
caused by the abrupt movement of the brain inside the
skull. These symptoms may indicate anything from a
mild injury with the temporary loss of brain function to
a more serious injury with permanent brain damage.
- Someone who experiences prolonged unconsciousness

after a head injury has sustained a more serious injury to the brain, which may include hemorrhage into the brain, blood compressing the brain, swelling of the brain, or spinal cord injury. These are real medical emergencies, and the unconscious person needs special treatment until emergency care arrives. Some tips to prevent further damage to the unconscious person are as follows:

○ Never move the person's head or neck! Keep their head and neck immobilized until medical personnel arrive. If the person has sustained spinal cord damage, moving the head may worsen the damage or may even be fatal.

○ When someone is vomiting, you may need to gently turn his or her whole body to the side to stop the fluid from getting into the lungs. In this situation the head and shoulders must be moved in the same direction at the same time. This is most easily done if you get another person to assist with the head as you roll the body. This maneuver is called a "log roll."

○ Watch the airway of the unconscious person, because he or she may develop airway obstruction and even stop breathing. Open the mouth of the injured person and look for food or fluid that may be blocking the airway. This material should be removed very carefully with your fingers. If the person is still not breathing, administer CPR (see Appendix A on page 350).

• Unequal pupils and weakness in an arm or leg are very important observations, even if the person's mental status has not changed. Since these symptoms may indicate complications of the head injury, they constitute a true emergency.

• Someone who appears to be okay shortly after a head injury may still be in danger. He or she may develop symptoms hours, days, or even months later. When this occurs, failure to obtain emergency treatment can be fatal. Be vigilant and on the alert for the person who becomes nauseated, very drowsy, and/or confused following a head injury, even if it seems that these symptoms are unrelated to the earlier injury.

All of the above red light warning signals may indicate bleeding and/or swelling in the brain or around the brain, requiring emergency medical intervention. A person is at a higher risk for these types of complications (even if the head injury is relatively minor) if he or she is over the age of 65, is on blood thinners such as aspirin, plavix, and coumadin, and/or has liver disease from chronic alcohol consumption—all of which increase the risk of excessive bleeding.

If the injured person is sent home rather than admitted to the hospital, and they go to sleep, ensure that their condition is stable by awakening them every hour for the first six hours after the injury to make certain they have not gone into an unconscious state. Then check them for consciousness every four hours for the next eighteen hours after the injury. Observe them closely for two or three days following the injury.

TIP 11

> If a person becomes loud, abusive, combative, or profane after a head injury, he or she may have a significant brain injury and is in need of emergency medical evaluation.

If you observe someone acting combative or abusive after a head injury, get that person to a doctor as soon as possible, because he or she may have a significant brain injury. A helper who does not realize that this behavior is due to brain injury may think the person is drunk, taking illegal drugs, or just rude. It is very important that combative behavior be recognized as a possible red light warning signal, as it may be the only indicator of brain damage that is getting worse.

(See Tip 16 for other causes of a sudden change in personality.)

Psychological Problems

TIP 12

> Fatigue, anxiety, and panic disorders may all be related to a medical condition known as depression, which is the most common of all psychiatric disorders. In its extreme form, depression can lead to thoughts about hurting oneself, or even suicide. You must know something about this disease in order to combat it. Effective medicine and psychotherapy are available to treat depression and related mood disorders, in combination with stress-relieving activities. There are also cutting-edge medical treatments such as deep brain stimulation surgery that have been very effective in certain situations.

From the medical perspective, the term "depression" does not necessarily mean feeling "down and withdrawn." Its symptoms may include fatigue, loss of appetite, sleeplessness, and/or headaches. You may experience anxiety or a loss of interest in the things you normally enjoy. If you are elderly, your number-one symptom of depression might be a feeling that you are losing your memory. These feelings do not mean that you are crazy or a weak person. They may merely indicate that you have a chemical imbalance in your brain, or other biological factors such as a genetic predisposition for depression. They could also be related to environmental factors (poverty, stressful upbringing, etc.) or behavior patterns such as drug use or excessive drinking of alcoholic beverages.

Certain areas of your brain have automatic centers that function without conscious thought to control the activities in your body, including your heart rate, changes in the size of your pupils or blood vessels, breathing, and sleeping. Normally when you experience an emotional event, these automatic centers create a specific spectrum of symptoms. For example, if someone frightens you, you may feel tightness in your throat, your muscles may become tense, and your heart rate may speed up. Other emotional challenges, like stress, may trigger one of your automatic brain centers such that you hyperventilate (rapid, deep breathing), have trouble sleeping, or experience headaches and an irritable stomach, all of which your brain will interpret as severe anxiety. These may sometimes be severe enough to be called "panic attacks."

If you have a chemical imbalance in one of the automatic centers in your brain, you may experience a variety of these symptoms without any emotional experiences to trigger them. For example, you may feel fatigued, as though you have been exhausted all day, even though you got enough sleep the night before. You may also feel anxious, with all of the organs of your body reflecting this anxiety, even though nothing has happened to make you anxious. Or you may feel depressed and withdrawn, without there being any reason for your anxiety. Note: A chemical imbalance can also result in bipolar disorder, wherein manic behavior cycles with depressed behavior.

Many effective medications can help restore the chemical balance in your brain, alleviating these symptoms. Unfortunately many people who are suffering from chemical imbalances do not seek medical treatment.

If you or a loved one have any of the symptoms of depression and have difficulty controlling them, make sure to seek help as soon as possible, because, in its most extreme form, this condition could turn suicidal. As such, it's important to watch out for the risk factors for suicide, which are listed below.

RISK FACTORS FOR SUICIDE:
- Being male (although more girls attempt suicide, more boys actually succeed)
- Chronic illness
- Family history of suicide
- Rural residence
- White or Native American ethnicity
- Advanced age
- Alcohol or drug abuse
- A gun in the house (firearms are the most common instruments of suicide in the United States)
- A previous suicide attempt
- A traumatic experience: a death, a divorce, a failed exam, rejection by friends, etc.

If you are having suicidal thoughts, there are several national phone numbers you can call to speak to someone immediately, including 1-800-273-TALK and 1-800-SUICIDE.

TIP 13

You have survived a heart attack and you have every reason to be happy. Your cardiac rehab is progressing well, but you don't feel like you want to do anything. Being around other people is a burden so you avoid them. What's going on? Call your doctor and find out. You may be depressed. Depression is more common in heart attack victims and reportedly poses an additional health threat beyond its psychological ill-effects. Depression may contribute to the development of many potentially life-threatening medical conditions such as heart disease, stroke, and diabetes.

It has been clearly established from multiple scientific studies that patients' outcomes following a heart attack can be adversely affected by depression (see Tip 12 for the symptoms of depression). There are changes in the body's chemistry when depression occurs that can affect the automatic control mechanisms of the body's vital organs. No one has determined how these changes reduce survival rates or increase the likelihood of heart attack complications, but there is overwhelming evidence that they do. Depressed heart attack patients are more likely to have a subsequent, fatal heart attack.

It is important for you to remember that there is no way to diagnose depression unless you discuss the condition with your doctor. Remember also that there are effective treatments for depression that may improve your odds of recovery.

Patients often think they feel down because they have just had a heart attack. They do not realize that the depression itself could possibly increase their risk of dying from another heart attack. So when you're feeling down after having a heart attack, talk it over with your doctor. It might save your life.

TIP 14

> Delirium, which is severe confusion and disorien-
> tation, means that something is wrong and is af-
> fecting the brain, which could be very serious.

Delirium is usually manifested by an altered state of consciousness consisting of confusion, distractibility, disorienta-
tion, and disordered thinking and memory. It often develops
over short periods of time (within hours or days), as opposed
to Alzheimer's dementia, which may take several years to be
recognized. It will generally fluctuate from hour to hour. The
person may merely seem detached from their surroundings or
they may begin to tremble and become agitated, or even have
hallucinations and a complete loss of contact with reality.

Many ailments can affect the brain, thereby causing delirium. They include:

- Infections (most commonly pneumonia, urinary tract
  infections, or infections of the brain)
- Side effects of medication
- Abnormal chemical levels in the blood
- Low oxygen levels
- Low blood pressure
- Poisoning
- Blockage of blood vessels going to the brain
- Swelling of the brain from high blood pressure

When in a state of delirium, a person usually cannot reason, and therefore getting him or her to medical care may be
difficult. He or she may be uncooperative and even combative.
But this situation is urgent and requires immediate medical attention. Call for emergency assistance.

TIP 15

Dementia, or the loss of memory and the ability to recognize things in senior citizens, is not always due to Alzheimer's disease or stroke. There is a curable cause of dementia that is often associated with an unusual way of walking and with urinary incontinence.

As they age, senior citizens may eventually develop abnormal personality changes, lose their recent memories, and/or become demented. There is a cause of these mental changes, called normal pressure hydrocephalus, which can sometimes be cured. Typically, a person with this disorder has difficulty walking. Their leg muscles work fine, but their brain does not remember how to use them—the result being that the person has lost the ability to purposefully initiate specific movements. In other words, they may not be able to coordinate well enough to walk. When they do walk, the pattern will seem quite erratic and awkward, and they will frequently fall. This condition is often accompanied by an inability to control the bladder.

The brain sits in a clear liquid that flows into the inner chambers of the brain. If something blocks the natural flow of this liquid, too much fluid may accumulate in these chambers. The pressure from the excess fluid damages areas of the brain, causing the symptoms described above. Possible causes for this excess fluid are a head injury, brain hemorrhage, or meningitis (an infection in the sac that surrounds the brain). It can also occur without any known cause. It usually appears in senior citizens, but can occasionally occur in younger people.

A diagnosis of normal pressure hydrocephalus can be made with special studies of the brain, including a CT scan or an MRI. If the liquid-filled chambers of the brain are enlarged, normal pressure hydrocephalus may be present. Spinal taps are also used when making a diagnosis. Fluid is drained to decrease brain pressure, followed by a reexamination to look for an improvement of symptoms. The condition can sometimes be reversed with surgery, wherein one end of a small tube is inserted in an inner chamber of the brain, and is then sewn in place down the neck through the body to the belly cavity, where the excess fluid can flow.

Family members of demented senior citizens should discuss with a brain specialist (neurologist) the possibility of a diagnosis of normal pressure hydrocephalus and the pros and cons of medical testing for it.

This discussion should also include evaluation of other potentially reversible causes of senility, including decreased thyroid function (hypothyroidism), increased parathyroid function (hyperparathyroidism), vitamin B_{12} deficiency, the side effects of medication, alcohol damage, or the effects of a blood clot on the brain (subdural hematoma).

Note: While many different conditions can cause a gradual onset of senility, any sudden change in memory, perception, or behavior in an elderly person could be a medical emergency such as a stroke, and requires prompt medical attention.

TIP 16

A sudden change in personality may not be the result of a primary psychiatric disorder but may occur as a result of chemical changes in the blood or as a side effect of certain medications. Personality changes can also be caused by tumors, a brain injury (which may be unwitnessed), a stroke, a seizure, decreased oxygen, or bleeding in the brain.

A sudden change in personality—including anxiety, apathy, confusion, bizarre or paranoid thoughts, excessive energy (mania), and irritability—may be one of the body's red light warning signals of a treatable chemical or physical abnormality in the body, including the brain. It is important to seek medical evaluation in order to treat the underlying illness. In many cases, medical treatment can reverse the personality disorder.

(See Tip 11 about combativeness after a head injury.)

EYES

Eyelids

TIP 17

> If one of your eyelids droops, you're seeing double, and/or your pupils are unequal in size, you may have a ballooning blood vessel (aneurysm) in your brain that could burst. Other causes could include nerve damage or possibly a brain tumor.

An eyelid that does not move normally, pupils that are unequal in size, and/or seeing double may indicate that the nerves controlling these functions are not transmitting impulses normally (see Figure 2). Any abnormality in the brain or surrounding structures that puts pressure on these nerves can cause the above symptoms. For example, a blood vessel that is ballooning out (aneurysm) at a specific location could press on these nerves. If this is the case, you need emergency medical evaluation—brain surgery may be required to prevent the blood vessel from bursting.

If one eyelid droops and the pupil of the same eye is smaller than the other, it may be evidence of a condition called Horner's syndrome, which means that a very specific nerve is being damaged. These symptoms are a major cause for concern if they are accompanied by a lack of sweating or

Figure 2. Eyes with Uneven Pupils.

flushing on that same side of your face. Alternatively, your symptoms could also be caused by a tumor or a defective artery in the neck that causes damage to a specific nerve that affects only one side of the face.

In any of these situations, you need to seek immediate medical evaluation.

TIP 18

> If your eyelids droop part of the time and you have double vision, or your jaw gets tired while chewing, you may have a serious neurological problem called myasthenia gravis.

Do people ask, "Why don't you open your eyes all the way? You look like you're sleepy"? Does your jaw get so tired at times when you are eating that you can't take another bite? If you have droopy eyelids, a weary jaw, difficulty swallowing, and/or general weakness, especially as the day progresses, you may have a potentially serious nerve disorder called myasthenia gravis.

With myasthenia gravis there is a blockage of the chemical that is needed for sending messages through your nerves to certain muscles in your body, and only a weakened nerve signal gets through. Weakened muscles make it hard to chew and cause your eyelids to droop. Other muscles, including breathing muscles, may also become weak. The weakness usually worsens with prolonged use of the muscle groups in question, and is often referred to as "fatigable weakness." If this ailment is left untreated, it could be fatal since you could stop breathing. Effective medications can control myasthenia gravis, so if you experience these red light warning signals, see your doctor as soon as possible.

Vision Abnormalities

TIP 19

When your line of vision becomes narrowed or you experience any defect in your field of vision, it may be an important symptom of a pituitary gland tumor, a brain tumor, a stroke, an injury to the retina of the eye, or advanced glaucoma.

When you look straight ahead, you can usually see objects on your right and left sides. These are your peripheral fields of vision. The loss of a portion of this peripheral vision will reduce your vision to that of a horse wearing blinders. A person with these symptoms will sometimes find themselves bumping into walls or furniture. This is a red light warning signal.

A simple test to detect one type of defect is to put your right hand over your right eye and your left hand behind your left ear. While looking straight ahead, move your left hand slowly so that it is reaching out in front of your face. You should be able to detect this movement out of the corner of your left eye even though you are looking straight ahead. Do the same while looking through your right eye. If either eye fails to pick up your normal peripheral vision, you may have a visual field defect.

Possible causes of defects include a stroke due to blockage of a blood vessel in the brain, an injury to the retina of the eye, glaucoma, bleeding in the brain, or a tumor in the area of the brain responsible for vision. A tumor of the pituitary gland, located on the underside of the brain, can also cause these symptoms. If the tumor gets large enough, it can press on the nerves from the eyes, causing the visual field loss. This type of tumor can also produce high levels of hormones, which may cause a milky white discharge from the nipples and may stop or alter menstrual periods. The growth can be controlled medically or surgically.

If you experience a sudden defect in your field of vision, you should go to an emergency room. In all cases, you need evaluation by an ophthalmologist (eye doctor) and/or neurologist.

TIP 20

If a haze, blur, cloud, or darkness appears over the field of vision in one of your eyes—even if it lasts for only a few seconds—it can be a sign that you are about to have a stroke. This symptom is often described as "a curtain being pulled down over one eye."

If you experience a blur, haze, mist, fog, or darkness over the field of vision in one of your eyes—usually lasting anywhere from a few seconds to a few minutes—it could indicate a partial blockage in one of the blood vessels leading from your heart into your neck or some of those supplying your brain. When this happens, it means that the blood vessel supplying the nerve to your eye or the part of your brain responsible for vision is not getting enough blood. Emergency treatment to prevent a stroke is necessary; a blood thinner may be given and/or surgery may be instituted to clean out the blocked artery.

You need to be taken to an emergency room immediately. Emergency treatment may prevent a stroke.

Eye Pain

TIP 21

> If you experience moderate to severe pain in one eye when you move both eyes, it could be an infection or tumor in the orbit of that eye (the eye socket).

It is important to make a diagnosis immediately. If it's an infection, it can instantly spread to your brain if not treated right away. This can occur in either adults or children, and vision can be lost quickly and permanently. Go to an emergency room immediately for evaluation and treatment. Ideally have someone drive you there.

TIP 22

> If you notice that normally straight appearing lines instead look wavy or distorted (for example, when looking at doorways, windows, or furniture), you may have a problem with the retina of your eye that could lead to severe vision loss. Don't ignore it!

You might not notice this problem unless you check each eye separately. Your eyes work together to give you your best vision, so if one eye has a problem, the other eye may compensate for it, hiding this important warning signal.

Cover one eye and look directly at something with straight

edges, like a desk or window. Then switch—cover the other eye and look at the same object. You can also do this by looking at a page of letters in a book. Look for straight lines that appear wavy, distorted, and/or broken. Look for a spot in the center of your vision that is fuzzy or darkened.

These may be warning signs of macular degeneration, a common problem in people over age fifty. Macular degeneration causes a loss of central vision. It does not immediately lead to complete blindness but can prevent you from driving, reading, recognizing faces, and performing daily tasks.

If you notice any of these changes, get a dilated eye examination from an ophthalmologist (eye doctor) as soon as you can. The doctor may be able to treat this problem and prevent further vision loss. Early treatment is necessary.

TIP 23

The sudden onset of seeing many spots before your eyes can be an urgent warning that you should seek medical evaluation.

Seeing spots can be caused by a variety of medical problems. Some spots are normal, like seeing blood vessels when you are staring up at a blue sky or seeing spots for just a second when you stand up quickly. Some are essentially meaningless, like a floater that drifts across your vision and moves away when you try to focus on it. However, some are important and may precede a serious event such as blindness.

One such condition is an outpouching of the blood vessels of the retina (the back part of the eye where vision is recorded and transmitted to the brain), called retinal microaneurysm. In a more advanced eye disease, for example, one caused by diabetes, new abnormal blood vessels grow and are at risk of rupturing. If these vessels rupture, blood can flow inside the eye, causing the sudden and severe loss of vision.

So, if you notice the onset of many spots in your field of vision, contact an ophthalmologist immediately. Since these symptoms may be associated with diabetes, diabetics should have their eyes checked every year to find and treat any abnormal growths of the blood vessels and prevent the complications that cause these symptoms.

TIP 24

You may notice little spots or strings floating across your vision. If there is a change in the number or appearance of the floaters or if flashes appear, you should call your eye doctor immediately. They may be the warning signs of a retinal detachment tear, or hemorrhage.

Most of us experience floaters from time to time and some people have more than others. They are caused when the clear jelly inside the eyeball shrinks with age. This jelly, called the vitreous, can tug on the retina of the eye, releasing a few cells or strings of cells. These are the spots and threads we see when we look at a white wall or a blue sky. The tugging can also cause little electrical currents to flash.

But if you see a change in floaters or any flashes of light, it might be a sign of retinal detachment, which could cause sudden, permanent vision loss or blindness. If you see your eye doctor (an ophthalmologist) immediately, you may be able to save your vision. Don't delay. If you can't reach an eye doctor, go to the emergency room.

EAR, NOSE, MOUTH, THROAT, AND NECK

Ear

TIP 25

> Unexplained gradual or sudden hearing loss in one ear, with a sense that the room is spinning around, and/or ringing in the ear may be an indication of a tumor of the nerve responsible for hearing or another problem near this nerve.

Hearing loss due to aging is a common, gradual process, which is often hardly noticed until someone else points it out. Another common source of hearing loss—noise exposure—is also gradual and occurs in both ears. Other people experience hearing loss because of their genetic inheritance.

But what about the loss of hearing in one ear that is accompanied by a feeling that the room is spinning around, and/or a ringing in the ear? A rare but serious illness that can cause these symptoms is a tumor of the hearing nerve (or near this nerve). Urgent medical evaluation is needed.

Another more common cause of hearing loss and this type of dizziness is an inflammation of the hearing apparatus in the ear. Early diagnosis and treatment may prevent permanent damage. Another cause of these symptoms may be Ménière's

disease. Even though the cause of these symptoms is sometimes not found, there may still be effective treatments, so it is
important to see a doctor for a thorough evaluation.

TIP 26

> Hearing the sound of your heartbeat inside your
> head, usually in association with episodic head-
> aches, could mean that you have a blood vessel
> malformation capable of causing a stroke.

It is common to hear your heartbeat in your ear when you lie
down and place your ear against a pillow. But if you notice the
onset of pulsating noise similar to a beating heart on one side
of your head, and if it is constantly present no matter how
your body is positioned, it is abnormal. It could indicate a
problem with your ear or a blood vessel abnormality inside
your head or neck (particularly if it is in association with
episodic throbbing headaches on one side of your head).

The rare type of blood vessel abnormality most likely to
produce this heartbeat sound is called a dural arteriovenous
malformation. Under normal circumstances, veins carry
blood to the heart, while arteries carry blood away from it.
This abnormality, often present at birth, is caused by the direct connection of an artery to a vein, which significantly increases blood pressure in the veins. As time passes, these
malformations may get larger and begin producing the heartbeat sound with such intensity that it can be heard in the ear
closest to the malformation.

If you experience these symptoms, seek medical evaluation
by a neurologist or a neurosurgeon. A blood vessel malformation may need to be repaired so it will not rupture and cause a
brain hemorrhage. A tumor is another possible cause of these

symptoms. A rare cause is a partial blockage of an artery in the neck. A more common cause is rapid or turbulent blood flow in the veins around the ear.

Nose

TIP 27

Nosebleeds are usually easily controlled but can be fatal in rare cases.

The majority of nosebleeds originate from just inside the nostril on the wall that separates the nostrils, called the septum. External compression, such as pinching the sides of the nose, just below the bony area, for a full ten to fifteen minutes with the head bent forward and applying an ice pack to the bridge of the nose usually helps stop the bleeding. Do not stop the compression during that time period to see if the bleeding has stopped. If compression does not stop the nosebleed, it may be bleeding from deeper within the nose. Lightly packing the nose with gauze or cotton can usually control this deeper type of bleeding. Allow the material to protrude from the nostrils so you can easily pull it out afterward. Sometimes soaking the cotton with medicines like Afrin or Neo-Synephrine can help, but you need to check the patient package insert to make sure that there are no contraindications for you to use them. (For example, if you have high blood pressure, it is best not to use these medications unless this is the only option to stop a severe nosebleed.) These steps will control the majority of nosebleeds. To avoid a recurrence, try not to blow your nose for at least six hours after treatment.

If you still have a nosebleed after you have tried all of these methods, seek medical attention immediately. Some bleeding sites, deep in the catacombs of the nasal passage, are particularly difficult to access and control. When injured, the major blood vessels located there are more susceptible to severe bleeding. Typically the blood will stream to the back of your throat, requiring constant swallowing. This problem poses a challenge even to an ear, nose, and throat specialist.

Nosebleeds are more severe in people with high blood pressure. Most result from a crack or ulcer on the nasal passage, often from dry air, chronic allergic congestion, or a growth called a polyp. If you have a disease or take a drug that impairs blood clotting, including aspirin, clopidogrel (Plavix), and warfarin (Coumadin), or if you routinely drink too much alcohol, you are at particular risk of severe blood loss from a nosebleed.

TIP 28

Infections of the upper lip or nose can be dangerous and may spread to the inside of the head.

You've heard of the Bermuda Triangle and its dangers, but you may not have heard of the "dangerous triangle." The body has one, and it has perils as well. The apex or tip of the triangle is at the forehead between the eyebrows. The angles of the triangle are at the corners of the mouth.

This triangle differs from other areas of the face and head in one very important way: Blood brought to this area by the arteries will return to the heart through the veins that travel inside the skull rather than the ones that reside outside the skull.

Why is this important? Germs that have gained entrance to the circulation in this location have a direct route to the brain and other structures inside the skull. Infections in the brain can quickly spread to the vital centers responsible for normal life functions, and can therefore be fatal.

An infected bump, boil, or any infection on the upper lip or inside or outside of the nose holds a greater threat of serious complications than many infections elsewhere on the face or head. Signs of infection are tenderness, warmth, swelling, and redness. When they occur, see your doctor as soon as possible. Due to the seriousness of infection in this locale, you should not delay seeking treatment by using home remedies, except for the most mild surface sores. Picking or squeezing the infected area can spread the infection. *Do not* pop pimples in this area.

Mouth

TIP 29

> Fruity-smelling breath may be the indication of a serious blood sugar problem that can happen when diabetes gets out of control, making your blood dangerously acidic.

Diabetes is a condition caused by abnormally high blood sugar. You usually get it when you have low levels of or an immunity to insulin, a hormone that is produced in the pancreas. The earliest signs of diabetes include frequent urination and unquenchable thirst. Diabetics also often lose weight rapidly (within days or weeks).

Insulin drives sugar from the blood into your body's cells so they can get nourishment. In untreated diabetes the body no longer burns sugar as its normal source of energy and instead burns fat. When this happens, acid compounds are produced as by-products, causing the blood to become acidic. Some of this acid is eliminated through the lungs, producing the characteristic fruity-smelling breath. When the acid by-products build up and the blood sugar rises, you may also experience extreme thirst, shortness of breath, and/or abdominal pain. Without treatment, coma and death may follow.

The diabetic rarely detects this strange-smelling breath odor. It is important that he or she is informed when it appears, since emergency medical evaluation is needed. Though most people have not smelled this odor before, it can be readily identified as an unusual smell. Unfortunately, since the acid in the person's blood can make them act like they are intoxicated, the smell may be mistaken for alcohol, causing the person to be misdiagnosed. (See Appendix C, page 383, for information about diabetes screening.)

TIP 30

A metallic taste on the tongue or a garlic odor on the breath may indicate arsenic poisoning.

The early signs of arsenic poisoning are sometimes a garlic odor on the breath and a metallic taste on the tongue. Later symptoms include vomiting and a burning, upset stomach. You may also experience other symptoms, including a burning and tingling in your arms and legs (which results from the damage to your nerves). Note: The early symptoms of arsenic poisoning can also be caused by certain medications like Biaxin, which tend to give you an abnormal taste in your mouth.

Arsenic poisoning has been known to occur in incidents of mail-order poisoning. No doubt you have also heard of food supplements or medications being intentionally laced with arsenic and distributed.

Call your local poison control center or the national poison control number (1-800-222-1222) for additional information and advice on appropriate evaluation and treatment if you suspect that you have been exposed to arsenic.

TIP 31

> A sore inside of the mouth, on the tongue, or in the throat that does not heal may be cancer. White spots in these areas may also be an early sign of cancer.

A sore inside of the mouth, on the tongue, or in the throat that does not heal within three weeks is considered cancer until proven otherwise. Many of these early cancers first appear as red sores in the mouth (called erythroplasia). White spots (called leukoplakia), which can be found in the same locations, are also potentially precancerous. Though leukoplakia are more common, erythroplasia are more likely to become cancerous.

Leukoplakia can result from the abrasive contact of the mouth's lining with the rough edge of a tooth or denture, but are more commonly caused by the use of tobacco or alcohol. These substances are very irritating to surface cells in the mouth, and can lead to the formation of leukoplakia. If this overgrowth continues, it can evolve into cancer, which can then spread to other parts of the body. An ear, nose, and throat specialist or a dental surgeon is the best specialist to evaluate both types of sores. Make an appointment as soon as possible.

Another cause of white spots in the mouth is a yeast infection. Yeast infections in the mouths of babies are common because babies have youthful immune systems. They can also occur in the mouths of adults with an abnormally weak immune system caused by diseases such as HIV infection. Additionally, yeast infections can appear as a side effect from taking antibiotics or steroids. For example, they can occur after the prolonged daily use of inhaled corticosteroid inhalers for asthma, chronic obstructive lung disease, or emphysema

(Asthmacort, Advair, etc.). If they persist, these white spots warrant evaluation.

TIP 32

Any ulcer (sore with superficial loss of tissue) in the mouth that lasts for more than three weeks should be evaluated by your doctor or dentist, an oral surgeon, or an ear, nose, and throat specialist to rule out cancer.

TIP 33

A blue or black spot or a nonpigmented growth in the mouth may be a sign of mucosal melanoma, a rare type of cancer.

At an early stage, mucosal melanoma can appear as a blue or black spot or a nonpigmented growth, usually on the roof of the mouth or on the gums around your front upper teeth. Other more common causes of a blue or black spot include stains from silver fillings.

A dentist or doctor, oral surgeon, or ear, nose, and throat physician can help determine the cause of your gum discoloration.

TIP 34

Chronically infected gums, known as periodontal disease, may cause serious illness or even death. Do not put off seeing your dentist.

Patients generally consider dental care only for cosmetic reasons, thinking it unessential for maintaining good health. It can be expensive, so it is often at the bottom of their priority list. Thousands of people go about their business not realizing that the poor state of their gums is risking the overall health of their body.

It is a fact that everybody's mouth houses bacteria (germs) that enter your bloodstream when your gums are manipulated. The body's natural defenses can often kill these bacteria when they enter the bloodstream. However, the germs occasionally survive and can infect heart valves that have been infected in the past, or can damage artificial heart valves. In addition, the condition of having chronically infected gums (periodontal disease) may contribute to damage to the internal lining of your coronary arteries (small blood vessels supplying nourishment to the heart) such that it leads to a heart attack.

Usually when you visit the dentist for some sort of procedure, you will be asked if you have a history of having an infected heart valve, have an artificial heart valve, etc. If you do, you are at increased risk, and may be given an antibiotic to prevent infecting your heart valve before starting dental treatment. However, recent studies indicate that people with chronically infected gums may continually be at a higher risk of a heart attack.

The important message to the general public is to get regular checkups by the dentist so that gum disease can be properly diagnosed and treated. Routinely brush and floss your teeth. Ask your dentist or dental hygienist to show you how to properly use a toothbrush and dental floss. Make proper dental care a priority.

TIP 35

Any development of persistent swelling or pain anywhere in the mouth or throat can be caused by many different conditions, including cancer, infection, or gland problems. You need to be evaluated by your doctor or dentist, an oral surgeon, or an ear, nose, and throat specialist.

Throat

TIP 36

Epiglottitis can block your airway. If you are gasping with a "seal-like" noise, often associated with a severe sore throat, you need to be seen by a doctor on an emergency basis.

Epiglottitis is an infection of the epiglottis (the flap over the windpipe that stops food from getting into the lungs when you swallow). It causes the epiglottis to swell, blocking the airway. An important warning sign of a potential life-threatening case of epiglottitis is drooling and/or the presence of noisy breathing.

When your condition gets much worse, there are depressed areas at the neck base, just above the breastbone, and in the spaces between the ribs. If these areas are noticeably sucked in when you inhale, it is possible that negative pressure in the chest cavity is being created by a significant blockage of the airway.

If you are experiencing noisy breathing or are struggling to inhale, you may be having difficulty getting air into your lungs.

Call for an ambulance (911 in most locations). You need emergency care. (See Tip 210 for information on epiglottitis in babies and children.)

TIP 37

> Persistent hoarseness for more than three weeks may be caused by cancer of the vocal cords or another serious illness. Seek medical evaluation by an ear, nose, and throat specialist as soon as possible.

Your voice is generated by the vibrations of your vocal cords, which are located in the area of the throat called the larynx (a structure in the upper part of the breathing tube). Changes in the vocal cords can cause hoarseness. Think of a vocal cord as a guitar string—the thicker the string, the lower the pitch. As the cord swells, the pitch of your voice will become increasingly lower, until it becomes nothing more than a whisper.

The two most common causes of hoarseness of the vocal cords are irritation from infection and swelling from excessive voice use. These conditions usually go away after a few days. Allergies and acid reflux from the stomach can also contribute to hoarseness. In the case of allergies, this can cause the hoarseness to come and go with the seasons.

Persistent hoarseness (lasting for more than three weeks), however, may be a tip-off to throat cancer, which causes permanent thickening of a vocal cord. This occurs more commonly in smokers and probably in people with chronic acid reflux from the stomach. A cure is possible with early diagnosis and treatment.

Persistent hoarseness can also result from the routine occurrence of fluid entering the lungs when the liquids you drink go up your nose as you swallow. This condition may be indicative of a nerve or muscle disorder, a stroke, or a tumor.

TIP 38

> If food or drink will not go down when you swallow, or swallowing causes you pain, you may have a partial esophagus obstruction that could lead to or be a sign of cancer.

Difficulty swallowing is a common problem. Most of the time it occurs when eating bulky foods like meat or corn bread. You swallow, and it sticks at a narrowed part of the esophagus (the swallowing tube that extends from mouth to stomach) before finally going down. You feel the food getting stuck in a region underneath the breastbone.

Narrowing most often occurs in the lower esophagus and is usually the result of stomach acid refluxing (backing up) into the lower esophagus, irritating it. If this happens over a long period of time, constriction or narrowing of the esophagus occurs too, and more foods get stuck when you swallow. The narrowing may be so gradual that you choose to stop eating difficult-to-swallow foods like steak without even realizing it. Or you may simply lose weight. At its worst, this condition can progress to the point of complete blockage, in which case relieving the obstruction may require emergency treatment.

A major reason to evaluate this problem early—long before complete blockage occurs—is to prevent the development of cancer of the esophagus, which can arise from this type of long-standing irritation. A gastroenterologist, a doctor who specializes in the stomach and colon, can insert a special tube with a small video camera into your mouth and down the esophagus. By obtaining and examining a small piece of the esophagus through biopsy, he or she can determine whether a long-standing irritation or cancer is present.

TIP 39

The symptom of a severe sore throat may lead to a throat infection that can close off your airway and cause you to strangle. Though this is rare, you need to watch out for any signs of infection.

Three major kinds of infection can endanger the airway: a pus pocket around the tonsils (peritonsillar abscess); an infection in the floor of the mouth, which spreads throughout the jaw and around the teeth (Ludwig's angina); and an infection of the epiglottis (the flap over your windpipe that keeps food from entering). You can prevent these infections by seeking treatment for your sore throat before it worsens.

Since sore throats are so common, how do you know when you may be in danger? Make sure your condition improves over a forty-eight-hour period. Never let it go longer before seeking medical attention. You might even want to get help earlier if your sore throat sets in after a dental procedure; your condition is more dangerous in this scenario because it can spread faster.

It is *always* an emergency if you experience hardness or swelling in the floor of your mouth and around the base of your tongue, if you have difficulty opening your mouth, or if you notice saliva drooling from your mouth. Also, more serious throat infections are often much worse if they occur on one side of your throat. When you open your mouth and look in the mirror, if the dangling skin hanging in the back of your throat (the uvula) shifts to one side rather than pointing downward, go to your doctor or the emergency room.

Keep aware of your symptoms, because it is possible for

your sore throat to improve after receiving antibiotics, only to later become worse. Without you knowing it, germs may be digging deeper into the tissues of your throat and setting up an abscess (pus pocket) that bulges into your airway, narrowing it. At this point the pain will usually increase and your fever will become higher, thus indicating that you need further medical treatment.

Note: Occasionally a sore throat that does not respond to treatment after a number of weeks is caused by a tumor located deep within the throat. These tumors can only be seen when the doctor uses a special small mirror or camera to look into your mouth.

TIP 40

If you have a severe sore throat with fever and a fiery red rash all over your body, seek medical evaluation right away. You may have scarlet fever. If this is the case, your tongue may also look like an intensely red strawberry, and your throat may turn red with white splotches.

Scarlet fever is caused by a rare type of the same germ that gives you strep throat. The germ releases a toxic substance into the bloodstream, which causes the red rash (your skin may also peel off as though you have been sunburned). The release of this toxic substance can lead to heart and kidney disease, so antibiotic therapy is needed as soon as possible to avoid life-threatening complications. Note: This disease was much more common before the use of antibiotics.

TIP 41

If you have a sore throat, followed by fever and joint swelling about two weeks later, watch out. You can get rheumatic fever from strep throat that was inadequately treated.

Rheumatic fever is a complication of a strep throat that usually occurs two to three weeks after having strep throat. It can cause the joints in your body to become swollen and painful. Fever and swelling are reactions of the body to the infection caused by the streptococcus germ. Rheumatic fever can also cause the heart muscle to become inflamed, and can thereby permanently damage the heart valves.

While rheumatic fever is most common in children who are between five and fifteen years old, it can also occur in adults. Adequate treatment of the initial sore throat is the secret to preventing rheumatic fever. If your doctor prescribes a course of antibiotics, make sure you take *all* of the medicine.

Other complications of a strep infection are acute glomerulonephritis (inflammation of the kidneys) and scarletina (see scarlet fever, Tip 40), which has the appearance of a red rash.

Neck

TIP 42

A lump found in the thyroid gland, at the front base of the neck (under the "Adam's apple" in men), may be cancerous.

If you detect an enlargement or lump at the front base of your neck, make an appointment with your doctor as soon as possible for testing and treatment. When your thyroid gland is larger than normal, you have a goiter. The three basic kinds of enlargement are:

- A general enlargement of the entire gland, often caused by a disorder of the immune system. It can also be caused by a deficiency of iodine (which is rare).
- A lumpy enlargement of the entire gland, which is usually harmless but may eventually lead to decreased gland function. Cancer is occasionally found in part of the gland.
- A single lump in the gland, which may be cancerous. Thyroid cancer can often be cured with treatment.

Any abnormality in the thyroid gland needs to be evaluated by a physician. (Also see Appendix C, page 371, for information about thyroid screening.)

TIP 43

A lump anywhere in the neck can be a sign of a serious illness.

The most serious neck lumps are often not associated with thyroid disease (in the front base of the neck). These lumps are only found on one side of your neck and are usually indicative of a lymph node that has become enlarged due to an infection. If the lump is located toward the front of your neck, it is probably the result of a throat infection. If it is in the back, it is probably the result of a scalp or ear infection. These enlarged lymph nodes are often less than an inch thick, and have a rubbery, semi-soft feel. They should shrink within fourteen days of treatment of the infection.

Lumps in the neck that are present for longer than fourteen days, are over one inch in size, are firm or hard in texture, and/or are not tender are more suspicious and may signify cancer of the lymph nodes or cancer that has spread from another site.

These are the general guidelines for examining lymph nodes, but there are exceptions. Seek advice from your doctor if any such lump persists.

TIP 44

Gradually increasing pain in the back of the neck or lower back over a period of several days, often accompanied by night sweats and a low-grade fever, may be caused by a serious infection. The pain may extend from the neck into an arm or from the lower back into a leg, followed by sudden weakness in that arm or leg. This requires emergency evaluation. You may have an epidural or intraspinal abscess. Seek medical care immediately.

An epidural or intraspinal abscess is an infection that occurs within the confines of the spinal canal, a space surrounded by the bone of the vertebrae extending from the head to the tailbone. This space contains the spinal cord.

Bacteria can enter the spinal canal via the bloodstream from a site elsewhere in the body, often the gums of the mouth or a skin infection. After gaining entrance to the spinal canal, the bacteria establish an infection in the wall of the canal. The body defenses react by walling off the infection and forming an abscess. The abscess rises like a boil, putting pressure on the spinal cord. First an arm or leg becomes weak, and then additional pressure may lead to a loss of function of the spinal cord and paralysis of all muscles below the level of pressure. An abscess in the neck area can paralyze both arms and legs. If it is in the lower back, it can paralyze both legs. Early treatment is essential to avoid permanent paralysis.

Take no chances. If you develop these symptoms, call 911 or have someone take you to an emergency room immediately.

ARMS AND HANDS

Armpits

TIP 45

> A lump in the armpit may be an enlarged lymph node, indicating a serious illness.

Lumps in the armpit are common. Most are tender sweat glands that have become clogged with deodorants—particularly those containing "drying agents." If these glands get infected, they may form large pus pockets that require drainage. Usually lumps caused by clogged sweat glands can be distinguished from other lumps because you cannot move them separately from the skin with your fingers. When you *can* move the lump separately, it usually indicates that it is deep beneath the skin and is a lymph node.

Enlarged lymph nodes in the armpit are often due to infections in the arm or hand. The most serious potential cause of an enlarged lymph node is cancer that has spread to that node.

Early medical evaluation of the cause of a lump in the armpit is important, especially since it could be a red light warning signal of a treatable cancer, like breast cancer.

Arms

TIP 46

> Paralysis of the arms or legs, weakness (espe-
> cially on one side of the face or body), tingling,
> burning pain, numbness, confusion, dizziness,
> double vision, slurred speech, trouble finding
> words, speaking "gibberish," etc., could be signs
> of a stroke, and you should get to an appropriate
> emergency center immediately. Early treatment
> may prevent permanent damage to the brain or
> even save your life.

A stroke may be caused by a blood clot that has formed in one of the arteries that supplies the brain with oxygen (see Figure 3). It can also be caused by a blood clot that has formed in a vessel somewhere else in the body, including the heart, and has traveled through the blood to a vessel in the brain. The area supplied by the blocked blood vessel will be rapidly damaged. The loss of oxygen affects the brain before any other body organ, and a few minutes of oxygen deprivation can result in the permanent loss of function.

The symptoms of a stroke depend on which particular area of the brain is involved. If a large vessel is blocked, such as the middle cerebral artery, a large area of the brain will be affected, causing paralysis of one side of the body as well as the loss of other functions such as understanding and speaking. If a smaller blood vessel is blocked, paralysis may be limited to one arm or leg.

The right side of the body is controlled by the left side of the brain, and vice versa. The left side of the brain is typically dominant for comprehension and verbalization. If you have a large stroke on the left side of your brain, it may make you

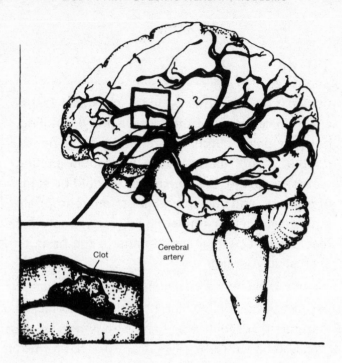

Figure 3. Blood Clot in Brain.

unable to comprehend or to speak (for example, you know what you want to say but are unable to express your thoughts in words) and it will paralyze the right side of your body. If the stroke is on the other side, you will be paralyzed on the left side of your body and it will usually not affect your ability to comprehend or speak.

A stroke can also result from the rupture of a blood vessel in the brain, which subsequently can hemorrhage. Cigarette smoking, uncontrolled high blood pressure, high cholesterol, and uncontrolled diabetes all increase your risk of having a stroke.

A stroke treatment that immediately dissolves blood clots in the brain is available at many emergency centers. If instituted soon enough, this treatment can potentially stop a stroke before permanent brain injury has occurred. At present, the commonly available clot-buster therapy needs to be given within three hours of the onset of symptoms in order for it to work, though newer medications that are being developed may work for longer after symptoms first appear. Also, at some hospitals, a catheter can sometimes be put into a clogged artery to mechanically destroy the clot or to inject medicine near the clot, thus dissolving it. There are reports that the symptoms of a stroke have been reversed six hours from onset with this specific type of treatment. This therapy is not appropriate for all stroke victims. For example, if the stroke is the result of a hemorrhage in the brain, clot-buster therapy or a blood thinner could actually worsen your condition.

Call an ambulance and get immediate transportation to an appropriate emergency room where clot-busting therapy is available. Hospitals will often make known that they are certified stroke centers. All stroke victims need urgent evaluation even if they are not able to get to medical care in the first three hours. Do not wait! Time is of the essence to save your brain.

TIP 47

A short episode of numbness on one side of your face, with slurred speech, weakness in an arm and/or leg, double vision, and/or "vertigo" (an unbalanced feeling), which lasts temporarily (usually minutes to hours), is a TIA (transient ischemic attack) if a certain area of the brain is not getting enough blood. Another symptom you may experience during a TIA is momentary blindness.

A TIA is an important red light warning signal of a stroke. When a loose blood clot in the circulation gets stuck in a narrow blood vessel traveling to the brain, it will restrict blood flow and cause abnormal functioning in the area of the brain that is not getting enough oxygen and nourishment. For example, it could create numbness of the face, slurred speech, or weakness in an arm, hand, and/or leg. If the blood clot dissolves quickly enough on its own, blood flow will return and the symptoms will subside. Note: Rhythm abnormalities of the heart can also cause decreased blood flow to the brain, resulting in these symptoms.

Persons with these red light warning signals require emergency evaluation and therapy because if the next clot is larger or the heart rhythm abnormality lasts too long, the affected brain tissue may be further damaged and a stroke may occur. Also, once a TIA has occurred it is more likely to recur unless treatment is instituted. (See Appendix C, page 392, for information about stroke prevention.) If TIA symptoms develop, do not wait to see if they resolve. Seek immediate emergency care.

Note: You might not be able to tell you are having a TIA (just as epileptics have no recollection of a seizure). It may be that only the person observing you can tell you are having a problem.

Hands

TIP 48

> Shaking hands or hand tremors may be the first signs of a serious illness, including an overactive thyroid (which is simple to treat) or Parkinson's disease (which is harder to treat).

The rhythmic shaking of a hand is often called a hand tremor. Besides hand tremors, you can also have tremors of your head and all of your limbs simultaneously, or tremors that are localized to only your head or one arm or leg. Your tremors may be fine and barely noticeable, or they may be coarse enough to shake the coffee out of a cup. Attempts at coordinated movements such as touching the tip of your nose with your index finger may worsen the tremors (the closer your finger gets to your nose, the worse the tremors get), and they will also be more apparent when you try to sign your name. These latter types of tremors are called intention or kinetic tremors and are most common with cerebellar (back brain) disorders that progress slowly and are not life-threatening. The most common hand tremors are called essential tremors. They are common with aging, have a gradual onset, sometimes run in families, and are not serious. However, there are many serious causes of hand tremors.

Trembling hands may be an early sign of an overactive thyroid. It is important to diagnose this disease as early as possible, as it can injure the heart. The tremor caused by an overactive thyroid is usually very fine and hard to see, but it can be made evident by a simple test: Extend one of your arms with the palm of your hand up, and place a sheet of paper on the hand. If your hand is shaking, it will immediately become evident. Other symptoms of an overactive thyroid include intolerance to heat, sweating, weakness, anxiety, and weight loss.

Another serious cause of tremors is Parkinson's disease, which is also characterized by slowness of action, and increased tone or muscle rigidity. This latter symptom is much more disabling because it impedes movement. The tremor caused by Parkinson's is initially found on one side of the body and then spreads to the other side. This kind of tremor is more pronounced when you are at rest. It is an asymmetric rest tremor. Sometimes it appears as though the individual is rolling a pill between his or her fingers. This tremor is accompanied by an expressionless face, stooping shoulders, and a shuffling walk. Parkinson's disease is a brain disorder in which a natural chemical known as dopamine is not produced in adequate supply by the brain. The average age of onset is about sixty years old. Parkinson's-like disorders are sometimes caused by multiple small strokes or as a side effect of certain medications.

A common cause of tremors in the young is substance abuse. Take note, though, that you do not have to be an alcoholic or crack addict to develop this type of tremor. The affected person could be a busy and stressed young executive, who works long hours without getting enough sleep, drinks too much coffee, drinks three or four scotch and sodas every night to "wind down," and/or heavily smokes. This person may begin to notice that his or her hands shake in the mornings. This symptom could be caused by any of these factors alone—caffeine, alcohol, or lack of sleep—and the combination only makes it worse. The shaking may signal the beginning of substance dependency, and it should encourage the person to develop healthier habits. However, the first sign of tremors may sometimes show up shortly *after* a person stops drinking. These are called withdrawal tremors, and they are not a major cause for concern. They will likely eventually go away, and, had you continued your unhealthy lifestyle, you would undoubtedly have developed far more (and longer lasting) symptoms and health concerns.

Certain prescription drugs can also cause tremors. In fact, strong tranquilizers cause them so often that additional medicines may be prescribed to prevent the tremors. Commonly used medication for certain stomach disorders (Reglan/metoclopramide) can also cause tremors, or even a full-blown

Parkinson's-like disorder. It clears very slowly when the medication is stopped.

It is important to seek medical evaluation early to determine the cause of your tremor, since treatment may prevent serious additional complications from the underlying problem.

TIP 49

> Smokers sometimes develop slow-healing sores on their fingertips, around their fingernails, or on their toes. These sores may indicate that a serious disease is blocking their arteries.

If you smoke and have sores on your fingertips or toes, you need to stop immediately. These sores may occur in one digit only. They will intermittently blanch white, are often painful, and are intolerant to the cold. The disease causing this red light warning signal is thromboangiitis obliterans (Buerger's disease).

This disorder can cause the blood vessels to narrow, impairing circulation and thus damaging the fingers and toes. This damage can be so severe that it leads to gangrene, which may ultimately require amputation of the arm and/or leg. Alternatively, dangerous blood clots could form in these narrowed blood vessels, potentially leading to fatal complications. Another common blood vessel problem caused by smoking is a decrease in blood flow to the sexual organs, which can lead to impotence.

If you notice that you have these symptoms, seek medical advice as soon as possible, and stop smoking.

Fingers

TIP 50

> Enlargement of the fingertips—such that they become wider, the nails become deformed, and they develop a clublike appearance—can be an important sign of a serious disease.

Enlargement of the ends of the fingers in a clublike fashion occurs subtly and without pain, therefore attracting little attention or concern. The important consideration is that they are a common sign of diseases that impair the oxygenation of the blood. It is thought that certain heart diseases, as well as some diseases of the lung, liver, and bowel—including cancer—can also be associated with these deformities. So if club fingertips appear, make an appointment with your doctor as soon as possible to find out why.

Fingernails

TIP 51

> Splinterlike reddish dark spots in the fingernails may be the sign of a serious infection in the heart.

Usually dark spots in the fingernails are due to an injury. But splinter hemorrhages in the nails may be due to fragments of material breaking off from an infected heart valve and then traveling to the tiny vessels in the fingernail beds (underneath the nails). As these tiny vessels become clogged, the damaged walls begin to leak blood into the surrounding tissue, forming the splinterlike reddish dark spots. Since these hemorrhages are not painful, they may go unnoticed. It is important to take note of them though, because the other initial symptoms of an infected heart valve are often subtle, such as slight weakness, weight loss, intermittent high fevers and/or chills, tiredness, or joint pain.

Heart valve infections usually occur in individuals who have a heart valve abnormality. Germs that gain entrance to the bloodstream are able to invade the diseased heart valve, multiply, and build a substance called vegetation. Fragments of this vegetation, which is full of germs, can break off and spread throughout the body via the blood. The speckling on your nails might be the first (and only specific) sign of this condition.

Germs commonly gain entrance into the bloodstream from ordinary dental work and may ultimately infect heart valves that have been damaged in the past. This is why, prior to dental procedures, dentists prescribe antibiotics to patients with a history of infected heart valves (see Tip 34). Antibiotics should also be given to these patients prior to any medical procedure that uses instruments, such as an examination of the colon or bladder. Since the use of unclean needles can cause infection of normal heart valves by introducing a large number of germs into the bloodstream, this condition is also often seen among intravenous drug abusers.

Get immediate evaluation if you have this finding—a heart valve infection (bacterial endocarditis) is a serious medical condition with a high mortality rate. It should be treated on an emergency basis in order to kill the germs before they cause serious damage to the heart.

TIP 52

> Fungus of the nails is often merely unsightly, but certain medications used to treat it have serious side effects, including liver toxicity.

The unsightly fingernails and toenails resulting from deforming fungus infections can deal a blow to one's vanity. They are ugly and keep getting uglier. Several prescription medications are highly effective in curing this type of infection, and they can usually do so within a few months (three months for fingernails and up to six months for toenails). The drawback is the potential side effects. Make sure that you discuss the pros and cons with your doctor before starting these medications.

There are many non-drug-treatment options that have worked well for some people: These include daily soaks for fifteen minutes in a 1:1 vinegar and water solution, or daily applications of Vicks VapoRub. While often more time-consuming and slower acting than prescription pills, these approaches are safer.

BREAST

TIP 53

> Any lump in the breast should be examined by a physician as soon as possible. If breast cancer is found and treated early, you have a greater chance for a cure.

Breast cancer is the most common cancer in women. Many lumps are harmless growths or are tiny balloonlike structures containing fluid, called cysts. But any breast change should be evaluated without delay by a doctor to rule out cancer.

Even though the mammogram (a special X-ray of the breast) is the best screening test to detect breast cancer, you can have a negative mammogram and still have breast cancer. Therefore your doctor should examine you first to try to locate a lump before ordering a mammogram. Alternatively, your doctor may choose to order a diagnostic test called an ultrasound, which uses special sound waves to take a picture of the lump. He or she may also insert a small needle to draw out any fluid or cells from the lump. For most women, examination of a piece of the lump (biopsy) under a microscope is the best way to make a definitive diagnosis of what is causing the abnormal growth.

Risk factors for breast cancer include:
- a previous history of breast cancer
- a family history of breast cancer (if your mother or sisters have had breast cancer, you are at a two to three times greater risk)
- increasing age (85 percent of breast cancers occur after the age of 40 and half of all breast cancers occur in women over 65). Note: Younger women can also get breast cancer.
- exposure to radiation
- not having children
- pregnancy at a late age (usually after 30)
- early menstruation (before the age of 12)
- going through menopause at a later age than normal (usually after 55)
- long-term use of hormone replacement therapy with progesterone as a component
- genetic predisposition (certain mutations of BRCA1 or BRCA2 genes)
- the use of oral contraceptives
- the regular consumption of alcohol

However, it's important to remember that the number 1 risk factor for breast cancer is being a woman. All women need to be conscientious about taking measures for early detection.

The key to beating breast cancer is early detection. Knowing what is normal for you may help you identify a lump, so many physicians feel that monthly breast self-exams are valuable. However, they should not take the place of routine breast exams by a physician and regular mammograms. A mammogram is the best test to pick up early breast cancer in the general population. (See Appendix B, page 364, for how to perform a breast self-exam and Appendix C, page 372, for information on breast cancer screening.)

Contact your doctor immediately if you detect a lump in your breast. Only one percent of all breast cancers occur in men, but any man with a breast lump should also be examined by a physician.

TIP 54

Changes in a breast, including redness and/or swelling, dimpling of the skin, orange-peel appearance of the skin, nipple retraction, or crusty appearance of the nipple may indicate cancer even if you cannot feel a mass. A thorough medical evaluation is necessary as soon as possible.

If you were born with retracted nipples—nipples that do not project outward—you may have more difficulty nursing babies. Otherwise, you should have no problems related to your nipples. However, retraction of a previously normal nipple may be caused by a growth located under the nipple, which could be cancerous.

Deformities of the skin of the breast that cause redness or swelling, dimpling, an orange-peel appearance, and/or a crusty appearance of the nipples indicate a progressive disease in the breast that may be cancer. These changes can be subtle, often occurring without pain. They are red light warning signals calling for immediate medical evaluation.

TIP 55

There are many types of fluids that can drain abnormally from your nipple. The following are the three main types: bloody discharge, white milky fluid, and green fluid. The type of fluid is indicative of the underlying breast problem. Clear fluids

> should also be evaluated by your physician be-
> cause they are occasionally a sign of breast can-
> cer.

Bloody discharge. A bloody discharge from the nipple that is sometimes watery and foul-smelling could be a serious matter. Most often, it originates from a localized growth (intraductal papilloma) in the lining of the tiny tube leading to the nipple of the breast. These tiny growths are so small that they cannot be felt by examining the breast. Although uncommon, intraductal cancer must be considered. A mammogram, biopsy, and/or surgical exploration of the nipple duct may be needed to rule out cancer. See your doctor as soon as possible.

White milky fluid. A milky white substance leaking from one or both of your nipples is called galactorrhea. Gently milk your nipple to see if you can draw out the fluid. Note the color, amount, and consistency. The fluid of galactorrhea has the consistency of water. The amount is usually small and is similar to the fluid secreted during pregnancy.

The pituitary gland, which is attached to the undersurface of the brain, secretes prolactin, the hormone responsible for lactation. Certain benign (noncancerous) tumors of this gland oversecrete the substance, causing the breast to leak this white watery discharge. Other signs that this might be occurring include the absence or alteration of your menstrual periods and problems with your peripheral vision (such as experiencing narrowed vision, like a horse wearing blinders). Tumors of this type are benign, but if untreated they can cause damage to surrounding brain structures, like the nerves to the eye.

Other possible causes for nipple discharge include certain medications, foreplay with the nipples, jogging without proper breast support, or various ailments including hypothyroidism (a low-functioning thyroid gland) or shingles (a painful rash caused by a virus). See your doctor for appropriate evaluation.

Green fluid. A green-colored, watery fluid coming from the nipple of one or both breasts is fairly common and usually benign, although it may persist. It often comes from small fluid-filled pockets in the breast, which are caused by hormones. The fluid is usually first noticed when you discover a stain on your bra. You can make sure it is coming from the nipple by compressing your breast. If a drop of fluid appears on the nipple's surface, dab it with a tissue to note the color. Your breasts may also be tender; this discharge usually occurs around the time of menstruation, which is the time of maximum breast engorgement. See your doctor for evaluation.

TIP 56

Male breast enlargement commonly occurs in adolescents, obese persons, or alcohol drinkers. It can be caused by a hormonal imbalance or certain medications, but on rare occasions may be a sign of cancer in the testicles or lungs or another serious ailment. It may or may not be associated with pain.

If you are an adult male and have noted an enlargement of your breasts, you may have a condition known as gynecomastia, which causes the breast tissue to get solid and lumpy, as opposed to the normal fat tissue near the nipples.

Some breast enlargement may be normal, resulting from the higher levels of the hormone estrogen found in young developing boys or the decreased levels of testosterone found in some elderly men (usually due to shrunken testicles). Since the hormone testosterone counteracts the effects of estrogen, normal adult men have very little breast tissue under their nipples.

The most common cause of abnormal breast enlargement is a side effect of medications, including diuretics, Digoxin, Dilantin, the tuberculosis drug INH, spironolactone, methadone, anticancer drugs, some antihypertensive drugs, Nizoral, Tagamet, theophylline, Zantac, and Flagyl. These drugs can upset the balance of testosterone and estrogen. If possible, you and your doctor may decide to alter your medications. The abuse of anabolic steroids, alcohol, and marijuana has also been reported to cause breast enlargement. Though rare, it can also be caused by Klinefelter's syndrome, a congenital condition that afflicts one in every five hundred men. It can lead to enlarged breast tissue and small testicles.

Less common causes of male breast enlargement include chronic liver disease, kidney disease, breast cancer, hypothyroidism, a pituitary gland tumor, and hormone-secreting tumors in organs such as the lungs and testicles. It is important that you seek medical evaluation to determine if you have any of these underlying ailments so that early treatment can be instituted. Occasionally, no cause is found for the breast enlargement.

CHEST AREA

Breathing Difficulties

TIP 57

Difficulty breathing and a wheezing sound while breathing, often following physical exertion, are signs of an asthma attack. Left untreated, an asthma attack can lead to severe chest muscle fatigue and death.

How do you know when an asthma attack is life-threatening? The most important consideration is how long it lasts. Since asthma makes breathing difficult, it requires much more energy to draw each breath, leading to fatigue. As the attack goes on, you will become increasingly tired, and your condition will thus become more life-threatening. During an attack, as the muscles for breathing become tired, the volume of air exchanged by the lungs will decrease. This decrease may be so subtle that you will hardly notice it. The result will be a drop in the oxygen level, accompanied by a rise in the carbon dioxide level in the blood.

Carbon dioxide is a by-product of body metabolism; it is carried by the bloodstream to the lungs, where it is exhaled out of the body. If the lungs cannot get rid of carbon dioxide, it will build up in your blood. A carbon dioxide buildup in the blood has a sedating effect on the brain, which may cause you to feel even drowsier. You may lose the motivation or energy to breathe.

In other words, if an asthma attack proceeds without proper treatment, you can get worse without realizing it. As your breathing worsens, your ability to think rationally also decreases and your brain will not recognize how ill you are becoming. This may result in you not being able to call for help. When respiratory failure develops, your condition may deteriorate rapidly. Death from respiratory arrest (cessation of breathing) can occur unexpectedly.

Urgent medical attention is necessary for a first-time asthma attack. It is also appropriate when an attack continues, does not improve, or gets worse. Signs that asthma is worsening include the need to use higher doses of inhalants, frequent episodes of shortness of breath (more than two to three times per week), or decreasing peak flow measurements when using a special monitor device (which you can get from your doctor).

If you suffer from asthma, you need to have an emergency medical plan. For example, you need to know where to go for emergency medical care, and you need a contingency plan for how you can keep your emergency medicines available to you at all times (no matter where you are). Note: Adult-onset asthma (especially in obese persons) may be caused by reflux of stomach contents into the esophagus.

TIP 58

> **Wheezing means you potentially have a serious lung problem.**

Wheezing is the noise produced by air as it is forced through narrowed air passages in the lungs when you breathe out. Narrowing of the air passages may suddenly occur due to a squeezing of the muscles (bronchospasm) in the wall of the small airways. This produces asthma, which may be the result of an inflammatory or allergic reaction, an inhaled irritant, or a reaction to medicines, infection, stress, and/or inhaling cold air. (See Tips 169 to 171 on allergies.)

Asthma attacks can be severe and life-threatening. Even if your wheezing is only mild, you could someday have an attack so severe that you would not be able to breathe. Therefore, if you wheeze, you should be evaluated for asthma. The treatment includes sprays and pills that can relax the muscles in the walls of the airways. (See Tips 57, 211, and 212 on asthma.)

Emphysema can also cause wheezing by destroying lung tissue, which results in narrowed air passages in the lungs. In emphysema there are also pockets of dead air space in the lungs, due to the disease's destruction of the lungs' tiny air sacs, called alveoli. This stale air takes up space in the lungs, limiting the amount of fresh air you can breathe in, and ultimately prevents you from getting enough oxygen in your blood. If the disease progresses, it can be fatal (see Tip 66 for more information on emphysema).

Alternatively, tumors in the lung and heart failure are both conditions that can block air passages and cause wheezing.

TIP 59

Deformities of the chest can impair breathing. They may worsen over time, so it's important that they are treated early.

Deformities of the chest are common birth defects that can affect the ability of the lungs to expand adequately. The chest wall is distorted, chest volume is reduced, and the heart may be displaced, encroaching on the lungs. There are three kinds of chest deformities that can interfere with breathing. Pectus excavatum is a sunken breastbone, scoliosis is a curved spine, and kyphoscoliosis is a hunchback condition with a curved spine. Of these, kyphoscoliosis is the common chest deformity that causes the most breathing problems.

If you have one of these conditions, then recurrent vertebral fractures, arthritis of the joints where the ribs connect to the sternum, and obesity would all pose special challenges for you. By further limiting the ability of your chest wall to expand, these factors would cause you to have more serious breathing difficulties. As you get older, the muscles of your thorax may become weaker and impair your ability to breathe. Indeed, with time, even a mild curvature of the spine may get worse and result in significant distortion of the chest. And an additional risk posed by all of these ailments is that they decrease the ability to cough up accumulated secretions and limit oxygen intake, thus increasing your chances for developing pneumonia.

If you have a chest deformity, have your lung function checked periodically by a physician. If you develop congestion, have it checked and treated right away. Note: It is very dangerous to create more problems for your lungs by smoking.

TIP 60

Excessive snoring, short episodes of "no breathing" during sleep, and/or daytime sleepiness may indicate that your oxygen supply is being cut off at night. This can result in serious health problems.

If you suffer from unexplained excessive daytime sleepiness (falling asleep at stoplights or while watching television) and are told that you snore loudly or intermittently stop breathing when you sleep, then you may have a medical condition known as obstructive sleep apnea (OSA). OSA is more often seen in

African Americans and obese adults with short, thick necks, small chins, and floppy airways. During sleep, part of the soft palate (the back of the roof of the mouth), the tonsils, or the base of the tongue is flip-flopping over your airway, causing you to snore and intermittently stop breathing for a few seconds. You may wake up without knowing why. The impact of intermittently cutting off the oxygen supply to the body has serious consequences—high blood pressure and permanent damage to the brain, heart, and lungs.

The diagnosis of OSA can be made by special tests ordered by your physician. Treatment often includes the use of a breathing assist device, called a C-PAP, while sleeping. The C-PAP pushes air through a mask you wear to keep your airway open. In some selected cases surgery or special oral appliances may also be indicated to correct the problem.

There are many simple things you can do to help ease your condition and minimize its negative side effects. Go on a diet if you are overweight. Since alcoholic beverages and sedative medications can worsen your condition, avoid them. Taking medications to treat insomnia when you have obstructive sleep apnea can actually be life-threatening. And, since OSA puts you in danger of falling asleep behind the wheel, don't drive until the problem is corrected.

This condition is an emergency if you stop breathing more than once every two minutes or you stop breathing for more than one minute at a time. The sooner you are evaluated and treated, the less the risk of serious complications.

TIP 61

Shortness of breath may indicate a serious heart or lung disease or a very low blood count (anemia).

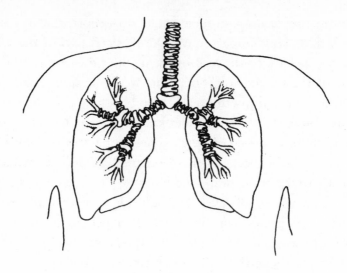

Figure 4. Lungs.

Your lungs are like a tree whose trunk and branches are tubes filled with air (see Figure 4). At the end of each branch are many tiny "balloons." When you inhale, the air travels from the trunk of the tree through the various branches and fills these balloons (the medical term is "alveoli") with oxygen. When you exhale, the balloons deflate, and carbon dioxide passes through the branches, to and then through the trunk and out of your mouth and nose. Very small blood vessels, called capillaries, run near these tiny balloons. At the site where the capillaries and balloons touch one another, the red blood cells flowing through the capillaries load up with oxygen and get rid of carbon dioxide.

The various causes of shortness of breath require completely different therapies. Many causes are either a result of swelling or blockage of the tubes carrying air to and from the lungs, or a result of a problem at the site where the alveoli and blood vessels exchange gases. Shortness of breath can also be the result of weakened breathing muscles or nerves. In many instances the doctor's first step is to give you oxygen through a mask. The second step is to treat the underlying ailment.

Many problems occur at the site of the tubes. Food can get stuck there, requiring the instant emergency measure of abdominal thrusts known as the Heimlich maneuver (see the section on choking in Appendix A, page 343). Alternatively, the tubes can swell from causes such as allergies, dust, and infections. While bronchitis (infection in the tubes) is treated with antibiotics, asthma (swelling of the tubes often caused by allergies) is treated with various medications to decrease the swelling and open the tubes.

If the disease is at the site of the alveoli and blood vessels, other therapies may be necessary. Blood clots in the vessels require a blood thinner, whereas a shortage of red blood cells, which carry the oxygen, may mean that you need a blood transfusion. A weak heart (heart failure) may cause a backup of fluid into the lungs, which requires medication to strengthen the pumping action of the heart or to rid the body of excess fluids (a diuretic). Also, a partial or total blockage of the heart's arteries (angina or a heart attack) can cause shortness of breath on exertion without any accompanying chest pain (see Tips 74 and 76). In this case, certain medications can be used to increase blood flow to the heart muscle, though other interventions may also be necessary to open clogged vessels. Pneumonia causes an accumulation of bacteria or viruses, white blood cells, and other by-products of infection, which clog up the vessels and alveoli. Antibiotics are used to treat bacterial infections. While viral pneumonias often resolve on their own, various supportive therapies such as oxygen or intravenous fluids may be needed. (See Tips 63, 65, 70, 72, and 248 for more on pneumonia.)

If you are merely breathing too rapidly and your tubes, alveoli, and vessels are in good working order, you may be hyperventilating, a condition that is often brought on by some sort of distress. When you hyperventilate, you exhale too much carbon dioxide. This makes you light-headed, and even more distressed, which causes you to feel that you have to breathe even more, thus worsening your condition. Hyperventilating is associated with headache, light-headedness, blurry vision, and muscle spasms, as well as numbness and/or tingling around the mouth and hands. Many things, including frightening situations, mouth breathing, fatigue, and repeated sighs can trigger hyperventilation. Frequent sighing and yawning may be a sign of long-term hyperventilation related to underlying anxiety.

The doctor can determine the cause of your shortness of breath by performing different procedures and tests, including listening to your lungs, checking the oxygen and red blood cell count in your blood, and taking various pictures of your lungs (X-rays, scans, etc.).

Since shortness of breath might be a symptom of a serious heart or lung disease, and the lack of enough oxygen can cause all the parts of your body to fail, immediate medical evaluation is appropriate.

TIP 62

> If you suddenly get short of breath after injuring your leg, you may have a blood clot in your lung. You need to be taken to an emergency room immediately.

A blow to your leg can damage the wall of a vein and cause the blood in that vein to clot. The swelling from the injury can also cause this problem, because it may slow blood flow in the vein such that clots form. Pieces of the clot can flow up the bloodstream to the lung. You are in need of emergency therapy to dissolve the clot or remove it. Immediate treatment can save your life. (See Tips 63, 64, 81, 175, and 249.)

Note: Sometimes the swelling in your leg is not noticeable or it is hidden because your leg is in a cast.

TIP 63

> If you develop a cough and/or shortness of breath after surgery—even a week or two afterward—you may have a blood clot in your lung, or pneumonia. You are particularly at risk if you first noticed swelling and tenderness in the back of your lower leg or in your groin, where a clot could have originated before traveling in the veins to your lung.

During and after surgery, especially if your surgery was in the belly or pelvic area or on the bones and joints, you are at a high risk of developing blood clots in the veins of your pelvis and legs because the blood flow will slow down in these areas. If a fragment of the clot breaks off and flows up the bloodstream to the lungs, you may experience sudden shortness of breath, chest pain on taking a deep breath, and a cough. (See Tips 64, 81, 175, and 249.)

It is important to notify your doctor immediately if you notice swelling and tenderness in your groin or leg at any time, including after surgery, even a week or two after you have gone home. Also, keep in mind that after surgery you are more susceptible to developing infections, such as pneumonia. (See Tip 248.) Pneumonia can also cause shortness of breath, coughing, and a fever. In both cases you need emergency evaluation and therapy.

TIP 64

> Sudden shortness of breath, especially if accompanied by chest pain and a cough with bloody phlegm, may mean you have a blood clot in your lung. Tumors and certain pneumonias can also cause these symptoms. You need emergency evaluation and treatment.

A blood clot in the lung occurs when a clot in a vein, often in one of the legs, breaks apart and a piece of it travels through the blood vessels into the lung. The clot may also originate in the right chamber of the heart. If the clot is small, a small area of the lung will be damaged. However, you should be aware that if you have had one blood clot, you are at a higher risk of getting another. The next one may be large; it could damage a more expansive area or even be fatal. The formation of a clot may take as much time as several days or as little time as a few hours. When the break-off occurs, however, it takes only seconds for the piece to travel to your lung.

Anyone who has had surgery, prolonged bed rest, or has been sitting for a long period of time (such as while traveling by car or airplane) is more prone to getting a blood clot in a leg, often with tenderness and swelling in the back of the lower leg. Clots often also develop in the veins inside the pelvic area, with tenderness and swelling in the groin. This problem may not be noticeable until after the hospitalized patient is home. Shortness of breath could be the first sign that something is wrong.

An injury to the leg can also be the cause of clotting in a leg vein, such that a clot from the injury site may travel to the lung. Please note: It is more usual for injuries to the leg to cause blood to flow out of the injured blood vessels into the tissue and then form large bruises or pockets of blood called hematomas. These pose little threat, since blood that clots outside of the blood vessels goes nowhere.

Certain diseases can cause blood to clot more readily. Birth control pills and/or smoking may also increase blood clotting and, if possible, should be avoided if you have a prior history of blood clots. Women on oral contraceptives who smoke are especially at risk of developing blood clots in their lungs. Pregnancy also increases your chances of developing a blood clot. Whatever the cause, blood clots are life-threatening and require emergency therapy. (Also see Tips 175 and 249.)

Tumors in the lung and certain pneumonias (including those caused by bacteria and tuberculosis) are some of the other ailments that can cause shortness of breath, chest pain, and a bloody cough. If you develop any of these red light warning signals, get to an emergency room immediately.

TIP 65

> If you have a smokers' cough, you are at much higher risk of developing a serious lung infection.

Tobacco smoke irritates the entire respiratory system, including the nose, sinuses, throat, windpipe, and lungs. This irritation injures the surface of these areas, reducing their ability to remove mucous secretions and defend themselves against germ invasion. These changes lead to more frequent infections of the nose, sinuses, throat, and lungs. Damage to the mucous lining causes persistent congestion and coughing, which is a prime setup for developing pneumonia. A chronic cough may hide a lung infection or other serious lung ailment.

To reduce your risk of developing serious infections, stop smoking. You will also feel better.

TIP 66

> If you currently smoke or have a history of smoking and find it difficult to breathe, or experience persistent coughing, you may have significant emphysema, which could eventually kill you. You should be evaluated by a physician. These symptoms can also be signs of new or other long-term lung diseases, including cancer.

Shortness of breath in a smoker can be the first sign of emphysema, lung cancer, heart disease, or pneumonia. Smokers are more likely to develop these diseases. Emphysema, which is most often caused by smoking, can lead to permanent lung failure and eventually death. Discovering that you have emphysema should be a stimulus to stop smoking.

Emphysema traps air inside of the microscopic air sacs that make up the lungs. When air enters these air sacs, it has trouble getting out, due to the spasm and destruction of the walls of the tiny air passages that lead to the air sacs, and the secretions in the air passages prompted by irritation from smoke. As a result, the tiny air sacs become overinflated, and they no longer empty all of their contents when air is exhaled. This means that there is a considerable amount of dead air (air poor in oxygen) in the lungs, which leaves less room for fresh air. Also, since these sacs are where the body normally obtains its oxygen for the blood, a reduction of available oxygen in the air sacs reduces the body's total supply of oxygen.

At first, you may not notice that your breathing is becoming impaired. Long before abnormalities appear on a chest X-ray or you have difficulty breathing, changes can be detected with lung-function testing. Lung-function testing involves breathing into a machine that makes several measurements, including the total lung volume as well as the rate of air flow into and out of the lungs. The primary measurement for diagnosing the severity of the emphysema is the amount of air exhaled from the lung during the first second. If you smoke, ask your doctor about a lung-function test. Pay attention to the results.

If you smoke and are short of breath, it is necessary that you see a doctor immediately to rule out emphysema, pneumonia, lung cancer, and other ailments.

TIP 67

> Shortness of breath when you lie flat in bed, which wakes you up in the middle of the night and improves when you sit up, is often a sign of heart failure.

The heart is one big muscle that pumps blood through your body. If the pump begins to fail, fluid can back up into your lungs and cause shortness of breath. Some people describe the feeling of shortness of breath as a feeling of drowning. In the early stages of heart failure, excessive shortness of breath comes only when you exercise, climb stairs, walk uphill, and/or are lying flat in bed or sleeping on one pillow. This is related to a shift in your body's fluids. When you are erect or sitting, fluid accumulates in the dependent parts of your body—your lower legs and your feet. People with heart failure who have excess fluid will often experience swelling of their legs, ankles, and feet during the day when they are in an upright position. This may go unnoticed because it produces no discomfort. But when you are lying flat, the fluid from your legs is returned into circulation and to the heart, which is too weak to pump it all, causing the fluid to shift to the lungs.

The scientific name for this condition is PND (paroxysmal nocturnal dyspnea), which means intermittent shortness of breath at night. You go to sleep, wake up short of breath, sit up, and breathe better, only to lie back down and get short of breath again. You may eventually need to sleep on two or three pillows. If the condition gets bad enough, you may have to sit up in a chair all night.

There are many causes of heart failure. When any symptoms of heart failure appear, including nighttime shortness of breath, it is urgent that the cause be found. Evaluation and treatment can be life-saving.

TIP 68

If you experience more shortness of breath than normal during and/or after mild exertion, particularly if you also have a rapid pulse, you may have a serious medical problem, usually in your lungs or heart.

Normally you get short of breath and your heart speeds up when you exert yourself, such as when you run up a flight of stairs. But if your shortness of breath and/or rapid pulse continue too long after rest (usually three minutes or more), or if they occur with very mild exertion, then you may have a heart-lung problem, a low blood count, or another serious illness. Seek immediate medical evaluation and therapy.

Cough

TIP 69

Coughing up blood may be a sign of bronchitis, pneumonia, blood clots, or cancer.

If you are coughing up blood, it is important to find out where it is originating. The bleeding may have an innocuous source—a small amount of blood from bleeding gums, a nosebleed, or a cut on your mouth may be trickling down and irritating your throat, causing you to cough it up. Or it may actually be originating in your lungs, which suggests the presence of blood clots or various infections, including tuberculosis. Also, you may have an abnormal growth in your lungs, possibly cancer.

You need to see a doctor immediately for evaluation and appropriate therapy. A thorough examination of your mouth and nose may help determine the cause of the bleeding. Alternatively, the doctor may need to look into your lungs with a tube, by taking an X-ray of your lungs, or by scanning them.

TIP 70

Coughing up dirty-looking phlegm may mean that there is pus in it from an infection.

When you get a cold or the flu, you usually cough up phlegm. It is important to note the color. Mucus produced by the lungs, airways, nose, and sinuses is usually clear and is often thicker than water. However, mucus is also produced in response to allergies, irritants like cigarette smoke, and illnesses such as a cold and the flu. "Dirty-looking" phlegm (usually gray or green) contains pus cells, which may be coming from a serious lung infection such as bronchitis or pneumonia. When the infection is confined to the air passages, you have bronchitis, and when it invades the substance of the lung, you have pneumonia. These infections may be caused by a number of different germs, including bacteria that require antibiotic treatment or viruses that usually disappear on their own (antibiotic treatment is not effective with viruses). Smokers, diabetics, or people with other serious medical problems often require antibiotics to clear up their dirty phlegm.

When your phlegm turns dirty, seek medical evaluation and treatment as soon as possible, especially if fever and fatigue are present or if you have other medical ailments. The doctor will determine what type of infection is present and if antibiotic treatment is needed.

Note: Also be aware that coughing up dirty-looking phlegm could be a result of mucus that has dripped down from a sinus infection.

TIP 71

A persistent cough lasting more than two weeks may be caused by something as simple as bronchitis or allergies, or by something as serious as tuberculosis, pneumonia, heart disease, or cancer. An annoying chronic cough can also be caused by reflux of stomach contents into the esophagus (the tube between the mouth and the stomach). You should be evaluated as soon as possible, especially if you cough up blood, which may then get into the lungs.

Everyone coughs from time to time, whether from postnasal drip, a cold, an allergy, or irritants in the air. Most of these minor illnesses run their course in fourteen days or less. If a cough lasts longer or is associated with additional symptoms, other causes must be considered by a physician. Some of these potential causes are life-threatening; they include lung infection, heart disease, and cancer. Smokers often cough constantly, so they may not realize when a more serious disease is present.

If routine treatments for coughs have failed, and more traditional causes have been ruled out, another possibility is reflux of stomach contents into the esophagus, which may be associated with a hiatal hernia. A hiatal hernia occurs when part of the stomach pokes through a hole in the diaphragm, which separates the chest from the abdomen. This condition can wake you up at night with the feeling that you are strangling. You may cough so hard that it takes your breath away, and you may even black out.

A hiatal hernia or other conditions can allow acid-containing fluid to back up the esophagus and then into the windpipe, which irritates the lining and causes repeated coughing episodes. This is called acid reflux. Acidic liquid is able to flow up the esophagus much more easily when you are lying down, so the reflux is usually more troublesome at night. If the cause of your cough is a hiatal hernia, you need to take medication for your stomach problem, not an antibiotic or cold medicine for your cough. It is important to address this problem—if your lungs become soiled by acid over a long period of time, scarring may occur, along with a reduction in lung function.

Treatment begins with prescription medicines designed to suppress acid formation in the stomach. Other practical measures are important as well. Before lying down, try to remain upright for two to four hours after eating or drinking. Avoid overeating at any time. Elevate the head of your bed by placing a brick under each leg of the headboard. This will provide enough of an incline to reduce the acid reflux yet not enough to disturb sleep.

Long-term coughing may also be the result of a postnasal drip, allergies, or asthma, which need to be ruled out as causes by your doctor. In addition, a chronic cough may be a side effect of medication, including a class of blood pressure and heart medications known as ACE inhibitors. If you take one of these blood pressure pills and develop a cough, tell your doctor.

TIP 72

A cough, fever, and chest pains with or without other common cold symptoms are often indicators of pneumonia. Failure to improve after forty-eight hours of treatment for pneumonia is a strong indication of a more serious infection requiring immediate medical evaluation. Note: These symptoms are sometimes indicators of blood clots in the lungs (see Tips 62 to 64, 175, and 249).

People often think pneumonia always follows a bad cold. That is, first you have the typical cold symptoms—congestion in the head and a sore throat—and then your symptoms spread to the chest, accompanied by coughing. Not so. The first symptoms may be the sudden onset of a cough, fever, and chest pains, with no cold symptoms whatsoever. If this occurs, you should see your doctor right away.

Once you start treatment for pneumonia, your condition should improve within forty-eight hours. If it does not, touch base with your doctor again. Seek immediate medical attention if you develop shortness of breath, since this may indicate that the therapy is ineffective at this point and that the infection in your lungs has reached a very serious stage. If you have had your spleen removed, pneumonia can very quickly become fatal.

Pneumonia is often caused by the bacterium pneumococcus. Alcoholics, smokers, senior citizens, and frail or disabled persons are particularly susceptible to this strain of pneumonia. While the vaccine for pneumococcal pneumonia may prevent the disease or help the body's defenses fight it, many other germs can also cause pneumonia, including staphylococcus, mycoplasma, and hemophilus.

These symptoms could also be caused by a rare condition called Legionnaires' disease, which is difficult to culture and identify. The illness often starts with diarrhea and possibly other flu-like symptoms. Then it goes on to involve the lungs. When this occurs you may have severe shortness of breath, fever, and a cough in which you bring up no phlegm (or only a small amount). This condition can be fatal if left untreated. The secret to survival is early diagnosis and appropriate antibiotic treatment. The disease is named Legionnaires' disease because it was first discovered at an American Legion conference. Several members of the American Legion contracted the disease because the germ had contaminated the conference room's air-conditioning system.

If the cough, fever, and chest pain are diagnosed as being due to blood clots in the lung, your doctor will start you on blood thinners and other therapies immediately. This treatment can be life-saving.

TIP 73

Cough, fever, and night sweats may be signs of tuberculosis.

Tuberculosis (TB) infections most commonly occur in the lungs but they can spread to other parts of the body. In the common course of the disease, an early cough is joined by other symptoms like weight loss, night sweats, and an overall ill feeling.

For a while, tuberculosis seemed to be a disease of the past. Improved medications and the isolation of infected persons helped decrease the prevalence of this ailment. But stronger forms of the bacterium have caused a marked resurgence of TB. Even powerful drugs are not very effective in killing some of these new TB germs.

TB can spread through nursing homes, attacking senior citizens, the debilitated, and AIDS patients, but in rare instances, there have been outbreaks of TB among healthy individuals. These outbreaks are more likely to occur in close quarters where air is recirculated through air-conditioning systems. People who have traveled extensively overseas are generally more likely to contract and spread TB.

These red light signals warrant immediate evaluation by a physician. If you have tuberculosis, adhere to your medical regimen, since the disease can be fatal. In addition to tuberculosis, other possible causes of these symptoms include various infections of the lung and cancers such as lymphoma.

Chest Pain and Discomfort

TIP 74

Learn to recognize the chest discomfort of a heart attack. Emergency medical care can save your life.

Your heart requires nourishment from blood that travels in three small but vital vessels on the surface of your heart. If one of these vessels becomes blocked by a blood clot (thrombus) forming at an area that has been narrowed by a cholesterol plaque, part of your heart muscle will be damaged. This process is a heart attack, and immediate emergency care is necessary since your heart may go into spasm and stop.

The pain and tightness of a heart attack occurs classically in the center or left side of the chest under the breastbone, and may extend into the right or left arm. Common variations include pain near the front base of the neck, or in the jaw (see Figure 5). Jaw pain sometimes may be felt as pain in the lower

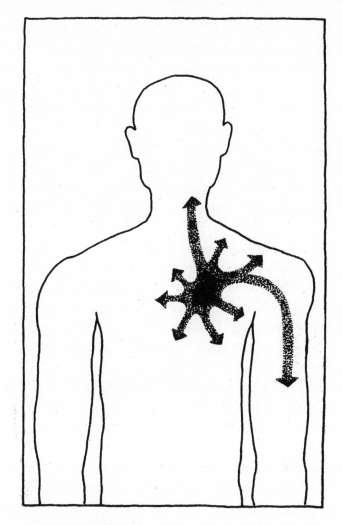

Figure 5. Chest Pain Warning of a Possible Heart Attack.

teeth. In some cases, the pain may instead appear across the entire chest or between the shoulder blades.

The character of the chest pain can be crushing or pressurelike, and is often described as a constricting or squeezing feeling. It can also resemble indigestion, and feel as though belching will make it go away. Or it may feel like a tingling or burning sensation. The severity of the pain does not correlate with the severity of the heart attack; mild or even slight pain can mean a severe heart attack. Some heart attacks are actually pain free, especially in women, diabetics, or senior citizens.

Intermittent pain, lasting usually twenty minutes or less, may be a symptom of angina, particularly if it occurs with activity and is relieved by rest (see Tip 76 for the explanation of angina), but if the pain lasts for thirty minutes continuously, you are more than likely having a full-blown heart attack. Other important symptoms include breaking out in a cold sweat, extreme weakness, nausea and vomiting, dizziness, feeling faint, and/or shortness of breath.

If treatment is started early enough (the sooner the better, especially if within hours), the doctor may be able to prevent damage to the heart. He or she may use any of a number of procedures, including dissolving the clot (clot busters), inserting a ballooning catheter to open the blood vessel, using a device called a stent to prop the blood vessel open, etc. (see Figure 6). If surgery to bypass the blocked blood vessel is necessary, the surgeon will attach a vein from your leg or an artery from your chest muscle to the blocked vessel above and below the blockage so that blood can flow around it. Sometimes treatment involves only the use of medicines. (Also see Appendix C, page 392, for information on heart disease screening.)

TIP 75

If you think you are having a heart attack with symptoms such as chest pain, chew one regular, full-strength aspirin (or four 81 mg low-dose aspirin tablets) immediately, unless you are allergic to aspirin. It could save your life. Also, get to an emergency room immediately.

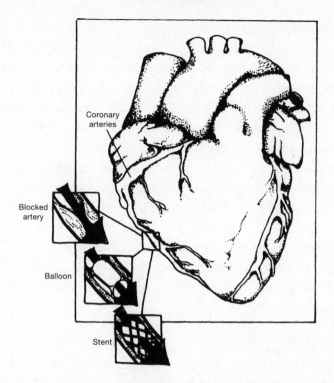

Coronary
arteries

Blocked
artery

Balloon

Stent

Figure 6. Heart.

It may seem ridiculous to take something as simple as an aspirin for something as serious as a heart attack, but it does
help prevent damage to the heart muscle during a heart attack.

Your heart has three small but vital blood vessels on its surface. These arteries provide the blood that nourishes the heart
muscle itself. If fatty substances such as cholesterol start to
clog up the vessels, they become narrowed and eventually only
a small amount of blood can pass through. It is like a small
pea stuck in a straw, with only a little opening around the pea.
Eating a lot of fatty and/or salty foods, smoking, high blood
pressure, and diabetes increase the chance that the pea ruptures, creating the perfect setting for a blood clot to form,
which can then, in turn, completely block the artery. This will
ultimately cause a heart attack, because no blood will be able

to pass through to provide oxygen and nourishment to the heart muscle. Part of your heart muscle will consequently be damaged, and you may develop chest pain. Depending on the location and degree of the damage to the heart, different things can happen: The heart may beat irregularly, the heart may become weak and lose its pumping strength, or the heart may stop pumping altogether.

Aspirin (not Tylenol or other pain medications) actually "unsticks" the components of the blood known as platelets, which contribute to forming the clot. If you chew an aspirin when you initially feel chest pain, the blood clot may partially dissolve or at least stop forming. Some blood will then be able to pass around the fatty blockage and therefore continue to deliver oxygen to the heart muscle, preventing a more serious heart attack.

TIP 76

> If you experience episodes of chest pain, tightness, and burning that extend to the neck, throat, jaw, and/or left shoulder and upper arm, usually lasting less than twenty minutes, you may be experiencing angina. This discomfort often occurs with exertion, but sometimes occurs during rest or sleep. It is often a precursor to a heart attack and needs immediate evaluation and treatment.

Your heart muscle has three small but vital blood vessels on its surface. When one or more of these blood vessels becomes partially blocked, the heart muscle does not get enough oxygen and nutrition. Subsequent changes in the heart muscle irritate its nerve supply, producing pain. Elderly patients, who are more likely to experience painless heart attacks than younger patients, are also more likely to experience angina without this classic squeezing chest pain.

Angina differs from a heart attack in that the artery supplying the heart muscle is not totally blocked by fat or blood clots, while in a heart attack the blockage is total. If you have a heart attack, the lack of oxygen and nutrition persists, the chest pain continues, and part of the heart muscle is irreversibly damaged.

The pain from angina often appears when you exert yourself, either mildly (shaving or walking up stairs) or more strenuously (lifting objects or exercising). It typically disappears with the cessation of exertion. However, it should be noted that angina can also occur without exertion, sometimes during rest or sleep.

Watch out for these symptoms—if you have angina, you are at a much higher risk of having a heart attack. The partially blocked artery that is causing your angina is susceptible to total blockage by a blood clot. Anyone having angina attacks should have a thorough heart evaluation, which may include an EKG while exercising, a heart scan, and a catheterization to examine the arteries that nourish the heart. (Also see Appendix C, page 392, for more about heart disease screening.)

There are many effective medical treatments for angina. It is urgent that you go to the emergency room in the following situations, which may be red light warning signals of an impending heart attack:

- The first time you notice you have angina
- Angina when you are at rest
- Angina that wakes you up at night
- A change in the pattern of your angina pain, such as becoming more severe, more frequent, or longer lasting

TIP 77

> If your father, mother, brother, or sister died at a young age (men before fifty, women before sixty) from a heart attack, you need to be checked for risk factors, even if you are only in your twenties.

The early death of an immediate family member from a heart attack is a warning sign that you are at a higher risk of having one. Other risk factors include:

- Diabetes
- Smoking
- History of prior heart attacks or strokes
- Known history of arterial blockages
- High blood pressure
- High cholesterol
- Obesity
- Being male
- Being a postmenopausal female

If you are at high risk of having a heart attack, you can reduce your risk by taking the following actions:

- Reduce the fat intake in your diet.
- Stop smoking.
- Seek treatment if you have high blood pressure.
- Exercise regularly.
- Adjust your lifestyle to reduce stress.
- Diet with the advice of a dietitian if you are overweight.
- See your doctor for a cardiac risk factor screening and possible medical treatment for elevated bad fats in your blood, etc. (Also see Appendix C for information on various preventive screenings such as for blood pressure, page 380; cholesterol, page 382; and diabetes, page 383.)
- Get treated for gum disease by a dentist.

TIP 78

Severe, prolonged chest pain under the breast-bone that extends to the back between the shoulder blades is uncommon but may indicate a rare, life-threatening condition.

This is the classic pain pattern of a dissecting aneurysm of the thoracic aorta. The thoracic aorta, the huge artery where blood flows from the heart, is the main thoroughfare in the distribution of blood to all parts of the body. The aortic wall is made up of three layers and is constantly subjected to pulsating pressure from the heartbeat, especially when your blood pressure is too high. This kind of stress can weaken and tear the inner layer of the aortic wall, allowing blood to work its way into the wall itself. This will cause the layers to separate in a process called dissection. An aneurysm occurs when the weakened wall of the heart balloons out. This constitutes a true medical emergency—you need to be taken to an emergency room as quickly as possible. If the aneurysm ruptures through the outer wall of the aorta, massive bleeding and death will follow. Note: There are inherited disorders that increase your chance of having an aortic aneurysm. If you have a family member who has been diagnosed with an aortic aneurysm, you need to be evaluated.

Other possible causes of this type of pain include a stomach ulcer that has broken through the stomach wall, pancreatic inflammation, and gallbladder disease. All of these conditions warrant immediate medical evaluation.

TIP 79

A sudden sharp pain on the side of your chest with shortness of breath may indicate a collapsed

> lung (pneumothorax). This and some other causes of these symptoms (see Tip 61) require emergency treatment.

When you breathe in, your lungs are full of air, and they still contain air when you breathe out. If there is a leak of air from the surface of the lung into the chest cavity, this leaked air can collapse the lung. If this happens, you will experience a sudden, sharp pain on the side of your chest, followed by shortness of breath.

A common cause of a collapsed lung is the rupture of a small balloonlike weakened area on the lung's surface (called a bleb). You may be born with such a weak spot, but it usually will not rupture until late adolescence or early adulthood. This occurs most commonly in tall, thin young men, particularly during exertion. Recurrence is frequent because those who have one weak spot on the lung often have many.

Alternatively, a smoker who has emphysema might experience this kind of rupture. It can also occur if the chest wall is punctured, such as in an accident. Air gets into the chest cavity, which presses on and then collapses the lung.

A collapsed lung constitutes a medical emergency, especially if the remaining lung is diseased. If the other organs in the chest, including the heart and major blood vessels, shift their position because of the collapsed lung, they may encroach on the remaining lung. Emergency treatment is necessary to reexpand the collapsed lung because this condition can compromise the function of the other lung, leading to an inability to breathe and, consequently, death.

TIP 80

Pain under the breastbone after a vomiting episode, especially if bright red blood is vomited,

> may indicate a tear in the lining of the esophagus.
> Usually, the person has retched or vomited multi-
> ple times before blood appears in the vomit.

The esophagus is the muscular tube that takes food from the throat, through the chest, to the stomach. Food does not just fall through the tube, but is squeezed through it by a wave of muscles in the wall of the esophagus. When vomiting occurs, the reverse happens: The stomach contracts, moving material into the esophagus, where the esophagus grabs it and—with a reversed wave of muscle contraction—hurls it out of the mouth. During episodes of severe vomiting, the squeezing of the muscle wall of the esophagus can be powerful enough to tear the lining of the lower esophagus near the opening to the stomach. A life-threatening hemorrhage or infection may follow.

The wall of the esophagus can also weaken. Continued vomiting may lead to rupture, which is often fatal. Early signs of this condition indicate the need for emergency medical treatment.

TIP 81

> Tenderness and pain in the back of your lower
> leg, chest pain, and/or shortness of breath, occur-
> ring after sitting for a long time (e.g., after a long
> airplane trip), or after lying in bed for an extended
> period of time, are symptoms of a potentially
> dangerous blood clot.

A blood clot can form in your leg during a long trip in a car or an airplane or when you are bedridden for even a short time. The sitting and lying positions cause more pooling of blood in the legs than standing does. When your legs are still, lack of

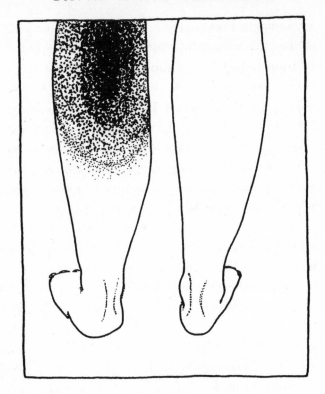

Figure 7. Leg Pain Location That May Indicate a Blood Clot.

leg-muscle activity results in less blood flowing up from the legs. The blood that pools in your legs is more likely to clot. When this happens, the back lower part of your leg, in the area of the calf, gets swollen, painful, and tender to the touch (see Figure 7). If this is accompanied by sudden chest pain or shortness of breath, a piece of a blood clot formed in your leg may have broken off and traveled through the bloodstream to your lungs. You need to be taken to an emergency room immediately, because this condition can cause life-threatening damage to your lungs.

The formation of blood clots can often be prevented if you take short walks to break up long periods of sitting. If you are taking a long trip, occasionally get up and stroll down the aisle of the airplane or stop the car and step outside for a break. Drink plenty of water so you don't become dehydrated. Don't drink alcohol, which causes you to urinate frequently and lose more fluid. If you are bedridden, try to take short walks, even if it is only to the bathroom and back. (See Tip 139 for other causes of blood clots forming in the leg.)

Note: If you have had blood clots in your legs before, you are at a higher risk for getting blood clots in the future. This is especially true if you have been prescribed blood thinners by your doctor and have not been taking them.

TIP 82

> Chest pain that gets worse when you take a deep breath (pleurisy) may indicate a blood clot, pneumonia, injury to the chest wall, a collapsed lung, a tumor in the lung, or other lung diseases.

Pleurisy is not a disease but a symptom. It is an irritation of the membrane (pleura) that lines the walls of the chest and the surface of the lung. The pleura is very smooth, slick, and moist, so as to decrease the friction between the lung and the chest wall during the expansion and deflation of the breathing cycle. If the pleura becomes irritated, swollen, or roughened, a sharp, stabbing pain will often occur when the lung and the chest wall rub against each other during breathing.

Pleurisy makes you feel as though your breath is being cut off. Pneumonia is a common cause; it inflames the tissue near the surface of your lung, which can then spread to the pleura. Note: It is possible to have pneumonia without having pleurisy.

A blood clot in the lung, a viral infection, a growth in the lung, an injury to the chest wall, a collapsed lung, lupus, and other diseases affecting the lungs may also cause pleurisy if the lining of the lung is inflamed.

If you experience chest pain that worsens with a deep breath, emergency medical evaluation and therapy are necessary.

TIP 83

Chest pain that is worse when you are lying down but gets better when you sit up and bend forward may be caused by inflammation of the sac that holds the heart. This inflammation may lead to the accumulation of fluid in the sac, which will interfere with the filling and pumping of the heart.

The heart is contained in a saclike structure called the pericardium. This compartment is located in the left side of the chest, and if inflamed, will cause pain in that area. Inflammation (swelling and irritation) of this sac is usually caused by a viral infection. It can also occur from a bacterial infection, the spread of a cancerous growth from the lung, the waste products released in the blood when the kidneys fail, or after a heart attack or some heart surgeries. Also, certain medications (procainamide, hydralazine, and the tuberculosis medicine isoniazid), can cause a lupus-like disease that may result in inflammation of the pericardium.

Both the severe chest pain and the often associated shortness of breath produced by this condition (called pericarditis) may be similar to the pain from pleurisy, pneumonia, or even a heart attack. The special characteristic of pericarditis is that the pain is often worse when you lie flat on your back. Sitting up and bending forward can ease the pain by relieving the pressure on the sac that contains the heart. This does not mean that you absolutely have pericarditis, but you should see a doctor immediately for evaluation.

A potential complication of this disease is the weeping of fluid from the sac wall into the compartment around the heart. If a large amount of this fluid accumulates, it can compress the heart such that it cannot effectively pump blood throughout the body, resulting in the failure of other organs. This is referred to as cardiac tamponade. It is important to have pericarditis diagnosed immediately so you can receive treatment and/or close monitoring of the ailment.

Irregular Heartbeats and Heart Sounds

TIP 84

> The red light warning signals that you may have a rapid or irregular heartbeat are: heart palpitations, fluttering, skipped or pounding beats, sudden spells of weakness, sudden spells of dizziness, a feeling like "squirrels running around in the chest," and a feeling like your heart is beating at the base of your throat. If you think your heartbeat is abnormally fast, slow, or irregular, take your pulse. An abnormal pulse can be a warning sign of many different life-threatening illnesses.

If you feel that your heart is beating abnormally, take your pulse. To do so, take the pads of your second and third fingers, place them on the thumb side of your wrist, and find the pulsations of the artery. If your hand is palm up, the pulse is between the bone and the first big tendon (see Figure 8).

Count the number of pulsations you feel in one minute:

- A normal rate is usually between 60 and 100 beats per minute. Normal ranges of resting rates vary from person to person. In other words, if your normal rate is 60 to 70, an abnormally high rate for you may be 90. Or if a normal resting rate for you is 85 to 95, then an

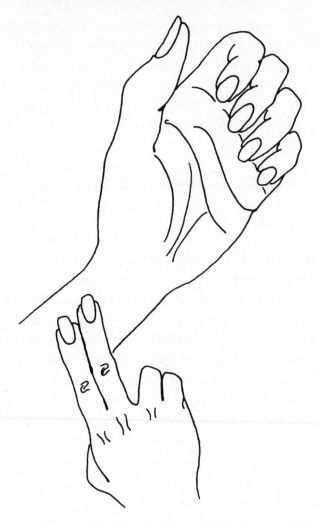

Figure 8. Taking a Pulse.

abnormally slow rate might be 60. It is a good idea to check your pulse a few times while at rest so that you get to know the general range of your pulse.

• A fast rate is a rate above your normal resting rate. Note: A resting rate above 100 is abnormal for anyone.

• A resting heart rate is considered slow when it is below

your normal range. For most people, a rate below 60 beats per minute is slow.

There are many benign reasons for an irregular heartbeat. It is normal for your pulse rate to rise to greater than 100 beats per minute with exercise, anxiety and stress, pain, or fever, and it may slow down significantly during sleep. It can also be influenced by herbal supplements/remedies or certain medications (such as Sudafed). In young, healthy people, irregular heartbeats are usually due to a small amount of abnormal electrical activity in a part of the heart; this can be brought on by stress, caffeine, or alcohol. In about 20 percent of the cases of irregular heartbeats in the young population, there is no explanation. These episodes of irregular heartbeats are usually harmless and will often go away when the heart speeds up during or after exercise.

However, a rapid pulse could be the body's red light warning signal of a life-threatening internal hemorrhage (usually accompanied by weakness and dizziness when you are switching from a lying position to a sitting position, or from a sitting position to a standing position).

Irregular, fast, or slow pulses can be dangerous and require immediate therapy in an emergency room. (Examples of some of the more common causes are listed in Tips 85 through 90.)

TIP 85

A rapid pulse may appear with the following symptoms: heart palpitations, fluttering, skipped beats, sudden spells of weakness, sudden spells of dizziness, and/or heart pounding. An elevated pulse is a common side effect of hyperthyroidism, dehydration, fever, anxiety, and certain medications. Also, a persistent rise in your pulse may be a sign that you are bleeding internally, often in the stomach or intestines. Any unexplained elevation in your pulse may indicate a need for medical evaluation and treatment.

Your pulse will normally go up when you run, climb stairs, et cetera, but a resting pulse around 115 or greater is always cause for concern, and depending on the cause, emergency medical treatment can be life-saving. A rise in pulse may be the first signal of a life-threatening hemorrhage in areas such as the stomach or intestines, followed by a drop in blood pressure. When blood loss occurs over a long period of time, a rapid pulse may be accompanied by fatigue and paleness.

TIP 86

The onset of a rapid pulse, especially if it starts and stops suddenly and occurs intermittently, may appear with the following symptoms: heart palpitations, fluttering, pounding or skipped beats, sudden spells of weakness and/or dizziness, and/or loss of consciousness. A sudden rapid pulse is most likely caused by an abnormality in the electrical system of the heart.

When your heart suddenly starts beating too fast because of a heart rhythm abnormality, its rate will usually be over 120 and can even be as high as 160 to 200. This rapidity can interfere with the pumping action of the heart, so that blood flow is compromised. You may experience symptoms of weakness, dizziness, light-headedness, and, if severe enough, sudden loss of consciousness. If you experience any of these symptoms, have someone take you to an emergency room. Make sure you stop consuming all caffeine, street drugs, herbal products (including teas), and over-the-counter medications until you discuss your condition with a doctor. Also tell the doctor you had been taking these products. If you pass out even for a short time, and/or experience chest pain or shortness of breath, call 911.

Sudden changes in your heart rhythm and a rapid or irregular pulse can be dangerous, particularly if you have previously experienced a heart ailment such as a heart attack, heart failure, or heart enlargement from high blood pressure.

TIP 87

An irregular, usually rapid pulse may appear with the following symptoms: a feeling like "squirrels running around in your chest," heart palpitations, fluttering, skipped beats, sudden spells of weakness, sudden spells of dizziness, and/or heart pounding. If your pulse suddenly becomes irregular (and usually rapid), you may be experiencing a serious heart rhythm abnormality known as atrial fibrillation.

If you have this condition, abnormal electrical impulses are originating from the upper chambers of your heart (the atrium), and are conducted to the lower chambers of your heart (the ventricles), typically in an irregular and rapid fashion. Your pulse is often very irregular and rapid, and can be very difficult to count. When the heart's electrical system is in this abnormal state, the upper heart chambers are no longer effectively squeezing blood into the lower chambers, and this may result in blood pooling, which can sometimes lead to a blood clot. When this occurs, pieces of the clot can break off and travel through blood vessels to the brain, where they may lodge in a vessel and block blood flow to a part of the brain. This part of the brain will be damaged, causing a stroke.

Atrial fibrillation frequently occurs in people with heart and lung disease, and in those with hypertension, but it can also occur in people who consume large amounts of alcoholic beverages or in people with an overactive thyroid (which is associated with shaking, tremors, exhaustion, and intolerance to heat). Please note, however, that atrial fibrillation sometimes occurs spontaneously in healthy people.

Treatment of this disorder may include taking a blood thinner to prevent the blood from clotting. The doctor can convert your heartbeat to a regular rhythm with medication or an electrical shock applied to your heart. If you feel the onset of an irregular and usually rapid pulse with the above symptoms, seek immediate medical care.

TIP 88

An electrical abnormality of the heart known as long QT syndrome can cause sudden death, especially in young adults, and even in children. The red light warning signals may include unexplained seizures or sudden loss of consciousness, often during physical activity such as swimming, when emotionally upset, or when startled by a noise. It's also reported that people with long QT syndrome may experience an irregular heartbeat with the following symptoms: heart palpitations, fluttering, skipped beats, sudden spells of weakness, sudden spells of dizziness, and/or heart pounding. However, it must be emphasized that these symptoms are very rarely associated with

long QT syndrome and are usually related to
other medical conditions.

The long QT syndrome, a serious heart rhythm problem that
occurs in young people, gets its name from the EKG readout,
as the syndrome increases the distance between the Q wave
and the T wave (which may only show up on an EKG during
exercise or on an ambulatory heart monitor). If someone has
this syndrome, he or she is at risk of developing a dangerously
fast heart rate, requiring cardiac shock or medication.

Even if you are young, if you have the above red light
warning signals, it is worthwhile for you to be evaluated by
your doctor as soon as possible, because it could be a warning
that you have long QT syndrome. It's very important that you
get evaluated for this condition if you have a family history of
drowning or of family members dying without any known
cause at a young age.

TIP 89

If you get an irregular pulse after you've experienced excessive fluid loss from diarrhea, water
pills, and/or sweating, that irregular pulse may be
the result of changes in the mineral levels of your
blood, such as the level of potassium. This may
have serious health consequences. The red light
warning signals may include: heart palpitations,
fluttering, skipped beats, sudden spells of weakness, sudden spells of dizziness, heart pounding,
and muscle cramps in the leg.

If you have lost an excessive amount of fluid from any cause, including sweating, taking water pills, or having prolonged or severe diarrhea, you may lose large quantities of certain minerals

such as potassium. The loss of potassium can result in abnormal electrical charges in your heart, causing dangerous irregular heartbeats. This can be life-threatening; emergency medical therapy and monitoring by a physician is necessary. Often special intravenous fluids are needed to replace these minerals.

On the other hand, heart rhythm problems can also occur if there is an *excess* of potassium or certain other minerals in the blood. If you experience these symptoms, you need to be taken to an emergency room immediately.

TIP 90

If your pulse drops below 50 beats per minute, there may be a serious impairment in your heart's pacing system that could cause serious symptoms such as light-headedness, dizziness, weakness, or sudden loss of consciousness. Although some well-conditioned athletes may normally have a resting pulse below 50, a pulse lower than 40 in an athlete is a reason to seek medical attention immediately.

Your heartbeat is regulated by specialized heart cells located in the upper chamber on the right side of the heart. If this area becomes diseased (or altered as a side effect of medication), it may begin to function abnormally, causing a sudden slowing of the pulse. Common medications that slow your heart rate include heart drugs like digoxin, beta-blockers like metoprolol or atenolol, and calcium channel blockers like verapamil or diltiazem.

The slow pulse may be so severe it causes you to pass out, or it may occur intermittently, with your pulse returning to normal for a while. If this is occurring even for short periods of time, you need to be taken to an emergency room immediately.

TIP 91

If you listen to your heart with a stethoscope and hear a swooshing sound, it may indicate a heart murmur. You should seek medical evaluation by your doctor.

A heart murmur is a swooshing sound coming from within the heart. Heart murmurs are quite common and frequently do not indicate a serious problem. For example, they may be the result of blood passing rapidly but normally through one of the four valves (doors) in the heart (see Figure 9). A large percentage of adolescents have murmurs that are not caused by disease. But a murmur may be abnormal when a damaged valve in the heart contributes to making the sound. It may also occur when blood travels through an abnormal hole in a wall that separates two heart chambers.

To understand why blood passing through a narrowed opening makes this sound, think about a garden hose. A garden hose makes little noise when water flows from it, but if you put a nozzle on the end, a swooshing noise is created as the water spews through the narrow opening. The same thing happens with the heart when blood flows through an abnormally narrow opening or rapidly through a normal opening. While listening to the heart with a stethoscope, the loudness, location, timing, and pitch of the murmur help the doctor to determine if and where the heart is damaged.

Certain heart murmurs must be monitored by your doctor to determine if the problem is worsening and if and when the abnormality should be corrected so that permanent damage can be avoided. For example, one common cause of a heart murmur is a ventricular septal defect, a birth defect in which there is an opening in the wall that separates the lower chambers of the heart. This opening causes an abnormal flow of

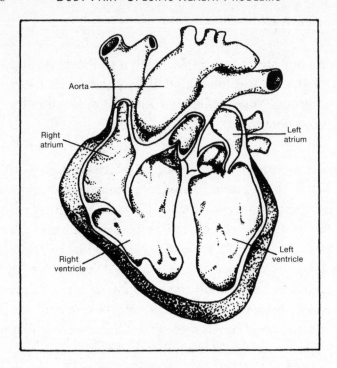

Figure 9. Inside of Heart.

blood, which can permanently damage the lungs. Diagnosis and treatment are essential. There are many other situations in which a murmur requires regular monitoring or medical intervention.

Both a damaged valve that has been infected in the past and an artificial valve provide prime targets for bacterial growth (bacterial endocarditis). Therefore, if you have these or certain other heart conditions and you are undergoing a procedure anywhere else on your body, it may be very important for you to take an antibiotic. For example, small amounts of bacteria can get in your blood during dental work or when tubes are put in your body to examine your bladder or colon. These bacteria may then grow on an abnormal heart valve or on an artificial valve in your heart. Appropriate antibiotics will kill any germs that get into your blood before they do damage.

BELLY, STOMACH AREA, OR ABDOMEN

How to Assess Belly Pain

Where, specifically, is your belly pain?
Many things can go wrong inside the belly cavity and cause pain. Some are serious and can endanger your life, while others may not require any treatment.

Draw an imaginary line horizontally across the belly at the level of the belly button. Draw a second line vertically from the lower tip of the breastbone through the belly button to the pelvic bone. This effectively divides the belly into four areas or quadrants: two upper, and two lower (see Figure 10). The location of your belly pain may provide an invaluable clue as to what is wrong, as it often (though not always) points to which organ is involved (see Figure 11).

The following ailments are commonly located in the upper half, the lower half, or in one of the four quadrants of the belly area (as seen from your perspective, if you were examining your own belly). Note: The less common causes of belly-aches are not mentioned here.

1. **The upper half of the belly area:** Stomach or duodenal ulcers and pancreatitis pains are commonly found in this region.

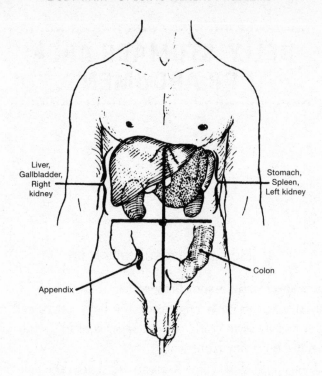

Figure 10. Quadrants of the Abdomen.

2. **The lower half of the belly area:** Pains from bladder or prostate infections, as well as infections and tumors in the fallopian tubes, ovaries, and uterus occur in this region.

3. **Your right lower quadrant:** A common and potentially serious cause of pain in this area is appendicitis. Other considerations include kidney stones, colitis, and—in women—problems with the fallopian tubes and ovaries.

4. **Your right upper quadrant:** The most common cause of pain in this area is gallstones, which may lead to infection in the gallbladder. Hepatitis (liver inflammation) may also cause pain in this area.

5. **Your left upper quadrant:** This area contains part of the stomach, part of the colon, and the spleen. A common cause of pain in this area is gas in the colon, which is

usually short-lived. Ulcers of the stomach can cause persistent pain in this area. Injuries (e.g., a spleen ruptured from blunt trauma to the belly) or diseases of the spleen can also cause pain here.

6. **Your left lower quadrant:** Pain from diverticulitis of the large bowel and from kidney stones can occur here. In women, infections in the fallopian tubes and ovaries are also considerations.

Is your belly tender when pressed upon?

Many serious causes of bellyache are accompanied by belly tenderness. It is important to test whether your belly is tender. Tenderness means that when you press down on a specific area of the belly with your fingers, the pressure makes it hurt. Most bellyaches from minor causes, such as a "stomach virus" or flu, are associated with very little belly tenderness. Though the serious causes of bellyache generally *do* involve tenderness, there are some exceptions. For example, kidney stones can be serious, but they cause a bellyache with little or no associated tenderness.

When belly tenderness occurs, it is usually most severe over the organ that is involved. If the inflammation or infection of the involved organ worsens and irritates the inside lining of the belly cavity, the pattern of the tenderness will change, spreading over the entire abdomen.

Does your belly pain get worse when you release your hand from the area where it has been pressed?

After you press your fingers down on an area of the belly, then suddenly release them, usually no pain occurs. But if this maneuver causes pain (called rebound tenderness), it usually means that the inside lining of the belly cavity is being irritated, perhaps from a specific disease that is spreading over the entire abdomen. This suggests a worsening of the problem.

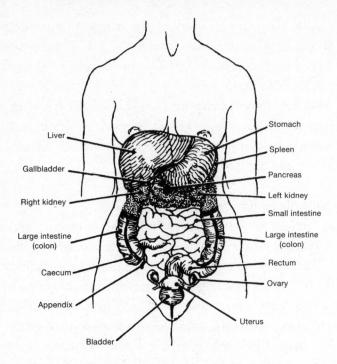

Figure 11. Evaluation of the Abdomen.

Can you feel any lumps or pulsations in your belly?

A hard area felt in the belly may mean the presence of an abnormal growth like a tumor or an abscess (a pus pocket). If the hard area pulsates with your heartbeat, it may be an artery that is ballooning out (dilating), known as an aneurysm. This condition warrants immediate medical attention. Firmness in the belly due to a muscle spasm of the belly wall can be mistaken for a problem originating within the belly cavity.

How would you describe your belly pain?

How the pain started, how it feels, and where it goes are important diagnostic considerations. It is therefore valuable for you to be able to describe these symptoms to your doctor.

What kind of pain do you have? Is it a cramping pain similar to the pain you feel when you get diarrhea or the urgent need to have a bowel movement? This kind of pain occurs when something contracts (squeezes) or goes into a spasm. Many of the hollow organs in the belly area—intestines, stomach, and gallbladder—have unique pain receptors called pressure receptors, meaning that anything that increases the pressure on the walls of these organs beyond a certain point will cause pain. On the other hand, these organs have no receptors that can detect cutting with a sharp object. For instance, the belly may be opened up under local anesthesia, with the individual awake, without causing pain. The bowel can also be cut under these circumstances. But if the bowel is grasped and squeezed, pain will occur. This makes sense when you consider that the danger to hollow organs is blockage, which can cause overexpansion, and possibly a rupture. Many diseases increase the pressure on the walls of these hollow organs, thereby causing cramping or colicky (spasmodic) pain.

Other kinds of bellyaches are dull, like a toothache. This often occurs when organs are infected or swollen. A sharper pain can occur in the belly when something ruptures, such as a cyst, dumping blood or other liquid material inside the belly cavity.

How the pain starts can be a very important consideration in diagnosing the problem. Was the onset abrupt? A sudden onset suggests that something ruptured (in the case of a sharp pain) or spasmed (in the case of cramping pain). Gradual onset with increasing severity suggests that something inside is irritated, inflamed, or infected, and is getting worse as the pain and swelling increase.

Where the pain extends is another important clue. Did it start in a certain area of the belly and remain there, or did it start in one area and spread to involve the entire belly? Pain that starts in one area and spreads suggests a progression of the problem.

Another type of pain is a sudden, sharp pain that occurs in one of the lower areas of the belly, and then sometimes spreads to one of the shoulders as well. This can occur if something like an ovarian cyst or a tubal pregnancy has ruptured and is causing blood or pus to irritate the diaphragm (the breathing muscle separating the belly cavity from the chest). If enough blood is released and it moves along the back wall of the belly cavity up to the diaphragm, then irritation of the nerve in the diaphragm will project a pain sensation to the left shoulder. While a similar pain is projected to the left shoulder from a rupture of the spleen, the bellyache will occur in the left upper area of the belly as opposed to the lower area of the belly. This type of pain rarely happens on the right side, because the liver prevents the blood from getting under the diaphragm on the right.

Pain in the belly that goes through to the back usually means something is wrong with an organ attached to the back of the belly compartment, such as the pancreas, the duodenum (first part of the small intestine), or the aorta (the large artery descending from the heart). Gallbladder pain often radiates along the back to the right shoulder blade. Keep in mind that if you have diabetes then there is damage to the nerves in your body, and you might not sense much abdominal pain.

Indigestion

TIP 92

Indigestion may be a sign of a heart attack. You should be especially concerned about:
- Indigestion with exercise or exertion
- Indigestion with a dizzy sensation
- Indigestion with a cold sweat
- Indigestion with numbness or pain radiating to the jaw or shoulder

- Indigestion with pressure in the chest
- Indigestion that does not respond to the usual medicines

Most of the time indigestion is not a serious disorder. But sometimes it can be a symptom of a heart attack. Though it is more often serious when associated with other symptoms, as listed above, it can still be the red light warning signal of a heart attack when it appears alone.

Under the above circumstances an immediate visit to the emergency room may save your life.

TIP 93

If you have long-term heartburn and belching that does not respond to an antacid or ulcer medication, it can lead to ulcers, bleeding, and/or narrowing of the esophagus (which may predispose you to cancer).

The tube that carries food from your mouth to your stomach is called the esophagus. When food backs up from the stomach into the esophagus (reflux) and the esophagus becomes irritated, you may develop heartburn. This condition often responds to an antacid or ulcer medication. However, if you have heartburn for weeks and it does not respond to conventional treatment, it is important to have it evaluated by your doctor.

Belly Pain

TIP 94

> Agonizing belly pain that worsens with any movement, accompanied by rigid belly muscles, especially in a person with a history of ulcers of the stomach or duodenum (the first part of the small intestine), is often a sign of a perforated ulcer.

Ulcer problems have a reputation for being long-standing, with frequent bouts of belly discomfort, including pain, indigestion, a feeling of fullness, nausea, and other symptoms. If you have ulcers, you may have gotten used to this discomfort by intermittently taking pills during severe bouts of pain.

This situation sets the stage for the ulcer to progress, eroding deeper and deeper into the lining of the stomach or duodenum (the first part of the small intestine, just below the stomach), until a hole is formed. When this perforation occurs, stomach contents are released into the belly cavity along with gas or air. Severe internal bleeding may also occur. This causes immediate, agonizing abdominal pain that worsens with any movement. Also, you may experience abdominal muscle spasms: The stomach contents will cause intense tissue reaction in the belly lining, resulting in a reflex belly muscle spasm with boardlike muscle rigidity. The belly area will thus feel like a solid board instead of soft to the touch.

This condition requires immediate medical attention at an emergency room.

TIP 95

An ulcer in the stomach or duodenum (the first part of the small intestine, just below the stomach) often causes pain in the upper-middle area of the belly, with or without bloody vomit and black tarry stools. It may wake you from sleep.

An ulcer is a sore on the lining of the stomach or duodenum. It can cause pain if it penetrates the wall or causes a spasm. (Some ulcers are painless.)

Inside the stomach the chemical hydrochloric acid and associated enzymes can change a piece of meat (or any food) from solid to liquid. The stomach and duodenum contain a mucous coating that covers the lining of their walls. This coating prevents the acid and enzymes from dissolving the stomach wall itself. Various substances—including nicotine, alcohol, caffeine, aspirin, some pain medicines such as ibuprofen (acetaminophen does not cause ulcers), and certain bacteria (see Tip 97)—diminish these defenses, causing ulcers to form. Also, people with hyperparathyroidism or hypoparathyroidism occasionally develop ulcers. (See Tip 187 for more about parathyroid conditions.) Note: Taking blood-thinning products, such as clopidogrel (Plavix) and warfarin (Coumadin), while you are taking aspirin increases the chance that you will bleed internally, particularly if you have an existing ulcer.

Bleeding into the duodenum may result in black tarry stools that are very sticky. Vomiting is also associated with the irritation caused by ulcers. Early medical treatment is necessary to prevent potentially life-threatening consequences, such as bleeding and perforation.

TIP 96

> Mild or severe upper-middle or left belly pain extending into the back with nausea and/or vomiting may be caused by pancreatitis. The pain is often less severe when sitting up and bending forward, while it worsens when lying flat on your back. Severe cases can cause diabetes, release dangerous chemicals into the blood, and produce internal hemorrhaging. Consumption of alcohol and foods high in fat content can cause this condition or make it much worse.

The pancreas is a narrow, bandlike organ one to two inches wide, extending behind the stomach across the upper belly area for three to six inches toward the left side. It has two major functions: to produce enzymes for the small intestine to digest food, and to make insulin, which is then dispatched into the bloodstream. If the pancreas gets inflamed, the release of its potent enzymes into the bloodstream or the surrounding tissues can make you very ill, causing internal bleeding and widespread tissue damage throughout the body. Destruction of the pancreas can also cause diabetes, since the hormone insulin is necessary to drive sugar from the bloodstream into body cells. Lack of insulin production causes hyperglycemia (high sugar levels in the blood).

The pancreas can become inflamed as a consequence of gallbladder disease. The gallbladder has a tube in common with the pancreas; if gallstones pass into this tube, they can block the outflow of the digestive chemicals from the pancreas. You can also damage your pancreas by regularly drinking alcohol; if your pancreas becomes inflamed, you should stop drinking alcohol forever. The mumps virus is another possible cause of pancreatitis. The pancreas can sometimes become in-flamed without any identifiable cause.

The symptoms of pancreatitis warrant emergency medical evaluation and treatment, in order to avoid serious complications. Blood studies can document damage in the pancreas.

TIP 97

A common, often curable, cause of recurrent ulcers of the stomach and duodenum is infection of their lining by a germ called *H. pylori*. The red light warning signals of this type of infection are episodes of upper-middle belly pain, with or without vomiting blood and/or passing black tarry stools.

For many years it was thought that stress caused ulcers. Relieve the stress, and the ulcer would heal, only to come again when the stress level was again increased. This is no longer considered totally correct.

The exact effect of stress on the development of ulcers has not been determined, but it is now known that a common cause of recurrent ulcers of the stomach and duodenum (the first part of the small intestine) is infection by a microscopic, rod-shaped germ called *Helicobacter pylori.* This discovery has, in many ways, revolutionized the treatment of ulcers. Antibiotics will eradicate the bacteria and prevent ulcers. Typically, the use of at least two antibiotics simultaneously, in addition to the medication used to shut off the acid in the stomach, treats the infection, achieves ulcer healing, and stops additional ulcers from forming.

Yet major questions arise. If an ulcer is caused by an infection, where did the infection come from, and how can you protect yourself from getting it again? At the present time, we have no definite answers to these questions. *H. pylori* occurs worldwide and is apparently acquired from the intake of contaminated food or water. But it is not known how to detect food contamination or how to kill the germ when preparing food. It is possible that it can be transmitted from one person to another within a household.

A doctor can determine if you have ulcers caused by *H. pylori* by looking into your stomach and duodenum with a special tube called a gastroscope. He or she will obtain a piece of the stomach lining (a biopsy) and will examine it for the *H. pylori* germs. In addition, there is a test that uses breath analysis to detect a by-product of the infection and, more recently, a blood test and stool test have been developed to detect the presence of the germ.

Of course, if you have an ulcer with heartburn (the backup of stomach acid into the esophagus), you should continue to avoid foods that cause these symptoms.

Ulceration can lead to serious hemorrhage as well as rupture of the stomach or duodenum, so it is very important to be evaluated and treated for this condition as soon as possible. If you are vomiting blood or passing black tarry stools, you should be seen on an emergency basis.

Persons with *H. pylori* are at increased risk of developing certain cancers: possibly an adenocarcinoma and definitely a MALT lymphoma.

TIP 98

If you experience upper-middle belly pain (with or without vomiting blood and/or passing black tarry stools), you may have an ulcer or inflammation in the stomach and/or an ulcer in the duodenum. Drinking alcohol may increase the risk of developing ulcers and also prevent the healing of ulcers that are already present. It can also make pancreatitis worse, increasing the possibility of fatal complications.

Alcohol is rapidly absorbed through the stomach lining and causes acid and enzymes to pour into the stomach in large volumes. The presence of excess amounts of these chemicals can lead to inflammation of the stomach, the formation of ulcers, and/or progression of ulcers already present.

When ulcers or inflammation of the stomach and duodenum (the first part of the small intestine) are a problem, abstinence from drinking is important. Alcohol may relieve the belly pain momentarily, but the condition will eventually worsen because alcohol consumption increases the risk that the ulcer will bleed and/or perforate in the abdominal cavity. Black tarry stools are often a sign of ulcers bleeding into the stomach or intestines.

Belly pain associated with pancreatitis from alcohol intake is potentially life-threatening. The pancreas, located in the upper belly, produces insulin to control blood sugar and the very caustic chemicals (or enzymes) that help in food digestion. When pancreatitis occurs, the substances that digest food begin to digest the pancreas itself. These caustic chemicals may also be released into the bloodstream with life-threatening consequences.

If you drink a large quantity of alcohol and suddenly develop nausea, vomiting, and severe belly pain, you are at risk of tearing the inside of your esophagus. This can cause severe bleeding and dehydration. Seek medical care to evaluate and treat this ailment and to get advice on how to stop drinking.

Belly pain with bleeding—vomiting blood or excreting black tarry stools—requires emergency medical care. (See Tip

125 for more information on black tarry stools and life-threatening bleeds.) Upper-middle and/or upper-left belly pain that extends to the back can be a sign of pancreatitis and also requires emergency medical care. (See Tip 96 for more information on pancreatitis.)

Note: The combination of drinking alcohol and smoking puts you at a much greater risk of developing these problems.

TIP 99

If you have upper-middle belly pain (with or without bloody vomit and black tarry stools), you may have an ulcer. Smoking makes stomach ulcers worse. It also increases your risk of stomach cancer.

Smoking may cause ulcers, and it definitely slows the healing of stomach and duodenal ulcers that are already present. Nicotine is an active drug that has a direct, injurious effect on the lining of the stomach and duodenum, and ulcers can consequently develop without healing.

Stop smoking, especially if stomach and duodenal ulcers are a problem. You are at a higher risk of hemorrhage, ulcers bursting into the belly cavity, esophageal and stomach cancers, and blockages in the arteries that supply the intestines with blood. Seek medical evaluation and treatment. If you are vomiting blood or have black tarry stools, you need emergency medical care. (See Tip 125 for more information on black tarry stools and life-threatening bleeds.)

Note: The combination of smoking and drinking alcohol puts you at a much greater risk of developing these problems.

TIP 100

Upper-middle belly pain, bloody vomit, and/or black tarry stools can be caused by certain pain pills. These medicines can cause ulceration of the stomach and duodenum, which may lead to the hemorrhaging and bursting of the stomach in the area of the ulcer. This problem has resulted in as many as 7,600 deaths in one year in the United States.

Aspirin, ibuprofen, Advil, Nuprin, Motrin, BC Powder, Goody's, and other similar medicines (known as nonsteroidal anti-inflammatory drugs, or NSAIDs) are heavily marketed for general pain relief and the relief of the joint pain caused by arthritis. The same medicines are prescribed by doctors in higher dosages for arthritis and other bone and muscle pains. Irritation and ulceration caused by long-term use of these drugs can be life-threatening when it results in hemorrhaging into the stomach or duodenum. You will develop bloody vomit, vomit that resembles coffee grounds in appearance, and/or black tarry bowel movements. Also, the ulcers can burst, causing corrosive chemicals in the stomach to leak into the belly cavity.

Take these medications only if necessary and only as directed. If you are experiencing belly pain, see your doctor immediately so that you can be evaluated and treated. There are other medications that your doctor can prescribe, along with drugs to prevent ulcer formation. Also, if you are already taking the blood thinners clopidogrel (Plavix) or warfarin (Coumadin), do not take any NSAIDs without first talking to your doctor. The combination of these medicines increases the chance of bleeding. If you experience belly discomfort and are vomiting blood, or if you note black tarry stools, seek emergency medical care. (See Tip 125 for more information on black tarry stools and life-threatening bleeds.)

TIP 101

Pain in the upper-right and/or middle belly area (with or without nausea and vomiting), often an hour or two after eating fatty foods, may be due to gallstones. If the upper-right belly becomes tender and the pain persists, and/or you develop a fever, the gallbladder may be infected.

The gallbladder is located in the upper-right area of the belly, under the liver. It serves as a reservoir for bile, a substance made by the liver to help digest fat and protein. When a fatty meal passes through the stomach and enters the first part of the small intestine (the duodenum), a hormone is released that stimulates the gallbladder to squeeze bile through the bile duct into the intestine. When bile is stored in the teardrop-shaped gallbladder, stones sometimes form. These stones may be forced into the gallbladder's narrow neck when it contracts (squeezes). As it attempts to force the stones through its duct opening, it develops spasms, causing severe pain in the upper-right area of the belly. Nausea, vomiting, and distention in the upper-right belly area are often present as well. The pain may be constant or intermittent, and may occur more often after eating meals high in fat content. Note: Gallstones are most commonly seen in obese women in their forties who have had several children.

If a gallstone is impacted in the neck of the gallbladder (like a cork in a bottle), the gallbladder will balloon out, become infected, and sometimes rupture. If a gallstone passes from the gallbladder neck into the common bile duct (a tube-like structure leading from the liver to the intestine) and blocks it, yellow jaundice will occur. Your skin and/or the white part of your eyes will turn yellow from the yellow bile backing up into your liver and bloodstream, spreading to all parts of your body. Blockage of the common bile duct can cause infection and/or even death.

Removal of the stones can save your life. Usually, the whole gallbladder is removed, using a fairly simple technique called laparoscopy, which involves inserting a special type of scope into the belly cavity.

If you experience symptoms even after your gallbladder has been removed, seek medical evaluation. In rare cases, gallstones can form in certain tubes inside of the liver. These can be removed with a procedure called endoscopy, in which a tiny camera device is inserted into the small intestine to help remove the stones.

If you experience upper-right belly pain often after eating fatty foods, with or without nausea and vomiting, seek medical evaluation as soon as possible. Fever indicates infection requiring immediate treatment. (See Tip 128 for more information on gallbladder disease.)

TIP 102

> Mild tenderness over the liver (the right upper area of the belly, just under the ribs), swelling of the ankles and/or belly, and yellow jaundice may be signs of hepatitis. Drinking alcoholic beverages to excess, and/or over a long period of time, can cause or worsen liver disease that leads to liver cirrhosis, liver failure, and death.

Drinking alcoholic beverages (whether liquor, beer, or wine) may cause injury to the liver. When an alcoholic beverage is consumed, the alcohol is rapidly absorbed through the stomach and small intestinal wall into the bloodstream. The breakdown of alcohol occurs mainly in the liver, where certain by-products cause alcoholic hepatitis, or inflammation in the liver cells. These cells may be destroyed and replaced with scars. The condition of a scarred liver is called cirrhosis. When enough liver cells are destroyed, liver failure and death follow.

The onset of liver cell inflammation from alcohol can be subtle, producing few symptoms. Instead of severe liver pain, you may feel mild tenderness over the liver and occasional nausea. As the inflammation and scarring progress, swelling will develop, first in the ankles and legs. Subsequently there will be swelling in the belly as fluid accumulates there. Liver failure will cause yellow jaundice and dark, tea-colored urine from the backup of yellow bile, which is made in the liver. This condition is readily diagnosable by a physician during a physical examination, with a blood test that measures liver enzymes, radiological studies, and sometimes a liver biopsy.

Liver inflammation is not a disease of "drunks." You do not have to be a heavy drinker to develop this condition. You may say, "I don't drink the hard stuff," or "I limit my drinking to beer," but this type of liver inflammation occurs in beer drinkers just as often as it does in liquor and wine drinkers. Alcoholic hepatitis, even when it is so severe that you turn yellow, can be reversed if you eliminate your alcoholic intake early enough and medical treatment is instituted. The consequence of restarting alcohol intake is often cirrhosis (scarring of the liver), causing liver failure and death. Cancer of the liver is also more common in patients with cirrhosis.

Individuals with any type of non-alcohol-related hepatitis (especially hepatitis C) are very sensitive to alcohol intake. It may increase liver inflammation and hasten the progression of liver destruction, resulting in cirrhosis. If you have liver disease, or if you have ever had alcoholic liver disease, do not drink any alcoholic beverages. Your doctor can help you stop. If you have cirrhosis, also be sure to avoid Tylenol (acetaminophen) and any other over-the-counter medication containing acetaminophen or any herbal product without first talking to your doctor. Many other medicines can further damage a cirrhotic liver. Always check with your doctor and/or pharmacist to make certain that all your medications are safe to take.

The symptoms of liver disease are red light warning signals that you need medical evaluation and treatment as soon as possible.

TIP 103

> An injury to the belly area can result in damage to the spleen, and a subsequent life-threatening internal hemorrhage many days after the accident. The warning signals may be worsening or recurring upper-left belly pain, often accompanied by left shoulder pain, and/or suddenly feeling weak or faint. These symptoms may be experienced many days after the injury.

The spleen is a spongy structure that is structurally similar to a grape, but is larger in size (it has a soft interior, and is covered by a capsule). Located in the upper-left area of the belly cavity, the spleen contains a large quantity of red and white blood cells. A severe blow to the belly area, from an incident such as an auto accident or a sports injury, may damage your spleen. Sudden weakness and/or fainting may indicate a life-threatening internal hemorrhage. If you have these symptoms after this type of injury, you need to be taken to an emergency room immediately. (See Tip 7 for more information on dizziness and life-threatening internal bleeding.)

Sometimes, however, the injury damages the capsule of the spleen, and there is a bulging out of the internal spongy material. The bulging contents may slowly continue to come out, eventually causing profuse bleeding. It can take several days for this to happen, so you may initially experience pain, and then the pain may go away and come back. Or you may develop an upper-left belly pain, which persists and worsens, and is accompanied by pain in your left shoulder—due to the nerve connections running on the inside of your back between the spleen and the left shoulder. Alternatively, you may suddenly become weak and faint hours or even days after the injury. It is very important to watch out for any of these symptoms after a blunt injury to the belly area. Recurring or worsening pain in the upper-left belly area, with or without left shoulder pain, deserves immediate attention at an emergency room.

If you are suffering from infectious mononucleosis, your spleen is more susceptible to rupture following a blunt injury to your abdomen.

TIP 104

If you are middle-aged or older and you have sudden lower-left belly pain with intermittent constipation or diarrhea, you may have diverticulitis. In most cases, the pain is persistent. Sometimes, though rarely, it can occur on the right side. If untreated, diverticulitis can cause the colon to rupture, requiring emergency surgery.

About 25 to 30 percent of Americans over fifty years old have diverticulosis (outpouchings in the colon wall). Diverticula are the small pouches that may be formed in the walls of the colon. As the colon squeezes the breakdown products of food to form stools, weakened areas of the colon wall bulge out, forming these dead-end paths. Note: Some doctors think that this disease is sometimes inherited.

Diverticula can become irritated and infected (a condition called diverticulitis) from stool that becomes lodged in these pockets and affects the integrity of the lining of the colon. If the infected diverticula burst, the infected material can spread throughout the belly cavity, causing pus pockets; drainage to the skin, bladder, etc.; scarring; and/or blockage of the bowel. Each of these conditions requires emergency surgery. Initially, the sole symptom of this condition may be mild lower-left belly pain. Diverticulitis can usually be treated with antibiotics. You can decrease your chances of developing diverticula by eating high-fiber foods (grains, fruits, and vegetables) and drinking lots of liquids to avoid constipation.

If you develop sudden lower-left belly pain, especially with a fever, seek immediate medical evaluation.

TIP 105

Mild lower belly pain or pain during sexual intercourse may be due to an infection of the female organs by a germ called chlamydia or other germs, including the gonorrhea germ. These bacteria can cause significant damage to the fallopian tubes and lead to infertility. They can also cause a life-threatening internal hemorrhage from a tubal pregnancy (ectopic pregnancy).

The symptoms may be few, but scarring from this type of infection can block the fallopian tube, through which the egg passes, causing infertility. Also, the scarring can interfere with the small fingerlike projections located at the end of the fallopian tubes, which pick up the egg when it bursts from the ovary each month. If it's not treated early, this may lead to infertility.

Fertilization normally occurs when an egg travels along the fallopian tube to its midportion and meets with sperm. After fertilization, the egg has approximately three days to travel through the rest of the tube into the cavity of the womb, where it grows on the wall and gets nourishment from the mother's body. If this trip is delayed by scarring from infections, the fertilized egg will attach in the wall of the tube and begin to grow there. Growth of the embryo can proceed only to a limited size (usually reached at six to eight weeks from the beginning of pregnancy) before the tube ruptures, with the potential of a life-threatening hemorrhage. Lower belly pain, weakness, dizziness, and a rapid pulse may indicate that this rupture has occurred. It requires emergency surgery.

It is important to know when your female organs are infected in order to prevent damage to your tubes, ovaries, and uterus. Mild discomfort in the lower belly or pain during sexual intercourse may be the only clues that infection is present, though it can usually be detected by testing at the mouth of the womb. Regular checkups with your doctor provide an opportunity for early detection. (See Appendix C, page 377, for more information about sexually transmitted diseases.) If you think you have had sexual contact with someone infected with chlamydia or gonorrhea, or if you have any of these subtle symptoms, tell your doctor as soon as possible.

TIP 106

Red light warning signals of a rare but serious infection called toxic shock syndrome are lower belly pain and a high fever, often with a bright red rash spreading from mid-body to all over the

body, and a "strawberry"-appearing tongue. Any
severe vaginal infection (sometimes associated
with the use of tampons) may lead to this ailment.

First observed in young menstruating women, toxic shock
syndrome is a rare but potentially fatal ailment. The onset of
the infection is sudden and it rapidly progresses from a high
fever and diarrhea with lower belly pain to a dramatic drop in
blood pressure and death.

This disease is more common in women who use tampons,
especially when they leave them in for longer than normal periods of time. (It is recommended that tampons be changed
every four to eight hours and not be used continuously
throughout the menstrual cycle.) Improper use may contribute to the development of the infection, which is caused by
a rare strain of commonly occurring bacteria. Severe vaginal
infections may be a clue that this ailment is present.

If treatment with antibiotics begins early, you can fully recover. If you have a high fever, lower belly pain, and a vaginal
infection, you should go to an emergency room.

TIP 107

The red light warning signals of lower belly pain,
lower back pain, and problems with urination—
such as slowing of the urine flow, increased frequency, a feeling of urgency to urinate, and/or
pain on urination—indicate many different possible ailments for men. Infections of the urinary
tract are important to recognize early since they
can cause serious kidney disease if left untreated
(see Tip 130). These symptoms can also be a sign
of prostatitis or, rarely, prostate cancer.

If you have an infected prostate gland (prostatitis), you may experience long-term pain and tenderness in the lower belly, pain in the lower back, or pain in the area behind the scrotum. You may also experience a burning sensation when you urinate and a slowing in the flow of your urine. When the prostate swells, it causes these symptoms by pushing against the urethra (the tube leading from the bladder through the penis to the outside). Prostatitis may appear with an inability to urinate and (rarely) with aching all over your body and a sudden high fever. The swollen prostate may be detected during a rectal exam, which would prompt further testing to make the diagnosis of prostatitis. Antibiotics are often the prescribed treatment.

A person with advanced prostate cancer may also find that he has difficulty urinating, and that he experiences a slowing of the urine flow, with dribbling after completion. The most common cause of these symptoms is a benign growth of the prostate gland, but pay close attention. When it *is* prostate cancer, there are usually few symptoms in the early stages. It can become advanced before it is detected. The PSA (Prostate Specific Antigen) blood test helps in the early detection of prostate cancer. All men age fifty and older (or forty and older for African-American men or those who have a first-degree relative with a history of prostate cancer) should receive a PSA test and a digital rectal exam annually. (See Appendix C, page 379, for details about this screening.)

Prostate cancer is much more common in men over sixty years of age, but it can also occur in younger men. In general, when you are old and get prostate cancer, the disease will act old as well in that it is usually slower growing and less aggressive than when you are younger. However, while it is less likely to spread and become fatal, there have been some cases of aggressive prostate cancer in older men.

If you are a man with lower belly pain and/or low back

pain, or urination problems, see your doctor as soon as possible for evaluation and treatment.

TIP 108

Lower-right belly pain and tenderness may indicate appendicitis. Appendicitis is a serious disease that can be fatal if the appendix ruptures.

Typically an early diagnosis of appendicitis allows it to be cured via surgery. But without proper treatment, the appendix can rupture, causing infection to spread throughout the belly cavity. This can be fatal.

Appendicitis is an inflammation of the appendix, a finger-shaped structure projecting from the first part of the colon. Swelling and inflammation at the spot where the appendix is attached to the colon can block its blood supply, leading to gangrene in its tip and, ultimately, its rupture.

Appendicitis often causes a bellyache. This pain may be vague and dispersed throughout the belly, and then will often (but not always) localize to the lower-right area of the belly, which will become tender to the touch. This usually occurs over a forty-eight-hour period and will continue to get worse until the appendix ruptures, at which time the pain may lessen. A sudden reduction of your pain may mean that your condition is actually worse, not better.

The pain of appendicitis is occasionally located in other areas, including the right side of the lower back (if the appendix projects up the back side of the colon) or the upper-right belly (if the first part of the colon is displaced to this area, as during pregnancy).

Other tip-offs that may accompany appendicitis include a low-grade fever (not usually over 101.5 degrees), loss of appetite, nausea, vomiting, diarrhea, and/or constipation. If you

suspect appendicitis, you should go to an emergency room for
immediate medical evaluation.

TIP 109

> Any woman who notices persistent and/or unex-
> plained bloating, abdominal discomfort or pain,
> and/or feeling full more quickly should be evalu-
> ated by a physician. While these symptoms have
> many common causes that are not serious, they
> could also be the first symptoms of life-
> threatening conditions such as ovarian or other
> types of cancer. Identifying the source early can
> improve the odds of successful treatment.

Bloating, pressure, and/or discomfort or pain in the abdomen
are possible symptoms of ovarian cancer. Others include feeling
full more quickly than normal, having trouble eating, and having to urinate often and/or urgently. These relatively common
symptoms are often caused by less serious conditions such as urinary tract infections or irritable bowel syndrome. The symptoms
may even be caused by totally innocuous conditions—like the
bloating regularly experienced around menstruation or the discomfort caused by an overactive bladder. However, you may want
to see a gynecologist to rule out ovarian cancer if these problems are new, severe, and occur continuously for several weeks.

Any woman who has reached sexual maturity should begin
to see her family physician or gynecologist on a regular basis
to be screened for ovarian cancer. It should be part of her routine health maintenance. During a pelvic exam, the doctor will
check the size and shape of the ovaries. However, ovarian tumors are difficult to identify early because the ovaries are situ-
ated deep within the body. If you have a high risk of this type
of cancer, your doctor will likely suggest additional testing.

Risk factors for ovarian cancer include:

- A strong family history of ovarian, breast, or colorectal cancer
- Increasing age (usually after menopause)
- Obesity
- Starting menstruation early (before twelve years of age)
- Having no children or having the first child after the age of thirty
- Going through menopause late (mid-fifties)
- Taking fertility drugs
- A personal history of breast cancer
- Undergoing estrogen and other hormone replacement therapy

If your doctor suspects ovarian cancer, he/she may use one or a combination of methods to evaluate you, such as a transvaginal ultrasound, CT scan, barium enema X-ray, colonoscopy, MRI, PET scan, laparoscopy (pictures taken of the ovaries and other pelvic organs through a tube placed in the lower abdomen), biopsy (tissue sampling), and blood tests. (For more information on ovarian cancer screening, see Appendix C, page 377.)

Bulges and Swelling in the Belly

TIP 110

If you have a pulsating bulge in your belly (more noticeable in a person of slender to medium build), it may mean that the aorta, the main vessel coming out of your heart, is ballooning out (aortic aneurysm). This is life-threatening if it leaks or bursts. It may also cause abrupt and/or worsening pain in the lower back, the side, or the abdomen. Sometimes the legs can turn blue and develop some pain. Often, an aneurysm is pain-less until it begins to leak and/or rupture.

The aorta, the large artery that leaves the heart, is the main passageway of blood to the rest of the body. It arches in the chest to follow the spinal column into the belly area, where it branches to both legs. If the wall of this blood vessel develops a weak spot, it can bulge out, much like the weak spots on an inner tube. The resulting bulge is called an aneurysm. The danger is that this aneurysm might rupture, causing sudden death from a massive hemorrhage.

The symptoms of an aortic aneurysm may be as subtle as vague belly pain or back pain, or a blood pressure difference be-tween both arms or an arm and a leg. On the other hand, symp-toms may be as obvious as the appearance of a pulsating palpable mass in the belly. The likelihood that an aneurysm will rupture increases as it becomes larger; when it reaches a certain size, it is important to get it repaired immediately, before it can burst.

Obviously this condition needs to be diagnosed before rupture. Therefore if you note a pulsating bulge and/or sud-den severe pain in your side, abdomen or lower back, you need to be taken to an emergency room immediately. Occasionally an aneurysm is detected during a routine physical exam, or during a routine abdominal X-ray. (See Appendix C, page 392.) Aneurysms are most often seen in smokers; in people with a family history of aneurysms (i.e., Marfan's syndrome); in people with high blood pressure, diabetes, and diseases where fatty deposits build up in the arterial wall; and in the el-derly. If you have an aneurysm and you suffer sudden, severe back pain, blood in your stools, and/or a change in the color of your legs, with or without sweating and/or weakness, you need immediate transport to emergency medical care.

Sense of Fullness

TIP III

If you have had ulcers, you feel full after eating small amounts of food, and you vomit frequently, you may have a blockage from scarring in the stomach or duodenum (the beginning segment of the small intestine). (See Figure 12.)

When ulcers of the stomach and duodenum heal, they are replaced with scar tissue. This tissue may shrink or contract, consequently strangling parts of the stomach or duodenum. Multiple ulcers produce multiple scars, sometimes causing blockage of the stomach or duodenum. This is an emergency.

During surgery the narrowed areas in the stomach or

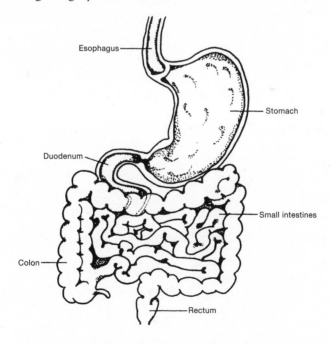

Figure 12. Intestines.

duodenum are opened and the scars are removed. Various segments of the intestines may need to be sewn together to bypass the blocked areas.

If you are feeling full or vomiting after small meals and have a history of ulcers, see your doctor for medical evaluation and therapy as soon as possible.

GENITALIA

Male

TIP 112

A usually painless lump or swelling in your testicle with or without a small lump in the groin could be serious. Testicular cancer is the most common cancer in young men. Most cases of testicular cancer are found between the ages of fourteen and thirty-four. However, they can occur later in life as well. Note: Testicular cancer is more commonly found in men whose testicle(s) did not naturally descend from the abdomen to the scrotum within the first year of life.

On the other hand, swelling, severe pain, and/or tenderness of the testicle can be the signs of another serious condition requiring emergency care.

If you notice a nonpainful, hard lump or swelling in your testicle, you need to see your physician for evaluation for testicular cancer as soon as possible. An ultrasound exam is an easy, painless way of detecting a tumor in the testicles.

Normally, within the first year of life, your testicles descend from your abdomen to your scrotum. If one or both do not descend, then your testicle(s) is surgically taken from your abdomen and placed in your scrotum. If this was the case with you, then you are at a higher risk of developing testicular cancer, even in the testicle that descended naturally. Let your doctor know so that he or she can monitor you closely. Other risk factors of developing testicular cancer include a family history of this type of cancer or a previous germ cell tumor in one testicle.

Many doctors believe that a self-examination of your testicles for lumps once or twice a month, beginning at puberty, may contribute to the early detection of cancer. However, self-examinations should not take the place of examination of the testicles by your doctor as part of your routine general physical exam. Discovering and treating testicular cancer at an early stage may save your life. Cure rates can be as high as 90 percent, depending on the type of cancer. (See Appendix B, page 367, for instructions on self-examination and Appendix C, page 378, for information about routine medical screening.)

Another cause of swelling in the testicle may be testicular torsion, in which the cord within the testicle gets twisted, cutting off blood supply to that area. This condition may also cause sudden and severe pain or tenderness. It can result from an injury to the testicles or strenuous activity, or it may occur spontaneously for no apparent reason. This is a true emergency and requires immediate medical attention. Treatment usually involves corrective surgery. If the blood supply is cut off for a long time, the testicle may be permanently damaged and may require removal. It is very difficult to save the testicles after six hours without treatment.

TIP 113

Irritation, redness, or tenderness occurring in the foreskin of the penis may be a sign of diabetes.

Blood testing to diagnose diabetes is important in men with these symptoms. Early therapy can decrease the complications of diabetes, including eye, heart, and kidney problems.

(Also see Appendix C, page 383, for information on diabetes screening.)

Male and Female

TIP 114

A nonpainful, raw-looking sore located on or near the penis, vaginal area, breast, or mouth may be an early sign of syphilis.

Initially syphilis begins as an ugly-looking sore with a hard rim around it, which heals on its own. During the next stage of the disease, you may notice a rash on your body (see Tip 151). This too will disappear on its own. The third and final phase of syphilis is when the infecting germ damages one of the valves (doors) in your heart and/or destroys brain cells, causing mental deterioration. Syphilis is curable if you receive antibiotics when you first notice the sore with the hard rim around it. Therefore if you have a nonpainful, raw-looking sore near the genitals and/or mouth, see your doctor as soon as possible. (Also see Appendix C, page 377, about syphilis screening.)

Note: Even if the signs of this disease disappear on their own, it is still very important to get treatment.

Female

TIP 115

> An early sign of a potentially serious infection of the female organs is a foul-smelling, thick, greenish discharge from the vagina, often accompanied by lower belly discomfort.

A discharge like this and/or severe lower belly pain that is tender to the touch, is often the first sign of a serious infection in the female organs. This infection can spread into your womb (uterus) and fallopian tubes, causing a condition called pelvic inflammatory disease (PID), and it can then also spread into your belly cavity.

Irritation of the vagina may be the only other symptom of PID. Alternatively, you may also have a fever of 101 degrees or higher, with weakness, nausea, vomiting, and generalized aching. As this condition progresses, pelvic pus pockets can form, and the infection can spread throughout the body. Scarring may occur in the area around the womb, which can impair fertility or even cause sterility. The scarring increases the risk of having a pregnancy in the fallopian tubes, which can burst, causing a life-threatening internal hemorrhage. (See Tip 192.)

Early medical evaluation and treatment of PID manifesting itself with a vaginal discharge (especially with lower belly discomfort) can prevent the dangerous spread of the infection.

TIP 116

> Yeast infections cause a red sore on the skin with a buttermilk or cottage cheese–type discharge from the vagina. These infections can also appear as white patches in the mouth. Repeated yeast in-

fections in the vagina, on the skin, or in the corners of the mouth may be a warning sign of diabetes or AIDS, so if you have repeated yeast infections, see your doctor as soon as possible.

Yeast infections in the vagina frequently occur after a woman takes an antibiotic, because the antibiotic kills the normal bacteria in the vagina, allowing the ever-present yeast to overgrow. Often a white, clumpy discharge (like cottage cheese) will occur. These infections usually clear up promptly after treatment with an antifungal medication.

Other common sites for yeast infections are on the skin near the groin, under the breasts, in the corners of the mouth, and even inside of the mouth. They are often accompanied by a burning sensation and a white discharge or plaque. These infections are usually also responsive to antifungal medication.

If you have repeated yeast infections, you should be tested for diabetes. High sugar levels in the blood, paired with a defense system that is defective in protecting against infection, will increase the incidence of yeast infections. Early diagnosis of diabetes with proper therapy can reduce your risk of serious complications, including kidney, blood vessel, and heart damage.

HIV infection can also create an environment for repeated yeast infections, because it weakens the body's immune system. Testing for HIV is appropriate for early treatment and preventive measures to limit the spread of the disease to others.

TIP 117

A wart in the genital area in women may be a warning sign of developing cervical cancer (cancer of the mouth of the womb).

A small, moist, fingerlike projection in the genital area may be caused by the human papilloma virus (HPV). The presence of HPV increases the risk that a woman will develop cervical cancer. Other risk factors include having a high number of sexual partners, intercourse at a young age, taking oral contraceptives, not using condoms, smoking, and increasing age.

It is important to see a physician on a regular basis for a thorough pelvic examination so that any malignant changes can be detected early. The Pap smear is the test used to check for abnormalities of the cervix. (See Appendix C, page 376, for details on routine Pap smear screening and HPV vaccinations.)

TIP 118

Any woman, particularly a postmenopausal older woman, who experiences redness, itching, white patches, and/or an ulcer that does not heal in or near the genitals, should seek medical evaluation. Cancer is one possible cause of these symptoms. Cancer in this region may not appear as a growth, but as an irritated or ulcerated area.

Thinning of the skin in the genital area occurs as a result of a decrease in the levels of the hormone estrogen and as part of the aging process. Cancer of the lips of the vulva (the outside of the vagina) usually occurs long after menopause. It is a type of skin cancer, but it may appear only as an irritated area, with or without ulceration. These red light warning signals need to be evaluated by your doctor as soon as possible. They may go unnoticed unless you see your doctor on a regular basis for checkups.

BOWEL MOVEMENT

Pain

TIP 119

Anal pain that does not improve with common hemorrhoid treatment needs medical attention. You could have a life-threatening abscess (pus pocket) around the rectum.

The anal area is very sensitive and can get quite painful when irritated. When severe pain occurs in this area, you will probably assume you have hemorrhoids. Most likely you will follow the basic treatment regimen of hot baths, foods or medications that soften your stools, and suppositories, expecting that the symptoms will go away. If the pain is actually caused by hemorrhoids, it will probably clear up with this treatment. But if you have formed a pus pocket (perirectal abscess), the waiting could be costly.

This type of pus pocket is formed when germs gain entrance to the anal wall and create an infection. The infection spreads through the anal wall into an open space between the muscles in the buttocks area. In this location the infection will not show up in the form of a boil or an abscess and will not come to a head. The germs will instead spread farther upward along the wall of the rectum, the pain caused by these abscesses increasing steadily. Surgery in which the pus pocket is cut open and drained is the only treatment to stop the spreading infection.

When you suffer from rectal pain, remember that it may not be caused by hemorrhoids. Do not allow the pain to persist too long before getting it checked by a physician.

Form and Frequency

TIP 120

> If you develop a change in your bowel habits (excluding a short episode of diarrhea) or begin to pass pencil-size stools, then you need to be evaluated. It could be an early sign of colon cancer. Other diseases affecting the intestines may also cause these warning signals.

The pattern of bowel movement frequency is an individual trait. Some people have a bowel movement every day, while others have one every other day or every third day. While any of these patterns may be normal for you, an important warning signal is when the pattern of your bowel movements suddenly changes. This is true whether they become more frequent or less frequent: It means that something is disturbing the normal function of the colon. In serious cases, that something could be cancer.

Another warning signal is a change in the diameter of the bowel movement. Usually the diameter of the formed stool that is passed reflects the diameter of the colon. A narrowing of the colon brought on by a constricting growth such as cancer may cause the stool to become consistently narrow in diameter.

Since early evaluation increases the chance of a cure for colon cancer or other diseases of the intestines, being sensitive to such minor changes in your body's function may save your life. When these occur, see your doctor. (See Appendix C, page 374, about early detection of cancer in the GI tract.)

TIP 121

> A bout of severe or prolonged diarrhea that results in severe dehydration can be fatal.

Severe or prolonged diarrhea can cause such severe dehydration (fluid loss) and loss of essential minerals that intravenous fluids and the replacement of minerals are needed on an emergency basis. Vomiting at the same time as the bout of diarrhea puts you at an even greater risk of dehydration. Also, emergency treatment may be needed even earlier in infants, the elderly, or people with chronic heart or kidney problems.

Sudden and severe infectious diarrhea can be caused by many different bacteria (*Campylobacter, Salmonella,* and *Shigella*) or by other germs called protozoans (*Entamoeba, Giardia,* and *Cryptosporidia*). They can make you sick with profuse, possibly bloody, life-threatening diarrhea.

One of the most severe types of life-threatening diarrhea is called pseudomembranous colitis, which is caused by a toxin from the *Clostridium difficile* bacterium. This type of diarrhea is often thick with blood and mucus and may look as though you are shedding the lining of your colon. It can result in dehydration accompanied by extreme toxicity, and may lead to death. This condition can also be caused by an antibiotic you've taken for an infection someplace else in your body—it may kill the normal bacteria that live in your colon, thus promoting the growth of the bacterium that causes pseudomembranous colitis.

Another bacterium that causes diarrhea is *E. coli*. Epidemics caused by one of the strains of *E. coli* result from eating under-cooked beef or ingesting water that has been contaminated. Also, though it is rare in the Western world, one of the most dangerous and infectious types of diarrhea is cholera. Before traveling abroad, particularly to developing countries, check with your local health department to find out about the appropriate preventive measures. Of course, if you have diarrhea and have traveled out of the country, it is very important to let your doctor know your travel history. In addition to germs, many illnesses can cause severe diarrhea.

In all cases of diarrhea you can become dehydrated (feeling dizzy, weak, etc.) and lose essential minerals, such as potassium. Therefore it is always important to replenish fluids and minerals as well as to diagnose the underlying cause of the diarrhea. Diarrhea that persists, contains blood, causes weight loss, is associated with fever, and/or wakes you up at night needs to be assessed by a physician immediately. If the dehydration progresses to the point that you feel dizzy when you sit up or stand up, or urine output stops altogether, call 911 or have someone take you to an emergency room immediately for evaluation and treatment.

TIP 122

> Bowel movements that occur less often than every three days usually mean you are consti-pated. Constipation can be a sign of various diseases of the colon, including cancer. Early di-agnosis and treatment can prevent serious com-plications.

After digestion is completed in the stomach and small intes-tine, food residues arrive in the colon. The colon is a muscular, walled tube five to six feet in length. It conserves body water by removing 90 percent of the water from the food residues (fecal material) as they pass through. If the transit time in the colon is too slow, too much water is removed, and the feces become hard. If the transit time is too fast, the fecal material will come out as diarrhea.

Constipation may be caused by weak muscles in the wall of the colon. Some individuals inherit this trait, while others weaken the muscles of the colon wall by using laxatives so frequently that they become dependent on them. Many medications, including certain ones for pain and blood pressure and those containing iron, can also lead to constipation. More serious potential causes include hypothyroidism (low thyroid gland function), many diseases of the colon, and cancer, all of which need to be tested for by a doctor. Early treatment of the underlying illness can often prevent serious complications.

Measures to relieve constipation are directed at improving the colon's ability to propel material through it. For example, increased water consumption helps prevent the fecal material from becoming too hard. Stool softeners also help. Some laxatives stimulate the colon wall to squeeze fecal material through more easily, while others irritate the bowel lining, which prompts the flow of water back into the colon to aid the flow of fecal material. The latter type of laxative is less desirable because it further weakens the bowel wall. The dietary fiber present in vegetables, grain, fruits, and pectin-containing fruit juices like prune juice, or in powder supplements can help facilitate the movement of feces through the colon, as can exercise.

If you have a bowel movement less often than every three days, or if you have experienced any change in your bowel patterns, see your doctor for an evaluation to determine the underlying cause.

TIP 123

> Cramping belly pain with a swollen belly, vomiting, and no bowel movement or passage of gas for more than twenty-four hours may mean that you have a life-threatening bowel blockage.

The bowel can be blocked either in the small intestine or in the large intestine. When it is blocked, fecal material and gas will back up. As the bowel attempts to force material through the blockage, you will experience severe cramping belly pain. If the location of the blockage is high up in the small bowel, vomiting will occur early on. If the blockage is low in the colon, vomiting will occur late or not at all.

Prior abdominal surgery is the most frequent cause of bowel obstruction. Scar tissue or adhesions occur after such surgery. Often these adhesions are "bandlike," stretching from one organ to another. These "bands" may cause entrapment of a loop of the bowel, kinking it sufficiently to block it. When left untreated, the entanglement may cut off blood circulation to the bowel wall, causing gangrene of the loop of bowel that is entrapped. If the blockage is not relieved by surgery, death can occur.

Colon blockage can also be caused by cancerous growths, severe inflammation and infection of the colon, and from thick, solid, hard stools accumulating in the rectum (an impaction). Impactions are commonly treated with enemas, but if this proves unsuccessful, blockages can often be removed by a health professional sticking a gloved finger up the rectum and carefully removing the hardened stools. This condition is more common in senior citizens or dehydrated bedridden patients.

If you are experiencing the symptoms of bowel obstruction, you should seek immediate medical attention.

Color

TIP 124

> Anytime dark or bright red blood appears in the bowel movement, early medical evaluation and treatment may save your life.

There are many reasons that you may pass blood from the rectum, but bright red blood that appears on your toilet tissue could be a sign of colon cancer. Detecting this cancer early could save your life. Colon cancer is one of the more common cancers. The thought that "It's only hemorrhoids" has put a lot of colon cancer victims in early graves. Remember, even if you have hemorrhoids, the rectal bleeding could also be from cancer; rectal bleeding should be considered a sign of cancer until proven otherwise.

Blood passing through the rectum can originate from anywhere in the gastrointestinal (GI) tract, from the mouth all the way to the anus. Possible sources of this blood are irritation and ulcers in the mouth, stomach, or intestines, as well as cancer in any of these areas. Even swallowing blood from a nosebleed can cause it to appear in your bowel movements. Usually the darker the blood, the higher up the bleeding site is in the GI tract. The stools can become black and tarry if the bleeding site is high enough. Sometimes the stools will look normal if there is a small amount of bleeding or if the blood has been absorbed into the rest of the body from the GI tract.

There are a number of procedures your doctor can perform to detect whether you are bleeding, and if so, where. A sigmoidoscope (a tube with a miniature video camera attached) can be passed into the anus to examine sections of the large intestine, and a colonoscope can be used to reach ALL of the large intestine (colon). Though these procedures sound intimidating, they are not nearly as uncomfortable as they might seem. An FOB (fecal occult blood) test—conducted by placing fecal material on a special card—detects blood in the stool that is not visible to the naked eye. A positive fecal occult blood test may indicate cancer or other less serious conditions such as hemorrhoids.

Also, when you bleed from the GI tract, you can develop anemia (a low blood count). This is a tip-off that you may have cancer of the colon, although there are many other reasons why you may have a low blood count.

If you have a close relative who has had colon cancer, a family history of colon polyps, a hereditary colorectal cancer syndrome, or a personal history of ulcerative colitis or Crohn's disease, you are at a greater risk for developing colon cancer. If this is the case, you should establish a program of routine colonoscopy, even if you are young and do not have any symptoms. Whether you have a family history or not, routine screening exams every five years and checking for microscopic amounts of blood in the stool every year may be life-saving. Colon cancer screening should begin no later than age fifty. Many doctors recommend that if you have a family history, you should get screened ten years earlier than the age your family member was diagnosed. For example, if your mother was diagnosed at age forty, you should start getting screened at age thirty. (Also see Appendix C, page 374, about early detection of cancer in the GI tract.) Early detection without any warning signs can lead to a cure; remember, this disease is not rare!

If you pass red or dark blood in your bowel movement, seek medical evaluation as soon as possible.

Note: A small amount of blood in the stools every day can lead to severe blood loss (severe anemia) with serious complications.

TIP 125

> Black tarry stools may indicate a hemorrhage from an ulcer of the stomach or duodenum. It is important to stop the bleeding and to rule out cancer as a cause.

When an ulcer in the stomach or duodenum (the first part of the small intestine) erodes into a blood vessel, hemorrhaging will occur. If the vessel is small, the blood loss may only be a trickle, but if the vessel is large, the bleeding will be brisk and life-threatening.

Bleeding a little from small vessels in the stomach or duodenum may go unnoticed. The blood can be spread out through the twenty feet of small bowel and the five to six feet of large bowel (the colon). This bleeding can be detected by conducting a fecal occult blood test, wherein a small amount of stool is placed on a special test card, which will change color if blood is present.

Blood originating from the stomach or duodenum often turns pitch black from chemicals (enzymes) in the small bowel. The stools can also take on a tarry consistency, especially if the bleeding is rapid. Belly pain caused by an ulcer may lessen when bleeding occurs because blood at the ulcer site coats the sore and protects it from the acid of the stomach. Nausea and vomiting are often not present unless there is a rapid flow of blood in the stomach.

There are other important warning signals of blood loss. You may become very weak from a low blood count (anemia) and, if the volume of blood loss is severe, standing up may make you feel weak and light-headed. Also, your blood pressure will drop and your pulse will rise. Under these circumstances death can occur rapidly unless emergency treatment is instituted.

If you have vomited blood, even if it only happened once and you otherwise feel fine, do not be complacent. Keep track of your pulse; if it is rapid (around 100 beats per minute), you must take immediate action. The pulse is the most sensitive measure of rapid blood loss, and if it is above 90, or higher than your normal pulse, emergency medical assistance is needed.

The safest approach is to always seek immediate medical evaluation and treatment when you first note that you are passing black tarry stools.

Note: You may get black, but not tarry stools from taking iron supplements or Pepto-Bismol, but the stools should return to their normal color within a day if you stop taking either product.

TIP 126

The passage of pale, putty-colored stools can be due to the blockage of substances normally secreted by the liver into the intestine.

Stools are normally dark, light brown, or green in color. If your stools become pale clay- or putty-colored, it means that there is a lack of bile (the substance that provides the normal pigment in stools) passing through the bile duct from the liver to the intestines. This indicates a blockage of the bile duct that can mean that you have liver disease, or that a gallstone or tumor is blocking the bile duct.

You should report this finding to your doctor as soon as possible, so that appropriate evaluation and treatment can be instituted. There is a potential for developing serious complications, including permanent liver damage.

URINE

Appearance

TIP 127

Any blood in the urine, even without pain, can signify a serious problem. Even if it's just one short episode and then your urine is clear, it is very important to be evaluated.

The most common causes of blood in the urine—kidney stones and a bladder or prostate infection—are usually accompanied by many additional symptoms. The agonizing pain of kidney stones or the burning discomfort and urinary frequency of a bladder or prostate infection will usually get people to the doctor early. But when blood appears in your urine without accompanying pain, especially if there is only a single episode, you may take a "wait and see" attitude. This attitude may have dire consequences.

If you see blood in your urine, tell your doctor as soon as possible. There are many causes of bleeding into the urinary tract, and one of them is cancer—which may be in the kidney, the ureter, the bladder, or the prostate. When they are still small enough to be curable, these cancers may not even cause pain. Blood in the urine may be the *only* clue for an early diagnosis.

Other causes of blood in the urine include infections, kidney stones, kidney disease (nephritis), an enlarged prostate, certain medications, trauma, and exercise (especially biking and jogging).

TIP 128

Tea-colored urine and/or yellow skin or eyes, with or without nausea and a sense of fullness, may indicate a chronic problem with gallstones. If untreated, this condition may cause liver failure, pancreatitis, bursting of the gallbladder, and/or a possible long-term risk of developing cancer of the gallbladder. Other possible causes of these symptoms are damaged red blood cells and many liver ailments, including hepatitis and cancer.

It is natural for urine to darken in color, especially in hot weather, when the body loses fluid through sweat and the urine becomes concentrated. If the urine turns a normal color upon drinking a half gallon of water, it could be that you were just dehydrated. However, if the urine contains excess bilirubin, no amount of fluid intake will affect the color, and it will be so dark it looks like tea. Bilirubin is normally processed in the liver and turned into bile. Bile is stored in the gallbladder and flows in a tube (the bile duct) to the intestines to help digest fat.

If gallstones form in the gallbladder and gain entrance to the bile duct, they often block the flow of bile to the intestines. The bile will then back up into the liver, causing inflammation. This results in a feeling of nausea and a sense of fullness. The backup of bile may also result in an accumulation of bilirubin in the blood. This yellow substance will turn your skin and eyes yellow and your urine a tea color. When the gallstone passes through the bile duct into the intestine, the urine will clear. But if another stone from the gallbladder gets stuck in the bile duct, these signs and symptoms will recur. If this continues to occur, the liver may become permanently damaged. Also, the blockage of the bile duct can cause the gallbladder to swell and rupture, resulting in toxic substances flowing into the belly cavity.

Another complication of gallstones can occur if a stone passes from the bile duct to a duct that is also connected to the pancreas. This tube carries very caustic digestive substances from the pancreas to the small intestines, and a backup of these substances can lead to the inflammation of the pancreas (pancreatitis), which may become fatal. (Refer to Tip 96 for more information on pancreatitis.)

It should be noted that liver ailments, including hepatitis and cancer of the liver, can also cause an excess of bilirubin in the blood, causing the characteristic tea-colored urine and yellow skin and eyes. Also, as red blood cells in the bloodstream contain bilirubin, any disease or side effect of a drug that breaks up red blood cells can cause bilirubin to accumulate in the blood.

If your urine turns tea-colored, or if your skin or eyes turn yellow, it is imperative that you seek medical attention.

TIP 129

A rare abnormal opening between the bladder and colon or other organs can cause you to pass bubbles while you urinate. This can make it seem as if you have a sputtering urine stream, as if your urine is being fired out of a machine gun. This condition can be caused by scarring or cancer. It may lead to serious infections. There are other

> causes of bubbles appearing in the urine, although in these cases, the urine appears foamy, like beer. It may be a side effect of a medication, or the result of a forceful urine stream or increased protein in the urine (proteinuria). Proteinuria can be found in people with conditions such as diabetes, hypertension, and kidney disease.

One of the most serious causes of "machine gun" urine flow is scarring or cancer resulting in connections (fistulas) between the bowel and the bladder. Also, these fistulas occur in persons with diverticulitis, ulcerative colitis, and Crohn's disease. The bubbles are caused by gas in the bowels passing into the bladder. If you urinated in the bathtub, bubbles would come up. The urine is foul-smelling, with debris from the colon. Seek evaluation and treatment by a urologist (surgical kidney and bladder specialist) as soon as possible.

Discomfort

TIP 130

> Discomfort and burning during urination, the recurrent feeling that you need to urinate, and frequent urination are all symptoms of a bladder infection. Repeated urinary tract infections may indicate a blockage in the plumbing system of your body and may cause kidney failure.

Bladder infections cause spasms resulting in frequent urination, a recurrent feeling that you need to urinate, and/or burning discomfort on urination. These infections are common and are treatable with antibiotics. Note: Women are more likely to have urinary tract infections. Due to the shortness of a woman's urethra (the tube connecting the bladder to the outside), a germ can enter her bladder more easily.

If a man has more than one urinary tract infection or if a woman has more than two in a row, there is an increased likelihood that an abnormality is impeding the free flow of urine. The abnormality may be in the tube that carries urine from the kidney to the bladder (ureter), in the bladder itself, or in the urethra.

A bladder infection that does not respond to antibiotic therapy is another red light warning signal. Anything that blocks, delays, or reverses the flow of urine can lead to a urinary tract infection that will recur unless the altered flow pattern is corrected.

Examples of such defects include:

- Kidney stones in the kidney or in the ureter (the tube that goes from the kidney to the bladder)
- A kink in the ureter
- A growth in any adjacent organ pressing on the ureter
- Vesico-ureteral reflux, a condition that allows urine to reverse its flow from the bladder back up into the ureter
- An abnormal valve in the urethra that partially blocks the urine flow from the bladder (most often seen in young boys)
- Urethral stricture, or narrowing of the urethra

If these problems continue uncorrected, they may cause recurrent kidney infections, resulting in kidney failure, the need to be routinely connected to a kidney machine (dialysis), or a kidney transplant.

Other causes of repeated urinary tract infections include disorders of the immune system and diabetes, which also require treatment.

If you experience painful, burning, or frequent urination,

you should see a doctor as soon as possible. Recurrent bladder infections or poor response to therapy indicate that you need a thorough evaluation by a urologist (surgical kidney specialist).

Frequency

TIP 131

> If you are having difficulty passing urine or cannot urinate at all, you need urgent relief. It is very important to determine the cause, which can be life-saving. Permanent correction is necessary to avoid kidney failure.

The inability to urinate requires urgent treatment. If you are not able to urinate, try sitting in a tub of warm water three to four inches deep. After a few minutes, try to urinate in the water. Though it is a more extreme solution, your discomfort can also be relieved by your being catheterized (having a tube placed into the bladder, usually by a doctor or a nurse). In situations when you can only partially empty your bladder, urine remains and accumulates there, which is a prime setup for infection. If left untreated, this type of infection can spread into the kidneys and destroy them.

What causes this problem of not being able to urinate? In men, an enlarged prostate gland may be blocking the flow of urine from the bladder, since the tube to the outside runs through the prostate. In both women and men, the urethra, the tube leading from the bladder to the outside of the body, may be narrowed by irritation and/or scars from an infection. Another cause of difficulty urinating may be the loss of strength in the muscles in the wall of the bladder, such that they are no longer strong enough to force urine through the urethra (the outflow passage). Diseases such as diabetes or multiple sclerosis can damage the nerves responsible for squeezing the bladder, while antihistamines and certain other over-the-counter medicines can constrict or partially close the bladder opening. This situation is self-perpetuating, as the longer the inability to urinate exists, the more the bladder wall expands, making it thinner and weaker, and this weakened wall is less able to squeeze urine out of the bladder.

If the passageway from the bladder to the outside of the body is blocked, effective treatment may include medication or a procedure to permanently unblock it. In men with an enlarged prostate, a PSA (prostate-specific antigen) blood test, an ultrasound, and/or a biopsy of the prostate tissue will help to determine if the enlargement is due to cancer. Early detection and treatment of cancer can be life-saving.

In conclusion, when you have difficulty urinating, see your doctor immediately or go to an emergency room for urgent relief. You need timely follow-up by a urologist (surgical kidney specialist) to evaluate and treat the underlying problem.

TIP 132

> Increased urination, weight loss, blurred distance vision, and/or increased thirst and appetite are highly suggestive of diabetes. The early stages of diabetes often have no symptoms, and the only way to know if you have it is to have your fasting blood sugar checked.

Weight loss is a sign of many disorders. But when you experience it along with an increased appetite and continuous thirst, you may have a certain type of diabetes. This condition also causes frequent urination, and may cause blurring of your distance vision.

Type 1 diabetes occurs when cells in the pancreas stop secreting insulin, the hormone responsible for transporting sugar in the blood to your body cells. Type 2 diabetes, on the other hand, is caused by a combination of insufficient insulin plus resistance to the action of insulin. When sugar increases in the blood, it will pass into the urine, pulling extra fluid along with it. You will drink more to replenish your fluids, and will continue to urinate a lot. The resulting changes in fluid and sugar levels often cause fluctuating blurry vision. The loss of sugar and water in your urine results in lost calories, dehydration, and hence weight loss. Due to the lack of insulin, the body cannot use the sugar as a source of energy.

Diabetes can be diagnosed by obtaining a fasting blood sugar test, which means you do not eat for at least eight hours before the test. A fasting blood sugar level of 126 mg/dl or higher suggests a diagnosis of diabetes. (See more about diabetes screenings in Appendix C, page 383.)

If you have diabetes, it is important to keep track of your blood sugar levels. You can use a glucometer with a test strip (available at pharmacies) to check the sugar in your blood. Also, your doctor can obtain a very helpful blood test, called hemoglobin A1c, to get an average assessment of your blood sugar level over a period of three months. This test is particularly valuable because the complications of diabetes are closely related to the long-term continuous control of blood sugar levels. Diagnosing this disease early is important so that treatment can be instituted to prevent complications. These include kidney disease, blindness, heart ailments, skin problems, and damage to blood vessels. Diabetes may also lead to the loss of toes, feet, or legs as a result of the buildup of fat deposits in the blood vessels, which blocks the supply of nourishment and oxygen to these specific areas of the body.

Type 1 diabetes is treated with insulin injections. A balanced diet with limited carbohydrates and minimal sugar intake is recommended. In addition, you should follow a healthy exercise program tailored to your needs.

In the case of type 2 diabetes, weight loss and exercise improve insulin action and are helpful. A special diet is also important, and sometimes medications are needed to control blood sugar levels.

If you experience increased urination, appetite, and thirst, often with weight loss, seek medical evaluation to determine if you have diabetes or if there is another cause for these symptoms.

MENSTRUATION (PERIODS), MENOPAUSE, AND PMS

Irregular Periods

TIP 133

Too much bleeding at the time of your period, an abnormally long period, or bleeding off and on between periods can be the sign of a serious disease.

Normally your body's menstrual periods occur every twenty-eight days, give or take seven days, and last approximately four days. If your periods occur less than twenty-one days apart or more than 35 days apart, if they last for more than seven days, or if you experience intermittent bleeding, then you have an abnormal bleeding pattern.

Abnormal vaginal bleeding can be an indication of cancer of the uterus (womb). Early diagnosis provides an increased opportunity for treating and curing the two types of uterine cancer—cancer of the cervix (mouth of the womb) and cancer of the endometrium (lining of the womb)—both of which can produce abnormal vaginal bleeding. Remember, this abnormal bleeding does not have to be heavy to indicate cancer; even a small amount of bleeding between normal periods or after intercourse can be significant.

Heavy menstrual bleeding can occur from common, usually noncancerous tumors of the wall of the uterus (fibroid tumors, or leiomyomata). These tumors can compress the blood vessels in the wall of the uterus and distort them, prompting heavy vaginal bleeding. They often need to be removed because they can cause severe pain and they have the potential to become so large that they press on other organs, such as the bladder or rectum. There are also medications that may shrink these tumors.

An overgrowth of the lining of the womb, though noncancerous, is another cause of excessive and prolonged vaginal bleeding. This condition, usually a result of hormone problems, causes irregular shedding of the lining of the womb and thus abnormal, often heavy, menses. It may be precancerous.

Women should begin yearly Pap smears when they become sexually active, but no later than when they turn twenty-one years old. Pap smears can detect cancer of the cervix early, even before abnormal bleeding occurs. (See Appendix C, page 376, for details on Pap smear/pelvic screening.) Note: Pap smears do not detect cancer of the endometrium, and the appearance of abnormal vaginal bleeding is usually the only clue that this type of cancer is present.

Birth control pills suppress eggs leaving the ovary and alter the hormone that causes the lining of the uterus to grow. Women who take them may experience sparse periods as a result of a decreased amount of uterine lining growth or increased bleeding due to changes in the hormone level. While scant bleeding is quite normal, heavy bleeding should not continue beyond two months. Report to your doctor any heavy bleeding that soaks more than one pad or tampon every two hours.

Fortunately most abnormal vaginal bleeding—whether it's too much or for too long—is not due to cancer. Usually the cause is more easily treatable. However, seek medical evaluation by your doctor as soon as possible, because even certain non-cancerous growths can turn into cancer. Also, continued blood loss can result in a dangerously low blood count (anemia), which may require blood transfusion or treatment with iron.

TIP 134

If you are not pregnant and you have irregular menses, miss your periods, and/or have fluid leaking from engorged breasts, you may have a tumor of the pituitary gland, which is located on the undersurface of your brain. Another sign that this may be the case is if you have limited peripheral vision.

The following signs may indicate that you have a tumor of the pituitary gland:

- The onset of puberty before the age of nine
- A sudden abnormal change in your usual pattern of menstruation—for example, missing periods for several months (when not pregnant)
- A feeling of "fullness" in your breasts or a milky white discharge from your nipples (when not pregnant)
- Limitations in your peripheral vision. You cannot see objects coming from either side when you are looking straight ahead. Your vision is like that of a horse wearing blinders (see Tip 19).

The pituitary gland produces hormones that regulate many other glands in the body. A pituitary tumor alters production of these hormones, which often results in changes in the activity of the glands that the pituitary gland regulates, such as the ovaries, which drive the menstrual cycle, and the breasts, which produce milk. A high level of prolactin, a hormone produced by the pituitary gland, suggests a tumor.

The above symptoms are all indications that a tumor may be growing in the pituitary gland. Early medical evaluation and treatment can cure this abnormal growth.

Note: Shingles (a painful rash caused by a virus), sexual foreplay with the nipples, hypothyroidism (low thyroid gland function), and medications such as Thorazine and oral contraceptives can also cause nipple discharge.

Missed Periods

TIP 135

Prolonged failure to menstruate in the absence of pregnancy usually means failure of one of the glands or the part of the brain involved in providing a normal menstrual cycle. It is important to determine if there is a serious underlying cause.

When an egg bursts from the ovary (ovulation), it leaves behind a remnant of the egg that produces hormones. These hormones make the lining of the uterus grow, preparing it to accept the fertilized egg. If fertilization does not occur, the lining of the uterus is shed via menstruation, and the cycle begins again. The menstrual flow consists of the shedding of the lining of the uterus (womb) mixed with blood. If any of the above events fail to take place, then the lining of the uterus will not grow, it will not be cast off, and there will be no period or menstruation.

Glands other than the ovaries are also involved in providing a normal menstrual cycle. The failure or abnormal function of these glands can cause missed periods, obesity, hair on the face, and acne. Prolonged failure to menstruate may be a sign that serious gland problems exist. Menstrual periods can be reinstituted with birth control pills, but it is still important to determine the underlying cause so that it can be treated.

Other hormone problems (such as excess estrogen) can also lead to a lack of ovulation. In this case the lining of the uterus will grow, but there will be no shedding or menstruation. Accumulation of the lining of the uterus may lead to a cancerous growth as early as six months after you start missing periods. It is also a common cause of infertility.

Keep in mind that you can fail to menstruate, have a negative pregnancy test, and still have an ectopic pregnancy. (See Tip 192.)

Prolonged failure to menstruate without pregnancy requires timely medical evaluation. Also, girls over the age of fifteen who have never had a menstrual period should be evaluated to determine the underlying cause and to implement appropriate therapy.

Pain and PMS

TIP 136

> Painful menstruation and PMS are not serious disorders, but some of the drugs used to treat them can have life-threatening, addictive effects.

Premenstrual syndrome (PMS) is a cycle of symptoms that may include a combination of the following: headache, breast swelling, bloating, and emotional symptoms. It usually begins sometime within two weeks of a menstrual period and it may continue throughout the period and up until a few days afterward. Menstrual pain appears to be caused by specific hormones called prostaglandins, which alter the muscle walls of the womb and its blood vessels. Specific over-the-counter medications (nonsteroidal anti-inflammatory drugs), including ibuprofen and Naproxen, stop the production of these prostaglandin hormones. Starting the medicine at the appropriate dosage a few days before your period is often very effective treatment for the pain. Your doctor may decide to prescribe a diuretic (water pill), an antidepressant, and/or hormones to treat the various symptoms of PMS, which include bloating, mood swings, and cramping. Exercise, diet modifications, and stress reduction techniques can also improve PMS symptoms.

Though you may be tempted to treat your symptoms with tranquilizers or narcotics, keep in mind that taking these on a regular basis is potentially addictive and can have a serious negative impact on your mental and physical well-being. Also, narcotics are not an effective way to treat either PMS symptoms or menstrual cramps because they do not affect the production of the prostaglandin hormones that are responsible for these symptoms.

Bleeding After Menopause

TIP 137

> Vaginal bleeding after menopause is a warning sign of possible cancer.

Menopause normally occurs in women at around the age of fifty and it signals the end of menstrual periods. Menopause happens because the ovaries run out of eggs and stop producing the estrogen necessary for menstruation. The menstrual pattern may become irregular before it stops altogether, which is called perimenopause, and it may also be accompanied by hot flashes. During a hot flash you will suddenly feel overheated and may even break out in a sweat that lasts for two to three minutes. When twelve consecutive periods are missed, you are in menopause, and any bleeding afterward is abnormal. The stage of menopause can be confirmed by certain blood studies, but it is often unnecessary to do these tests.

Recurrent vaginal bleeding after menopause is abnormal and may be an early warning sign of cancer, especially endometrial cancer (cancer in the lining of the womb). When this occurs, you should seek prompt medical evaluation. Early diagnosis and treatment may improve your chances of survival.

Starting at age thirty-five, women who have a family history of hereditary nonpolyposis colon cancer (a risk factor for endometrial cancer) should get annual screenings for endometrial cancer by getting an endometrial biopsy. Other risk factors for developing endometrial cancer include:

- Obesity (being more than sixty pounds overweight)
- Menstruating before age twelve
- Reaching menopause after age fifty-two
- Not having children
- Ovarian disease (polycystic ovaries)
- Use of Tamoxifen (a medication used to treat breast cancer that acts by interfering with the activity of the hormone estrogen)

GROIN

TIP 138

A bulge of tissue often located in the groin area or around the belly button may be a hernia. Hernias are potentially dangerous and usually warrant repair.

Hernias are most common at the belly button or in the groin. A hernia occurs when a hole opens up in the muscles that constitute the belly wall or other muscular walls. Belly contents push through the hole, particularly when the pressure inside the belly cavity increases with activities such as lifting, straining, and coughing. The hole often gets larger over time, increasing the possibility of belly contents pushing through. If a segment of intestine pushes through the hole, it may become so kinked that it blocks the flow of the bowel's contents. This kink could also cut off blood supply to the bowel, potentially leading to gangrene (death of part of the bowel). This condition can be fatal and warrants emergency surgical treatment.

When a bulge is noted, it is important to determine if the contents inside the bulge can be pushed back in. As long as they can, no immediate danger exists, but you should still consult your doctor about possibly repairing the hernia. Don't ignore a hernia because you think it's small; it can still be very serious. Should the bulge become stuck, especially if it is tender and painful, urgent medical evaluation is needed.

HIPS, BUTTOCKS, LEGS, AND ANKLES

Hips, Buttocks, and Legs

TIP 139

Swelling, pain, and tenderness in the groin or leg may indicate the presence of blood clots, which can travel to the lungs.

Irritation of the walls of the veins is a prime setup for blood clots, because the blood can back up in these vessels. One sign that blood clots may be forming is if the back of the lower leg often hurts and is tender to the touch. This condition is known as phlebitis, meaning "inflammation of veins."

There are many causes of phlebitis, including:

- The pooling of blood in the legs along with certain dilated and damaged veins near the surface of the skin (varicose veins)
- An injury to one of the legs
- Sitting for long periods of time (often during a trip in a car or airplane)
- Lying in bed for an extended period of time (being bedridden at home or in the hospital)
- Cancer of the lung, colon, or blood, which may produce chemicals that attack the veins of the legs and cause

phlebitis (this is sometimes the first indication that a cancer exists)

- A generalized inflammation of blood vessels that develops with diseases of the connective tissue, such as lupus

Phlebitis is potentially deadly because a large piece of the blood clot in a vein of the leg might break off and travel through the blood vessels from the leg to the lungs. A clot in the lungs produces shortness of breath and an inability to oxygenate the blood, which can be life-threatening. (See Tips 62 to 64, 81, 175, and 249.) It is therefore urgent that you see a doctor for evaluation and treatment, including a blood thinner if appropriate.

TIP 140

Pain in your legs, hips, and/or buttocks when you walk could be from arthritis but could also be from clogged arteries. When occuring in the leg, it is usually only in one. When the blockage of the arteries is total, gangrene of the leg and infection can occur. This infection may then spread to the rest of your body.

Pain in the legs during activities such as walking that is relieved during rest is usually due to insufficient blood flow to the legs. During activity the leg muscles require more blood, and when they do not receive it, you feel pain. The distance you can walk before the pain occurs is determined by the degree of blockage in the artery to your leg. A severe blockage may bring on the pain after walking only a few feet, and a less severe blockage may allow you to walk without pain for as much as a quarter of a mile. In very rare cases, the pain occurs at the first attempt to walk but then disappears after you have been walking for a while. If the blockage is in the arteries of the thighs, then the pain will be in the calves. A higher blockage will cause pain in the hips, buttocks, and thighs—this type of blockage is more commonly seen in patients who smoke, or have diabetes or high cholesterol.

If a blood clot forms in the markedly narrowed area of the artery, then a complete blockage of the artery will follow, with severe leg pain. If the blood flow is interrupted for too long, causing gangrene, there is risk that a life-threatening infection will spread throughout the body. In this scenario, amputation of the leg may be necessary.

If you experience pain in your leg when you walk, you should seek medical evaluation as soon as possible. It is best to correct the problem before total blockage occurs. Circulation may be restored by cleaning out the blockage: The artery can be reopened at the narrowed area with a small tube tipped with an inflatable balloon. Surgical repair is also possible: One end of a small piece of blood vessel can be sewn to the blocked vessel above the site of the obstruction, while the other end is sewn below the site of the blockage. This will allow blood to bypass or detour the site of the obstruction. A third approach is to inject a substance into the blood vessel that can dissolve the blood clot.

TIP 141

A deep, aching pain that starts in the lower back or buttocks and travels down the back of the leg can be due to the irritation of one of the nerves in the spine. If left untreated for many weeks or months, the compression of the nerve root can lead to nerve damage, causing permanent weakness, numbness, or even regional paralysis.

The soft disks between the cords of the vertebral bones in the back provide cushions for the spine. As we age, these disks can become brittle, a condition known as degenerative disks. When they bulge or tear, the disks may press upon large nerves as they leave the spinal canal, causing symptoms in the parts of the body where the strained nerve usually travels. If this happens in the neck area, symptoms of weakness or numbness may travel into the arms. If it happens in the lower back, pain may travel into the buttocks and down the back of the leg, making it difficult to lift up the toes. This can cause the foot to slap the floor while walking.

In the great majority of cases of degenerative disks and disk herniations, the symptoms will resolve on their own in six to eight weeks. When this does not occur, your doctor may need to see you in order to prevent permanent damage. Even when the pain resolves, it is important to continue to maintain good back care. This may include plans for long-term weight loss, core body exercises like yoga and pilates, as well as swimming and water aerobics. Also, be sure to use back healthy techniques when lifting heavy objects (e.g., lifting from a squatting position "with the legs" instead of bending forward).

Note: While a stroke can also cause weakness or numbness of a limb, unlike nerve root compression, strokes are usually pain free.

TIP 142

Unexplained and persistent bone pain, particularly if it wakes you in the middle of the night, warrants evaluation by a doctor. It may be cancer originating in the bone or another cancer that has spread to the bones.

You need to be able to distinguish this deep, aching kind of bone pain from pains in the joints, which are usually due to overexertion or arthritis. In the early stages of bone cancer, the pain may be intermittent, but it will often get worse at night. As the cancer develops, the pain will become more severe and constant, and may also worsen with movement.

Cancer originating in the bone can involve the bone itself or the core of the bone where blood cells are made. It is best to have these serious problems ruled out when you have severe bone pain before seeking therapies such as spinal adjustments, manipulations, acupuncture, etc. Early treatment of cancer can make a difference in your outcome.

Ankles

TIP 143

> General swelling of the ankles can be the sign of a serious disease.

Standing too long causes swelling of the ankles, especially if you are overweight or pregnant. If this is the cause, the swelling is not significant and should clear after a night of rest. On the other hand, lower leg swelling may be an important sign of a serious disease, including inflamed or blocked varicose veins. It may indicate that you have heart, liver, or kidney disease; a low-functioning thyroid gland; or cancer elsewhere in your body. Alternatively, it may appear as a side effect of a medication.

You can determine the severity of the swelling with a simple test: The first step is to be up and about (out of bed for at least an hour). Next, while standing, press your thumb firmly over your shinbone for five to ten seconds, then release it. If the imprint of the thumb remains, significant swelling is present. The deeper the pit, the worse the swelling. If the swelling does not disappear after one night of rest or leg elevation, it is important to seek medical evaluation.

SKIN

Bites

TIP 144

The bite of an animal with rabies can be fatal. Therefore, if you are bitten by a dog, cat, raccoon, fox, skunk, horse, bat, or any other warm-blooded animal, you need immediate medical attention.

Note: You can also get rabies from exposure to the saliva of a rabid animal (via contact with an open wound or your mucous membranes). For example, bats flying in the room of a sleeping person or near an awake, unattended child have been reported to have spread the disease to the individual, even when there has been no evidence of a bite.

Animals with rabies, including dogs, cats, horses, skunks, bats, foxes, and raccoons, can transmit their disease to you through a bite. The virus can also be transferred if the animal's saliva comes in contact with an open cut on your body or with your mucous membranes—for example, your eyes or mouth. If you get the appropriate immunoglobulin and vaccination shots after contact with a rabid animal, you can avoid developing the disease.

Fortunately the time between your exposure to the disease and the appearance of symptoms is normally within two to twelve weeks (though this can happen over a shorter or much longer period of time). If you are bitten by a pet that appears healthy, observe the animal for ten days and begin to get post-exposure rabies treatment only if it begins to act strangely. If the pet is rabid or suspected rabid, you will need immediate treatment, which involves receiving a series of shots. If you are bitten by a wild animal, such as a bat, raccoon, skunk, fox, or most other carnivores, the animal should be regarded as rabid unless it can be captured and proven negative with laboratory testing. If the animal is not captured, immediate vaccination should be considered. This is crucial, since untreated rabies is almost one hundred percent fatal.

If you are going to be traveling to developing countries in Asia, Africa, and Latin America, especially if you plan to spend time hiking, consult with your health-care provider about getting a preexposure vaccination against rabies. In these countries, dog rabies may be more common and preventive treatment can be difficult to obtain. Keep in mind that preexposure vaccination does not offer full protection; however, it reduces the amount of postexposure therapy needed and allows you to go a longer time before getting it.

Of course, whenever you get bitten by an animal, follow standard first-aid protocol; wash the area immediately with soap and water, apply antibiotic ointment, etc.

TIP 145

If you have had a severe allergic reaction, the next time it could be worse—even life-threatening. Swelling of the lips and throat and difficulty breathing after a bee sting or exposure to another allergen are red light warning signals. Skip di-

> rectly to Tip 169 if you are currently experiencing these symptoms.

Serious allergic reactions can get worse with every episode. Vital areas of the body can become more sensitized, resulting in increasingly severe reactions with each exposure. Such sensitization can lead to massive swelling, with closure of the windpipe, shock, and death.

If there is any possibility that you might be at risk of a severe allergic reaction to any biting or stinging insect, food, cosmetic, plant, dye, and so on, carry an emergency treatment kit with you at all times (see Tip 169). An immediate shot of adrenaline after a life-threatening reaction—with sudden shortness of breath, wheezing, and weakness—could save your life. Some treatments can reduce the severity of these allergic reactions. Consult your doctor or an allergist.

TIP 146

> Human bites are serious. The bitten area can become infected, requiring treatment by a physician.

Believe it or not, there are more germs in a human mouth than that of a dog. If someone's teeth go through your skin, even if it is a shallow cut on your hand from punching their mouth, watch out. The wound may look fine for the first forty-eight hours, only to develop redness and swelling later on, followed by pus. Immediate antiseptic cleansing and the removal of the damaged tissue from the wound as soon as possible by a health professional can often prevent the spread of infection. Also, get a tetanus shot if you have not had one in the past ten years.

TIP 147

> Antivenom shots may save your life if you are bit-
> ten by a poisonous snake. The area of the bite is
> often swollen and painful.

If the snake's poison gets into your bloodstream, death may be
sudden unless you can get immediate treatment. Examination
of the snake (dead or alive) can determine if it is poisonous,
helping the doctor decide what treatment is necessary. Do not
attempt to capture or kill the snake if it puts you in danger of
another bite, but, if safe to do so, bring the snake or its rem-
nants to the doctor's office. At the very least, try to get an accurate description of the snake.

The following steps should be taken at the time you are
bitten, if they will not cause excessive delay in getting you
medical care:
- Stay calm.
- Try to immobilize the area that has been bitten.
- Wipe the wound with a clean cloth to remove poison left
  on the skin.
- Do not apply a tourniquet, cut open the bite, or suction
  or tamper with the wound in any way.
- Seek emergency medical care.

TIP 148

> The bite of a tick can cause staggering, a lack of
> coordination, or even paralysis. These symptoms
> usually clear when the tick is removed.

A tick bite on the back of the neck near the base of the skull
can cause "tick paralysis." The tick attaches, burrows its head

through the skin, feeds on your blood, and regurgitates a toxin into your skin.

If you stagger and become uncoordinated for no apparent reason, examine the back of your neck and other parts of your body for a tick. Whether or not you find one, it is important to seek immediate medical evaluation and treatment if you have these symptoms. If you *do* find a tick, it is important to remove the entire insect. This can be done by putting alcohol on the tick to relax it, and then stretching the skin and pulling the tick off with tweezers. Doctors recommend placing the tweezers at the base of the head (where the neck would be) pulling gently, and the tick should become loose.

Discolorations

TIP 149

> Changes in your pattern of bruising, little black or red dots on your skin (which may look like pin-size bleeding spots), nosebleeds, gum bleeds, rectal bleeds, or bleeding too long after a cut are all indications that you may have blood-clotting problems from an ailment or as the side effect of a medication (such as aspirin or other pain pills).

Blood clotting requires a cascade of many different chemical reactions. If anything interferes with this cascade of reactions, your blood may not clot normally. For example, certain clotting substances are made in the liver, so if you have a liver ailment, you may bleed more easily. Also, hemophiliacs are born without a specific clotting factor and need to be given a replacement for it.

Particles in your blood called platelets prevent blood from leaking out of the capillaries, your tiny blood vessels. Platelets also release chemicals that aid in the clotting process, so if you begin to bruise or bleed easily, it could be the result of a low platelet level. This latter condition might be a side effect of a medication you are taking or the result of a disease that destroys platelets, such as an enlarged spleen or hemolytic-uremic syndrome, which is more commonly seen in children. (See Tip 214.)

These symptoms require immediate medical attention, since it places you at a higher risk of bleeding in your brain (a stroke) or bleeding internally at some other site in your body.

TIP 150

In rare cases, a darkening and thickening of the skin around the back of the neck, armpits, and groin of an adult (usually over forty years of age) can be the sign of a serious disease, including certain cancers and/or diabetes.

If you notice that your skin is darker than your normal skin color in places such as the back of the neck, the armpits, or the groin area, you may have a harmless skin condition known as acanthosis nigricans. In rare cases it can be the symptom of a dangerous disease. Two extreme possibilities are cancer of the stomach or of the colon.

Acanthosis nigricans is commonly found in dark-skinned individuals or obese people with high levels of the hormone insulin who are at risk of developing diabetes. (See Appendix C, page 383, about diabetes screenings.) Weight reduction may improve diabetes, but not necessarily the skin discoloration.

If you have this condition, you should see your physician for an evaluation to determine if you have any of the serious associated diseases.

TIP 151

Dark spots (brown in African Americans and Asians, pink to dusty red in Caucasians) on the palms of the hands and/or soles of the feet may be a sign of syphilis or Rocky Mountain spotted fever. If treated early, fatal complications can be avoided.

While the telltale dark spots of Rocky Mountain spotted fever are usually accompanied by a high fever and severe headache (see Tip 162 for additional information on Rocky Mountain spotted fever), dark spots may be the only sign that the syphilis germ is living in your body. Also, since Rocky Mountain spotted fever is caused by a germ transmitted by a tick bite, finding a tick on your body is an immediate tip-off that you may have contracted the disease. Syphilis, on the other hand, is a sexually transmitted disease (STD). It is important to diagnose and treat early because the damage it may do to the body organs cannot be reversed. It is particularly dangerous in pregnant women, as it can be passed to the fetus and cause life-threatening complications for the baby.

Urgent treatment of either ailment may be life-saving.

TIP 152

Turning blue often indicates that you are getting an insufficient oxygen supply. This is commonly seen in children with inherited heart abnormalities and people with lung disease, but it can also occur as a side effect of certain medicines and from other causes. If your skin turns blue, you need immediate medical evaluation and possibly treatment.

Most people think that when the skin turns blue, it is from an inability to breathe. It is true that cutting off your oxygen supply will make you turn blue in a hurry. But there are also other possible reasons for this skin discoloration.

Normally oxygen attaches to a protein called hemoglobin in your red blood cells. This occurs as blood travels through the vessels in your lungs. The oxygen is then transported throughout the body by the red blood cells for use by all of the body's organs. This gives a normal pink color to the skin of Caucasians and to the mucous membranes (the lining of the mouth, nose, eyes, and so on) of all people. If the oxygen supply to the blood is cut off for any reason, then the hemoglobin circulates without oxygen, giving the skin a blue appearance, called cyanosis.

As mentioned, certain medications and other maladies can also lead to this red light warning signal. They can alter the hemoglobin in some of your red blood cells such that they are unable to carry oxygen, turning your skin a bluish color.

If your skin and/or lips turn blue, you need to be evaluated by a doctor immediately to determine the underlying cause. Your organs may not be receiving sufficient oxygen, which can have a long-term negative effect on your health. In many cases therapeutic intervention can reverse the disorder.

TIP 153

A low count of red blood cells (anemia) can cause paleness, fatigue, and a rapid pulse with or without shortness of breath. In certain cases you may feel dizzy or pass out. Diagnosing and treating causes of a low blood count can be life-saving.

There are many reasons why you could have a low blood count, including:

- Poor nutrition
- A disease that destroys the bone marrow, where red blood cells are made
- A drug that causes red blood cells to break apart
- Cancer in the colon with a slow bleed
- Heavy menstrual flow

It is important to seek medical attention to diagnose the cause of your low blood count because, in many cases, early treatment can cure the underlying ailment. This is also important because—apart from the possibility of a serious underlying condition—a very low blood count can do significant damage to your organs all on its own. Red blood cells have the vital role of supplying oxygen to your brain and heart. For that reason, when your blood count is dangerously low, an immediate emergency blood transfusion may be needed to save your life.

The doctor can easily tell how low your blood count is by drawing a sample of your blood and performing a simple test. (See Appendix C, page 384, about blood test screenings.) If you have symptoms of fatigue, shortness of breath, and/or pale skin, you should see a doctor right away to determine your blood count and get a thorough evaluation. If you also have a rapid pulse, the bleeding may be sudden, requiring immediate transport to an emergency room.

TIP 154

> If you notice a serious skin sensitivity to the sun, check the side effects of the medicines you are taking. Other possible causes include lupus and other diseases.

Hundreds of medicines can make your skin sensitive to the sun. There are two main types of reactions:

- **Phototoxic reaction.** This type of reaction occurs immediately after you begin taking the offending medication, because it causes the skin to be much more sensitive to the ultraviolet light of the sun. This can create such an intense sun sensitivity that a normally harmless amount of sunlight may burn your skin.
- **Photoallergic reaction.** This type of reaction is due to an allergic sensitization of the skin by a drug. It appears after being on the medicine for a while (24 to 72 hours, or even as long as a few weeks). Skin exposed to the sun may develop eczema, hives, small fine bumps, hard plaques, or blisters. There is a chance that these reactions will continue to recur for some time after the drug has been discontinued.

Note: Even visits to sun-tanning salons can cause these symptoms.

Since so many different medicines can cause these reactions, consult your doctor to determine if a drug you are taking may have these side effects. You can also consult with your pharmacist and ask for a copy of all of the package inserts for the medicines you are taking (both prescription and nonprescription) to see if skin sensitivity to the sun is a side effect, and, indeed, if there are any other side effects.

Both phototoxic and photoallergic reactions can be very serious and may even be fatal. If you develop a reaction, you should discuss it with your doctor as soon as possible to determine the safest way to deal with it (for example, by changing medicines). Don't make these decisions alone.

(See Tips 169 to 171 about other life-threatening allergic reactions to medications.)

Freckles, Moles, Bumps, Warts, Lumps, Plaques, and Patches

TIP 155

Irregular-shaped, dark, multicolored, enlarging, bleeding, itching, or painful moles need to be frequently checked for early detection of malignant melanoma. Early treatment can be life-saving. Being seen within days or a couple of weeks is much better than within months. The sooner, the better.

Moles that can turn into cancer (malignant melanoma) may be raised, like regular moles, or flush with the skin surface, like large, dark freckles. They often begin as an abnormal growth of pigment cells, which then darken with exposure to the sun. Pigmented lesions on the pads of the hands and soles of the feet (more commonly seen in African Americans), and dark streaks under the fingernails or toenails can also be signs of melanoma. There is even a rare type of melanoma that has no pigment.

If you have a mole or moles with any of the following features (which suggest they are cancerous), see your doctor or a dermatologist right away:

- Asymmetrical shape—not a smooth, round circle, like a regular mole
- Multicolored appearance with shades of brown, black, gray, red, and white
- Large size (greater than the eraser end of a pencil)
- Growth in size over a period of time (unlike regular moles, which do not grow)
- Itching, pain, or bleeding
- Any kind of change in a mole

The incidence of malignant melanomas is increasing in the population at large. They are most prevalent in adults over thirty years of age and are actually the most common cancer in people who are between twenty-five and thirty-five. The following increase your risk of developing this cancer:

- You have been diagnosed by a physician as having certain types of moles that are precancerous.
- Members of your family have had a malignant melanoma.
- You are light-skinned and easily sunburned.
- You have been exposed to a great deal of sunlight, especially in childhood and adolescence, and have had multiple sunburns in the past.
- You have many moles of any kind.

Monitor your moles on a regular basis, including those in the genital area, where changes are often missed (the use of a mirror may be helpful). Avoid tanning beds. If you are at a high risk of developing a malignant melanoma, your dermatologist or primary care doctor should assist you in monitoring your moles. If you detect a suspicious mole, see your doctor or dermatologist as soon as possible so that it can be removed early and examined under a microscope. A simple removal of the mole is all that is necessary if it is less than .75 millimeters and without special features as seen under the microscope by a pathologist. If there is a need for further surgery, consider getting a thorough evaluation by someone who specializes in melanoma treatment.

Try to preempt this problem by using sun protection routinely after six months of age. The UVB sun protection factor should be SPF 30 or greater, and the container should indicate that both UVB and UVA light are blocked. (Also see Appendix C, page 380, for routine screening information.)

TIP 156

> A pearly bump on the face or other area of the skin exposed to the sun is a potential sign of skin cancer. Early treatment is important.

If you have spent lots of time in the sun, and have developed a round, pearly bump on your face, you may have a skin cancer known as basal cell carcinoma. The face, like other areas of the skin exposed to sunlight, is a common site for this type of tumor. Basal cell cancers are usually slow-growing and do not spread, but there are exceptions. Basal cell carcinomas are most often diagnosed in people forty years of age and older. However, they can also be found in people as young as in their twenties. Albinos are particularly at risk of getting this skin condition.

A diagnosis is made when your doctor cuts off a slice of the bump and inspects it under a microscope. Surgical removal can usually cure this condition. If you suspect you may have skin cancer, do not wait. See your physician early.

TIP 157

> Freckles on the lips, in the mouth, or on the inside of the lips are associated with growths in the intestines, which can become cancerous (Peutz-Jeghers syndrome).

In the unusual, inherited condition called Peutz-Jeghers syndrome, freckles occur on the lips and on the inside of the mouth. They may be present at birth, develop over time, or even disappear over time. It is important to determine whether they are associated with dangerous polyps (growths) in the intestines.

If you have freckles that follow this pattern, an evaluation by a doctor may be appropriate to find and remove any polyps. This may help you to avoid intestinal bleeding and to prevent cancerous growths. Sometimes the polyps may already be malignant, in which case early surgical removal can be curative.

Let your doctor know if you have this warning signal, especially if you have a family member who has had cancer of the colon. (See Tip 226 for more information on this disorder in children.)

TIP 158

A flat deposit or plaque that is yellowish to white in color may appear in the skin above or under an eye, at the side of the nose, or in another area on your body, such as under the elbow. It can be the sign of a serious cholesterol problem.

The deposit or plaque will usually be oblong in shape rather than round like a cyst, and will be about a quarter of an inch wide. If you have one of these, it will usually not cause you any discomfort. The plaque is inside of your skin, though, so you will not be able to remove it by squeezing out its contents.

The plaque is probably a fatty deposit, and as such, it may be a warning sign that you have a dangerously high blood cholesterol and/or triglyceride level. The cholesterol can invade the wall of an artery, eventually resulting in total blockage of the vital blood vessels that provide nourishment to the heart or brain, causing a heart attack or stroke.

These yellow, cheesy-looking plaques are a warning message that you should heed. See your doctor and have your blood checked for cholesterol and other fats. Plaques can be removed for cosmetic reasons, but they may recur, unless the underlying problems are resolved. Most importantly, high cholesterol and other fat levels in the blood should be lowered with diet and/or medicines. (See Tip 174 for more information on an elevated cholesterol level, especially in senior citizens. Also see Appendix C, page 382, for information on cholesterol screenings.)

Infections

TIP 159

> Occasionally a skin infection will spread very rapidly, often causing red streaks or red, tender, swollen areas on the skin. The infection may also be associated with fever and feeling ill. It can be fatal.

A wound that has become infected with germs is red and slightly swollen. Infected cuts or abrasions are common and, if kept clean, will usually improve within twenty-four hours. But if the redness of an infection spreads and there is more swelling and pain, watch out. Certain nasty germs, such as streptococci and staphylococci, can spread rapidly. Red streaks running up an arm or leg from the site of the infection indicate a rapid and dangerous spread of germs. If you have diabetes or are taking prednisone, you are especially vulnerable to these types of infections.

If your infected wound is getting worse, consult your physician immediately. Your doctor can do tests to determine which antibiotic will be the most effective to combat the infection.

Itchy Skin

TIP 160

> Itching all over without any sign of a rash can in-
> dicate cancer, liver disease, kidney disease, a psy-
> chological problem, an infection, a blood or
> glandular illness, or a potentially serious reaction
> to a medication.

Most of the time itchiness has an obvious explanation, such as
dry skin. But seemingly unwarranted itching can be an early
sign of cancer, including lymphoma and leukemia, particularly
when associated with a low-grade fever. A diffuse itching,
caused by the accumulation of substances normally broken
down in the liver, may also be the first sign of liver disease.

Therefore itching all over your skin may indicate the need
for a thorough medical checkup. If it is a sudden onset, particularly after you begin a new medicine, notify your doctor
immediately before continuing to take it. The itching may be
an early sign of an allergic reaction. If this is the case, a second
dose could be life-threatening.

Rashes

TIP 161

> A bull's-eye red rash, with or without joint pain,
> could be a sign of Lyme disease from a tick bite.
> However, other skin conditions can also appear
> as red circles. Any bull's-eye rash requires diag-
> nosis by a physician.

The initial event in Lyme disease is often this skin rash: a reddened area, circular in shape, with more intense redness at the center. The rash itself will clear up without treatment, but the disease will spread to other areas of the body. You may initially have flu-like symptoms and/or a fever. As the disease progresses, you may also develop joint pain, weakness, and fatigue. Eventually the brain and heart will be damaged.

If you have this type of rash, contact your doctor immediately. Treating Lyme disease with antibiotics during the rash phase is very effective and will usually cure it. When the infection spreads to other parts of the body, treatment becomes more complicated. Chronic Lyme disease can be a very disabling illness.

Although Lyme disease is not very common, it does pose a threat, especially in the Midwest and along the Atlantic coast. The tick that transmits the disease is smaller than most, so the bite often goes unnoticed.

TIP 162

Rocky Mountain spotted fever is identified by a high fever and a rash that appears as little red/purple pinpoint blood spots or splotches. The rash usually begins on the wrists and ankles or the palms of the hands and the soles of the feet and then spreads over the body. It is transmitted by ticks, so you will reduce your risk if you use insect repellent and remove any ticks from your body after each day spent in the woods.

Rocky Mountain spotted fever germs gain entrance to the body through the bite of a carrier tick, and then spread throughout the body. Within fourteen days, you will develop the rash and a fever, often accompanied by weakness, chills, a headache, and a generalized flat rash. This rash has an unusual appearance and pattern that does not often occur in other acute illnesses associated with a fever. Since this disease can be fatal, immediate medical attention is necessary, even if the tick is not found. In 10 percent of cases, there is only a high fever and possibly a bad headache with no rash until it's too late for you to be saved. If you develop an unexplained fever in the summertime, especially if you live in areas where cases of Rocky Mountain spotted fever are commonly reported, seek medical attention. In the United States, these include North Carolina and Oklahoma.

Also, ticks need time to spread disease, so check your body for ticks immediately after you return from the woods. Dousing a cotton ball with rubbing alcohol and holding it over the tick will relax the creature so that you can pluck it safely off of your skin with a pair of tweezers. Make certain you remove the entire tick by placing the tweezers at the base of the head (where the neck would be) and pulling gently.

TIP 163

> Everyone with hives (a rash that is widespread, raised, red, swollen, intensely itchy, and may look like giant mosquito bites) ought to have at least one medical evaluation, because hives can occur with blood cancers.

Hives are most commonly the result of a generalized allergic reaction to foods, pollen, or medication. Exposure to heat and cold, sunlight, stress, and infections can also influence the development of hives. The recurring nature of hives is the most frustrating feature. Once they appear, they may improve, only to pop out again a few days later, without any known reexposure to the precipitating factor.

Certain blood-borne and other cancers can cause hives, such as leukemia and cancer of the lymph system. Although this rarely occurs, it is advisable to check with your physician, who may do more extensive testing if he or she is suspicious that a serious condition is causing the hives (also see Tips 154, 169, and 170).

Sores

TIP 164

> If you have had a draining sore for months, and it will not heal—particularly if it is on your neck (usually around the angle of the jaw), your fore-arm, or your foot—you may have a serious body-invading fungus infection. There are many other treatable causes of nonhealing sores that also re-quire immediate medical evaluation and treat-ment, such as scrofula, which is a cousin of tuberculosis.

Fungus infections are always life-threatening in anyone who has an impaired immune system. Most of them are limited to the skin and nails, but some can invade the body and spread to the internal organs. It is important to see your doctor as soon as possible for tests on the material draining from the wound so that early treatment can be instituted. Note: The most common presentation of a fungus infection is generally a rash, but the type of deep draining sore that is described above is more common in people with impaired immune systems.

Yeast infections are also fungal. They are usually confined to the vagina, around the corners of the mouth, or in the mouth. A life-threatening blood-borne yeast infection is more common in patients with poor defense mechanisms, including people with AIDS, people who are receiving chemotherapy for cancer, and people taking steroids and other drugs after receiving an organ transplant. Yeast infections are usually responsive to antifungal agents.

TIP 165

> An ulcer on the skin that does not heal after a maximum of one month could be skin cancer and needs to be evaluated.

Occasionally people attribute a sore or ulcer that does not heal to an injury, when actually it was not caused by trauma. Any ulcer that does not heal within a month should be evaluated by a doctor to rule out cancer or another underlying disease.

BACK

Back Pain

TIP 166

> Back pain that originates just above the belt line on one side of the lower back, often accompanied by blood-tinged urine, indicates kidney disease that may require immediate medical attention. The pain is sometimes associated with fever and urination problems and is worsened when you gently tap the affected area.

This type of back pain is sometimes accompanied by fever and/or pain and difficulty urinating. Also, pain is more likely to occur on the sides of the back and in the abdomen than exclusively in the center of the lower back (see Figure 13).

It is important that you seek medical evaluation and treatment for this type of back pain as soon as possible. It may be caused by a kidney stone, which often requires medical intervention for removal. Also, if there is a kidney infection, antibiotics are required. (See Tip 130 for more information on evaluation and treatment of urinary tract infections. Also, see Appendix C, page 376, for information on preventive kidney screenings.)

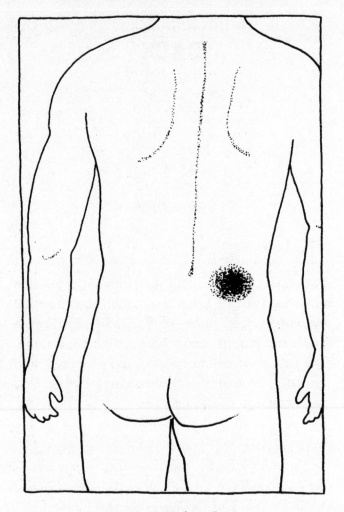

Figure 13. Kidney Pain.

TIP 167

The sudden onset of severe back pain could be a compression fracture, which occurs when there is general weakness in the bones caused by a loss of bone density. It is more common in senior citizens and requires increased bed rest.

Sudden agonizing back pain can be the result of a softening of the bones and a vertebral fracture. Weak bones are more susceptible to fractures and collapse.

Osteoporosis (a loss of bone mass and softening of the bones) develops gradually and usually without symptoms. It often begins in older women after menopause, since the ovaries produce less estrogen, causing the bones to lose more calcium. All postmenopausal women should be evaluated for osteoporosis. Keep in mind, however, that it can also begin earlier in life, especially in patients with lupus, rheumatoid arthritis, and/or those who are taking steroids. It is more common in people who are small in size, are not physically active, are Caucasian or Asian, and who smoke. The early diagnosis and treatment of osteoporosis is an important preventative measure. Vitamin D and calcium supplements can often be very helpful if taken in the proper doses. (See Appendix C, page 384, for more about bone density screening.)

Bones that bear weight, such as the vertebrae of the spine, are the first to experience a change from the softening, which is why older people tend to lose height. If a vertebra collapses in what is called a compression fracture, it can produce agonizing pain.

Confinement to bed, often resulting from fractures of the spine, hips, and legs, is the enemy of senior citizens, as it may lead to an early death from blood clots or lung infections. Lying still creates an environment where blood is more stagnant and more likely to clot, so doctors often recommend that elder patients with fractures use a brace so that they can get out of bed and move around, rather than being sedentary.

Ideally, seniors should attempt to avoid fractures in the first place. New treatment options are available to increase the thickness (mass) of the bones and thus strengthen them. This preventive therapy may be appropriate for those with osteoporosis and vitamin D deficiency. However, the side effects and costs of the treatment must be considered before starting it. If you have osteoporosis, you should discuss the pros and cons of this therapy with your physician.

TIP 168

> Severe back and, in certain cases, leg pain, especially when accompanied by a fever, may mean you have a serious infection rather than a backbone problem such as a disk herniation or spur. If the pain is caused by an infection, often the lower back will be tender to the touch. Senior citizens and/or debilitated people are more vulnerable to these massive infections.

At first the symptoms may seem mild: some redness around a cut on your leg (which only appears to be a minor infection), pain during urination, and/or a chest cold that just seems to get worse. Afterward you develop a major symptom: an overwhelming and agonizingly severe pain in your lower back and legs. The pain is so severe that you don't mention your earlier symptoms when you visit your doctor—they seem so minor in comparison. The doctor can easily assume your back pain is being caused by a run-of-the-mill muscle strain or lumbar disk disease and may make the wrong diagnosis. This error could have dire consequences.

Though it happens rarely, minor infections can spread rapidly through the bloodstream to locations throughout the body. Fever and severe back pain, frequently accompanied by leg pain, may be the signal that this has happened. Sometimes if a massive infection has overwhelmed the body's defense mechanism, there will be no fever. It is crucial that the victim is immediately treated by a doctor, with life-saving intravenous antibiotics.

An important message here is that you should always carefully report all of your symptoms to the doctor, even if they seem minor.

Note: Sometimes a minor infection will not spread throughout the body but will advance into a serious pocket of pus, called an abscess, which often needs to be drained by a surgeon. (For an example of this, see Tip 119.)

....

PART TWO

....

General Symptoms and Signs

(More Common in Adults):

Not Body Part–Specific Conditions

ALLERGIC REACTIONS

TIP 169

A serious, life-threatening allergic reaction, especially starting with a swollen, tingling, or numb tongue, lips, and/or throat and breathing problems may progress rapidly, becoming fatal within minutes. Hives and/or itching may also occur in the upper body. The allergic reaction can be reversed if medical treatment is started immediately.

Allergic reactions are common. They can follow exposure to just about anything, but they usually occur from foods, certain plants, bee stings, or medicines. They are not dose-related—you can have a serious reaction following even a tiny exposure. And you can also develop allergic reactions to things you were not allergic to in the past.

Most allergic reactions result only in an itchy rash and swelling. Occasionally the swelling will become severe when it occurs in locations where there is loose skin, like the area around your eyes or groin. This massive swelling looks bad but is generally not dangerous; it responds well to medical treatment.

Sometimes, however, allergic reactions occur very rapidly and become life-threatening. The main cause of death in these cases is an inability to breathe, because severe swelling has blocked the airways. In addition, there is a collapse in blood pressure from the sudden dilation (expansion) of blood vessels throughout the body. If you exhibit the following symptoms within thirty minutes of exposure to an allergen, then you are in danger of a full-blown allergic reaction and need to get to an emergency room immediately, or need to receive an epinephrine shot on the spot:

- Swelling of the tongue and mouth
- Hoarseness, a "lump in the throat" feeling, difficulty swallowing
- Breathing problems, a cough, chest tightness, wheezing, and croup
- Dizziness, with a cold sweat and/or profuse sweating
- A pale or blue appearance
- Abdominal cramps and/or vomiting
- A loss of consciousness

Be prepared! If you have had a severe allergic reaction in the past, it may be worse next time. Know the early symptoms of a severe allergy attack so that you can tell if you need immediate life-saving medical treatment. Also, ask your doctor for a home epinephrine kit—it contains a single shot of the drug epinephrine, which you can inject into your muscle. This medicine opens your airways and tightens your blood vessels, thus saving your life. However, the effects of the shot wear off within a few hours, and you will need to be admitted to an emergency room for observation and/or further treatment.

To prevent allergic reactions, you need to first become familiar with your allergies. Make a record of all allergic reactions you have experienced and what caused them. The following are some of the most common substances to which people are allergic (called allergens):

- **Foods:** shellfish, soybeans, nuts, milk, eggs, MSG, sulfites
- **Insect bites:** bees, wasps, ants
- **Drugs:** penicillin (most common), aspirin, sulfa-based drugs, ibuprofen or other nonaspirin pain medicine
- **Radiographic contrast material:** the fluid injected into you during a study such as a CT scan (a special computerized X-ray), an IVP (a special X-ray of your kidneys), angiography (special X-ray study of your arteries), etc.

An allergist is a medical specialist who can help you identify your specific allergies and teach you how you can avoid exposure to them. (In some cases he or she may recommend that you begin getting weekly allergy shots that will help immunize you to your allergies.) Inform any doctors and medical staff involved in your care of all of your allergies, especially if you are allergic to any medications or to the contrast material injected into you during X-ray procedures. Consider purchasing an engraved bracelet listing your allergens; your pharmacist should know where you can obtain one. This may be useful in emergency situations.

There is a rare but potentially fatal ailment called angioedema that presents itself similarly to an allergic reaction. The red light warning signal of this condition is the isolated and painless swelling of a random body part—the tongue, the mouth, a hand or a foot, et cetera—without itching. People who have angioedema can spontaneously develop swelling in the windpipe, cutting off their air supply. These swellings are rare and often occur for no known reason, though they have been occasionally associated with high blood pressure and heart medications known as ACE inhibitors (check with your pharmacist or doctor to determine if any of the medications you are taking fall into this category). Urgent evaluation and treatment of this type of swelling is necessary. (See Tips 170 and 171 about allergies to medications. See Tip 231 for more information on allergies in children.)

TIP 170

> Allergic reactions to medication commonly occur in the form of a rash or an upset stomach. Other symptoms include a low-grade fever, aching joints and muscles, and a sore mouth and tongue. Though rare, life-threatening reactions may occur.

People can have reactions to both prescription and over-the-counter medications, including headache pills, aspirin, laxatives, and sinus pills.

Severe allergic reactions to medications are rare, and they usually only occur immediately after starting (or restarting) a medication. In life-threatening situations associated with weakness, shortness of breath, wheezing, vomiting, and/or dizziness, emergency epinephrine shots are necessary.

A skin rash is one of the most common reactions to medication. This type of rash is generally very itchy, and its appearance will vary from patches of small red bumps to hives. It may occur anywhere on the body. It will usually not result in serious complications if the offending medication is stopped soon after the symptoms appear. Contact your doctor immediately so he/she can decide whether it is safe for you to stop the medication and start alternative treatment. Besides helping you to control the situation (and prevent future allergic reactions), he or she can also prescribe treatments to alleviate the rash.

However, while rashes are a common side effect, there are many other possible reactions. For example, another common one is a sore tongue or mouth. Anytime this occurs, it should be considered a reaction to a medication until proven otherwise.

You may also experience stomach irritation in reaction to a medication. This is quite common with over-the-counter pain medicines. Make sure you notify your doctor immediately and stop the medicine, because stomach ulceration can occur and may lead to a life-threatening hemorrhage. (For more on ulcers caused by medication see Tip 100.)

In some cases, symptoms of an allergy to medication may be quite vague, including fatigue, a low-grade fever, and aching all over the body. It may seem like the flu, but if your condition gets worse after a week, it is time to go back to the doctor, because you may have developed a severe toxic effect from the medication.

Many medications can also ultimately cause a severe inflammatory reaction in the kidneys or liver, which could result in kidney failure and/or chemical hepatitis. It is prudent to be on the lookout for this phenomenon when starting a new medication. Always consult your physician immediately if you think a medication is causing any of these reactions.

To further protect yourself, avoid the following bad combinations of these common medications. Do not take any ibuprofen (Advil) if you are currently taking an NSAID [Daypro, Indocin, Ketoprofen, ketorolac (Toradol), meloxicam (Mobic), naprosyn (Aleve)], or if you are on blood thinners, such as Coumadin. Do not take any aspirin while taking Coumadin without first checking with your doctor. Note: In certain cases, *low-dose* aspirin (81 mgs) can be taken with Coumadin. In addition, review the package insert available from your pharmacist for information on side effects and drug interactions relating to all of the medications you are taking.

TIP 171

> On rare occasions certain medications can cause fatal reactions, starting with a rash with targetlike lesions. This distinctive symptom is usually accompanied by sores in the mouth, nose, eyes, anus, and/or genital region, and a low-grade fever. Though extremely dangerous, this condition is treatable and curable if caught early.

This condition is called Stevens-Johnson syndrome, and it can cause a severe allergic reaction that may damage a large area of the skin, causing it to blister and slough off. When this condition develops, seizures, coma, and death can follow, so early diagnosis and treatment are essential. If you develop a rash after starting a medication, get in touch with a doctor (preferably your own physician) immediately.

TIP 172

> Weakness and/or tingling sensations in the legs, which usually progresses to the arms and upper body and causes breathing difficulties, may ultimately lead to paralysis and death. This rare ailment, known as Guillain-Barré syndrome, sometimes follows certain infections, vaccinations, or surgeries.

When Guillain-Barré syndrome develops, the body's immune system begins to attack its own nerves. The syndrome eventually interrupts the transmission of nerve impulses to the areas of the body controlled by these nerves. This will gradually result in the onset of paralysis in the legs (usually starting from the toes and moving up the body), accompanied by an increased difficulty in breathing. Death may occur if medical treatment is not instituted.

Most people recover with proper treatment, but rehabilitation is lengthy. One form of treatment is plasma-pheresis, a process that cleans the blood of bound antibodies causing these nerve problems. High-dose immunoglobulin therapy (administering proteins that normally attack invading germs) can also help. If this latter procedure is done before the muscles for breathing are affected, it may prevent you from being put on a ventilator.

If the symptoms of Guillain-Barré syndrome occur, see your doctor immediately, or get to an emergency room.

BLOOD AND
BLOOD PRESSURE

TIP 173

Even a mild elevation in blood pressure can put you at risk of having a heart attack, stroke, kidney disease, or heart failure.

It is a common misconception that mild high blood pressure (hypertension) is not serious. Optimal blood pressure is 120 over 80 or less. If the upper number (the systolic blood pressure) is above 120 or the lower number (the diastolic blood pressure) is above 80, you are at a higher risk of stroke, heart disease, and kidney failure than those with lower blood pressure. Just because your blood pressure has been normal your whole life doesn't mean you should stop having it checked. As the arteries in your body stiffen with aging, the systolic blood pressure (the top one) will continue to increase and you may need to begin taking medications. Mild to moderate elevations do not usually cause noticeable symptoms, but they are still dangerous to your health. Hypertension is known as a "silent killer." Slight elevations such as 140 over 90 are often ignored for months or years, which may cause damage to the heart, brain, or kidneys, eventually resulting in a stroke, kidney failure, heart attack, or heart failure at an early age.

Any elevation should be monitored with repeated blood pressure recordings. You should be evaluated by a doctor to determine the most effective therapeutic approach for controlling your blood pressure. (See Appendix C, page 380, for more detailed information about blood pressure and preventive screenings.)

TIP 174

> Treatment of high cholesterol and other abnormal blood lipids (fats) is important, even if you are a senior citizen.

Elevated cholesterol and other blood fats can create fatty deposits (plaques) that may block your arteries, resulting in a heart attack or stroke. These plaques can also create blockages in the blood vessels of the legs. Many people think that the time to diet and/or take medication to prevent this from happening is when you are young. Senior citizens often believe that the damage is done and there is nothing they can do about it. This defeatist attitude is absolutely wrong. The combination of lifestyle changes and cholesterol-lowering drugs can slow or stop the buildup of plaques and, in some cases, even reduce the amount of plaques that are already present. Microscopic photographs taken inside the arteries show that cholesterol deposits will sometimes even shrink with treatment.

It was originally thought that the gradual buildup of fats in an artery's walls would totally block it, at which point no more blood would pass through the vessel. If the blood vessel was responsible for the nourishment of the heart, a heart attack would result, and if it was responsible for the nourishment of the brain, a stroke (with symptoms such as paralysis, speech loss, etc.) would result. But recent research indicates that the fat does not totally block the blood vessel, but only partially blocks it. Total blockage is actually caused by a chemical reaction at the site of the fatty deposit, which results in the formation of a blood clot. Therefore if you slow the formation of and/or shrink the fatty deposits, the likelihood of blood clotting diminishes, reducing the risk that you will have a heart attack or stroke. This is confirmed by the scientific finding that both young and old people live longer after lowering their cholesterol and other blood fat levels.

The medications now used to treat these problems are very effective. Liver toxicity is a potential side effect, though, so your doctor should monitor your liver function with certain blood tests. Also, if you develop muscle pain or weakness while on these medications, you should discuss these new problems with your doctor.

(See Appendix C, page 382, for more detailed information about cholesterol and preventive screenings.)

TIP 175

It's always important to know why you have had blood clots (phlebitis). The cause may require long-term therapy. Also, it may be related to an undiagnosed disorder that needs to be diagnosed and treated. Ask your doctor if he/she can determine the cause of your blood clots.

Phlebitis, or what doctors refer to as deep venous thrombosis, is when you have blood clots in the veins, most often in the legs. It is a true medical emergency and warrants immediate medical attention. However, when you get out of the hospital and all of the anxiety has subsided, you need to find out why you had phlebitis, so that repeat episodes can be prevented. Also, it needs to be determined if there is an urgent underlying problem that has to be addressed. Do not put it off.

The process of blood clotting is a complex series of chemical reactions. There are a number of things that can go wrong, increasing the risk of dangerous blood clots. For example, it is possible for substances called abnormal antibodies to promote excessive clotting of the blood. Though antibodies are made by the body's immune system, these antibodies can do harm by causing the blood to clot inappropriately. Their presence can be determined by blood tests. If you have them, you are under a continual risk of another blood clot, and there is a need for prolonged anticoagulation (blood-thinning) therapy to prevent recurrence of the blood clots. You may also need long-term treatment if the reason you got the blood clot is heart failure or if your work involves long periods of sitting still, since either circumstance puts you at a much higher risk of developing future blood clots.

More serious conditions can also lead to increased blood clotting. One of the possibilities is cancer—many types of cancer cause few or no symptoms and sometimes the only tip-off to their presence is an episode of phlebitis.

Don't let this happen to you. Ask your doctor why you had blood clots. (Also see Tip 139 for a full description of the symptoms of phlebitis and Tip 249 about preventive measures for anyone with phlebitis who is hospitalized for any reason. Also see Tips 62 to 64 and 81 for symptoms relating to blood clots in the lungs or leg.)

TIP 176

The best method to control blood spurting from a blood vessel due to a severe laceration is to put direct pressure on the wound and pressure on another blood vessel between the wound and the heart. Some examples of good secondary pressure points are between the shoulder and elbow,

> the groin area, and behind the knee. This approach is better than using a tourniquet. Also, elevate the wounded area above the heart if possible.

Very few things are more frightening than seeing blood spurting from a severed artery after a serious injury. The best way to reduce bleeding is to apply direct pressure. Gauze dressing is the ideal material to press against the wound, but if gauze is unavailable, any type of cloth will suffice. Continued compression will cause the artery to constrict, and clotting will follow. Even bleeding from a large artery can be controlled in this fashion until emergency care arrives.

Do not attempt to wash the wound or remove any debris. If there is anything sticking out of the wound, wrap material and apply direct pressure around it. If it is a head injury, do not apply direct pressure, since there may be a skull fracture that can be made worse. Wrap material snugly around the head to cover the wound.

Avoid the temptation to look under the bandage to see if the bleeding has stopped; you may break the clot and make the bleeding worse. Once direct pressure has been applied, leave the gauze in place until it is removed by a health professional. If it bleeds through, apply another cloth on top of the first one.

If too much blood is lost, an individual may go into shock (this condition is characterized by a sudden drop in blood pressure, cold/clammy skin, paleness, etc.). If this happens:

- Call an ambulance (911 in most locations).
- Lay the victim on his/her back and elevate the legs. However, if you suspect a neck injury, DO NOT move the victim.
- If he/she stops breathing, begin CPR (see Appendix A, page 350, for CPR guidelines).
- Keep the victim warm.

If you are assisting an injured person, avoid contaminating your eyes, mouth, or an open wound with their blood. Wear gloves when available and wash yourself well for fifteen minutes as soon as possible.

TIP 177

> It is important to have the right level of potassium in your blood. Both low and high potassium levels can make you feel very weak and cause muscle cramps. In more serious cases, either condition can lead to a fatal heart rhythm problem.

Potassium is a mineral found in a wide variety of foods, such as bananas, tomatoes, and orange juice. You can usually get enough of the potassium your body needs from the foods you eat.

Potassium moves in and out of muscle cells, creating the electrical currents that make your muscles move. This is true for all muscles in your body, including those in your arms, legs, and torso. Low potassium levels in your body can cause profound muscle weakness, spasms, and cramps. The heart is the most important muscle that depends upon potassium. When potassium levels become too low or too high, abnormal electrical currents will travel throughout the heart. The sudden discharge of these abnormal currents can cause it to pump irregularly, which may lead to a sustained heart spasm, followed by death.

You can lose potassium when vomiting or having diarrhea. This loss is normally replaced through ingested foods and beverages, but long periods of vomiting and diarrhea can result in dangerously low potassium levels, which can be checked with a simple blood test. Taking potassium pills or liquids may be necessary to avoid a life-threatening abnormal heart rhythm.

High blood pressure can be associated with low potassium levels. Most water pills (or diuretics) used to treat high blood pressure, swelling, and heart failure can cause you to lose extra potassium in your urine. If you are taking a diuretic for any reason, you should have your blood potassium level checked by your doctor on a regular basis. Depending on your potassium level, it may be important for you to take supplemental potassium pills or liquids.

Another rare cause of profound potassium loss can be an overactive adrenal gland (located on top of each kidney), which causes high blood pressure. This condition requires a special medication or the surgical removal of part of the gland to maintain a normal potassium level.

On the other hand, very high potassium levels can cause heart-pumping irregularities, associated with certain medications, including the blood pressure pill known as an ACE inhibitor. These high potassium levels can also be caused by kidney disease. You should not take extra potassium pills without having your blood potassium levels monitored by your doctor.

In conclusion, if you experience muscle weakness and/or cramps, especially after diarrhea; are vomiting, taking water pills, taking potassium supplements, or taking the category of blood pressure pills called ACE inhibitors; or if you have a history of kidney disease, you should tell your doctor so he or she can monitor your potassium level. Note: There are many other possible causes of muscle cramps.

DEHYDRATION

TIP 178

If you are taking steroid medications (including cortisone, prednisone, hydrocortisone, or methylprednisolone) and you get sick with any illness, you must be on the alert. These steroid medications may make it difficult for you to recover from the new illness. Symptoms indicating that steroids are complicating another illness include (but are not limited to) fatigue, dizziness, muscle cramps or weakness, and/or salt craving, which may require emergency care. These symptoms can also occur if you suddenly stop taking the steroids after taking them every day, or if you develop a disease in the adrenal glands.

The glands on top of your kidneys, the adrenal glands, are small but very important in helping your body to function normally. They produce steroids and other essential hormones, and maintain the balance of salt and water in your body. Steroid-type medications can decrease the production of natural steroids by the adrenal glands, because the steroid medication usually substitutes for your natural steroid hormones.

When you get sick, however, and your body needs more of these hormones, these glands are often so suppressed that your body develops symptoms from a lack of steroids. This can also happen if you have been taking steroids for a while and you suddenly stop taking them; the natural hormones may not be immediately available, causing you to become very ill. Muscle weakness, fatigue, muscle cramps, nausea, vomiting, and dehydration can develop very rapidly. In some cases, your blood pressure can drop to such low levels that death may result.

Though rare, disease can occur in the adrenal glands, which will directly affect their functioning. Also, since the pituitary gland, which is located under the brain, produces hormones that control the adrenal glands, any malfunction in the pituitary glands may also lead to the improper functioning of the adrenal glands. This will cause you to have the symptoms of dehydration.

Emergency medical treatment can save your life when you do not have enough steroids in your body.

FEVER

TIP 179

> Anytime your body temperature exceeds 99.8 degrees Fahrenheit, you have a fever and something is causing it.

Having a fever does not mean feeling hot. It means an actual elevation of your body temperature, which is usually between 98.6 to 99.4 degrees. Normally your temperature is higher in the evening, though it still should not be over 99.4. (It begins to decrease again during your nighttime rest due to total body inactivity.) To allow for inaccuracies in taking your temperature, a good arbitrary level to set as being abnormal is 100.4 degrees with an oral thermometer. Therefore anytime your temperature is above 100.4 degrees, you have a fever, and you need to know why. Note: The elderly generally run about 0.5 degrees cooler than younger adults, and they can sometimes have even a severe infection without an elevated temperature.

Fever is an indication that your body is combating an illness caused by a virus or bacterium. But cancer and various autoimmune diseases (where the body fights against itself) can also cause fever, which may be the only clue that illness is present. You should seek medical evaluation if you have a persistently elevated temperature, even without an apparent cause. Early treatment of these illnesses often reduces the risk of serious complications. Note: A fever over 103.5 degrees often indicates a serious infection and should be evaluated immediately.

The rise-and-fall pattern of the body's temperature may provide a clue as to the cause of the fever, so keeping a chart monitoring temperature levels at various times may be helpful in diagnosing the problem. Also, when you have a fever, your temperature is often elevated in the evening but normal in the morning. You should never consider yourself well until your temperature has been normal for at least a twenty-four-hour period.

An oral temperature is very accurate. However, if a person is unable, for any reason, to hold a thermometer under his or her tongue, there are other options for measuring a temperature, including under the arm, in the ear, on the forehead, and rectally (the most accurate). A comprehensive discussion of these alternatives is in Appendix D, Taking a Child's Temperature, on page 393. (In many cases, the issues apply to both children and adults.) To convert Fahrenheit to Celsius, subtract 32 and divide by 1.8. To convert Celsius to Fahrenheit, multiply by 1.8 and add 32.

TIP 180

Fever and continual drenching sweats at night suggest the presence of an infection such as tuberculosis or an AIDS-related infection. Occasionally these symptoms occur with cancers, such as lymphomas and leukemia. There are also many other potential causes of night sweats.

Long-term infections are notorious for causing fever at night. When fever occurs, and your body's temperature then returns to normal, drenching sweats result. They may be so profuse that you have to change your pajamas. This sweating is part of the body's cooling mechanism, as it helps get rid of the heat of a high fever.

A common cause of night sweats is tuberculosis (TB), a disease whose other symptoms include weight loss and a cough, sometimes with bloody phlegm. TB is more likely to occur in people with weak immune systems (such as those with AIDS), those traveling to countries with a high TB infection rate, and those who have been exposed to TB patients. Drug abusers, patients who have had their stomachs surgically removed, and those who have been exposed to silica (the major component of sand, used in making glass) are also prime candidates for TB.

Night sweats are also one of the early signs of an HIV infection, the virus that causes AIDS, and they can occasionally be caused by cancers such as lymphoma. Other causes of night sweats include menopause, certain medications, low blood sugar, hormone disorders, and certain neurological conditions. Sometimes there is no identifiable cause.

Persistent night sweats and fever are red light warning signals that you should see your doctor for medical evaluation as soon as possible.

MEDICATION

TIP 181

> If you stop taking a medication suddenly, you may develop serious complications. Therefore it is best to consult your doctor before stopping or decreasing the dosage of your medication.

Some medications cause serious problems if you suddenly stop taking them. A few important examples are high blood pressure pills, steroid-based pills, and most antidepressants:

- If you suddenly stop taking certain blood pressure pills, not only will your blood pressure rise but in certain cases it may actually rise to such a high level that you have a stroke. For example, stopping the drug clonidine (Catapres) may result in a very high "rebound" blood pressure, possibly along with other side effects. Also, if a patient suddenly stops taking beta-blockers (metoprolol, atenolol, propranolol, carvedilol), he/she may experience angina or a heart attack as their heart rate speeds up.

- Steroid pills may actually suppress your body's normal production of steroids. Therefore when you stop taking them, your body may react to the very low level of internally produced steroids. Your doctor should decrease the dosage slowly over time in order to allow the body to start producing the normal amount of natural steroids. (See Tip 178 for additional information on symptoms after stopping steroids.)

• SSRI antidepressant medications can have severe withdrawal reactions if stopped abruptly, such as extreme anxiety and the feeling of shock waves rippling up and down the arms. Always discuss with your doctor the timing and method for stopping these medicines.

Since many medications can have a negative impact on your body if they are suddenly stopped, always consult a doctor immediately if you feel as though you should not or cannot follow the prescribed directions for taking your medication.

PASSING OUT, LOSS OF CONSCIOUSNESS

TIP 182

> If someone has passed out, it is extremely impor-
> tant to know whether they lost consciousness be-
> cause of a seizure. Seizures can be recurrent and
> warrant specific treatment. They can also be a
> sign of an abnormality in the brain or an emer-
> gency life-threatening condition such as very low
> blood sugar or a serious electrolyte abnormality
> in the blood.

A seizure means there has been a sudden alteration of the electrical function of the brain that produces a sudden change in
behavior. A seizure can occur in a normal brain if its metabolism is disturbed, such as with low blood sugar, lack of oxygen,
low sodium, high fever, or certain drugs.

A generalized convulsive (grand mal) seizure involves a sudden loss of consciousness with rhythmic jerking of the entire
body, which can also be accompanied by biting of the tongue,
and urination, followed by a period of sleep before regaining
consciousness. However, not all seizures follow this pattern.

Seizures occur in a variety of ways, since the brain has so
many different functions. The spectrum is so wide that it

ranges from merely experiencing a strange smell to acting funny. If the electrical currents released by your brain are less intense and are confined to a small area of the brain, a minor seizure will occur. The results of this minor seizure depend on the area of the brain involved. For example, you may just smack your lips or stare without being aware that you are doing anything.

The term "epilepsy" refers to a chronic brain disorder characterized by recurrent unprovoked seizures, which is either inherited or acquired. It usually, but not always, begins in childhood. The seizures caused by epilepsy may continue throughout life.

The first phase of a seizure is sometimes a special feeling called an "aura," which may be an unusual smell, a rising sensation in the belly, or just not feeling right. The seizure—major or minor—is in turn followed by confusion, lack of memory of the event, fatigue, and sometimes a period of deep sleep, often with heavy snoring, before normal behavior returns. This sequence of events—aura, altered consciousness (with or without jerking), followed by a period of sleep or changed awareness—distinguishes seizures from fainting or other causes of sudden unconsciousness. The jerking phase of a seizure usually lasts only a few minutes, while the period of postseizure sleeping and/or symptoms such as fatigue, muscle soreness, confusion, combativeness, or agitation may last much longer. If the jerking phase does not stop after several minutes, or if it keeps recurring, and the person does not begin returning to his or her normal self, the condition is life-threatening. Call an ambulance.

If you witness a person who is having a seizure lose consciousness, turn them on their side, away from dangerous objects. Do not attempt to put anything in their mouth. Call for emergency care, unless the person is a known epileptic and you have been advised otherwise.

A common cause of seizures in children is a high fever. As the brain matures into adulthood, it becomes less susceptible to this happening. (See Tip 201 for more information on seizures due to fevers in children.)

Seizures can also result from a brain injury, brain tumor, stroke, a life-threatening low or high blood sugar level, abnormal electrolyte levels in the blood (such as one might experience after prolonged vomiting), or a sudden loss of blood flow to your brain. These conditions all need to be treated on an emergency basis, so all first-time seizures require an immediate visit to the emergency room to determine the underlying cause or causes.

Seizures can sometimes occur without an apparent cause. A normal adult with no previous history of seizures, no family history of epilepsy, and no current illness can suddenly have a major seizure. What do you do if medical tests do not reveal any cause? You will often need to take medicine to control the seizures, since you cannot risk a recurrence while driving or in another potentially dangerous situation. If you have not had a seizure in many years, you should discuss with your doctor whether you should continue to take the seizure medicine. Only your doctor can make this judgment, based on your individual circumstances.

In most states, driving is not permitted for up to six months after a seizure. It is also important to take other safety precautions, such as avoiding heights (not using ladders, climbing trees, working on rooftops), avoiding swimming or taking baths unsupervised (showers are safer), and avoiding being in front of open flames (such as campfires and barbecues).

TEMPERATURE CHANGE

TIP 183

> Prolonged exposure to cold can cause fatal body hypothermia.

The body's protective mechanisms maintain its temperature at around 98.6 degrees, which is necessary for carrying out normal body functions. Internal control mechanisms help maintain body temperature by routing blood away from the surface of the body (the area just beneath the skin) and the extremities (the arms and legs), and by shivering to generate heat. If the body still cannot contain warmth, the body temperature drops and symptoms begin to appear. They are:

- Confusion and forgetfulness
- Sluggishness and fatigue
- Lack of coordination
- Slurred speech
- Shivering (when shivering stops, the condition is getting worse)
- Heart palpitations (heartbeat is irregular, slow, or fast)

If the body's temperature continues to drop, it can lead to coma and death. Older adults are at the highest risk of becoming ill from their body temperature dropping.

If you encounter someone who is hypothermic:

- Get the person to a warm room. Do not immerse them in a tub of hot water or place them in front of a heater or fireplace. The sudden exposure to excessive heat may worsen their condition.
- Remove any wet clothing.
- Cover the person with blankets.
- Warm the person with close body contact, but do not rub their skin.
- Offer the person warm fluids if they can drink. Do not give them an alcoholic beverage.
- Seek emergency medical assistance.

Note: A hypothermic person can sometimes be revived even after prolonged cardiac arrest; it is thought that the low body temperature can prevent cell damage for an extended period of time.

TIP 184

Fatigue, dizziness, and/or headache are the first symptoms of heat exhaustion and they may progress to a life-threatening case of heatstroke if you do not respond appropriately. Working or playing in the hot sun can be dangerous, as can a lack of proper ventilation and air-conditioning in the summertime (particularly for the elderly). Anyone who appears to act confused after being in a hot environment needs to be cooled down and taken to the ER immediately.

It is hard to tell when you are in danger of heat exhaustion. When you are active on a hot day, the body uses its cooling mechanism to release sweat, because the evaporation of sweat on the body's surface allows it to shed heat. The body is generally able to keep an even temperature this way, but environmental factors like high humidity and the absence of a breeze can make it difficult for the body to cool itself. Also, individuals with fewer sweat glands are in greater danger of heat exhaustion, as are senior citizens and young children, who have less effective cooling mechanisms.

Fluid loss and a rise in body temperature can result in a serious derangement of body chemistry. Symptoms of heat exhaustion include any combination of the following:

- Nausea
- Dizziness and/or headache
- Weakness, fatigue
- Paleness
- Incoordination and/or confusion
- Muscle cramps
- Vomiting
- Low or no urine output
- Pounding heartbeat
- Fainting

If you have any of the above symptoms, it is urgent that you do the following in order to avoid heatstroke:

- Rest.
- Move to the shade or indoors with air-conditioning. Sit in front of a fan.
- Place a wet towel over your face, arms, and legs.
- Spray yourself with cool water.
- Drink cool, nonalcoholic beverages, such as apple juice or Gatorade, to replace your electrolytes. Note: Eating a

banana may help replace potassium in the body if you don't have access to Gatorade.

• Seek medical assistance, especially if your symptoms include a feeling of confusion. Call 911 or get somebody to take you to the ER immediately. You may need to be given intravenous fluids or other therapy in order to cool down quickly.

The most effective method of handling heat exhaustion is to prevent it. Take frequent breaks from exercise and exposure to heat. If you get tired, rest and cool off for a while.

TIP 185

Your thyroid gland does not have to be enlarged in order to be overactive or underactive. The variety of symptoms accompanying an overactive or underactive thyroid gland require early diagnosis and treatment to prevent serious complications.

The red light warning signals of an overactive thyroid are: intolerance to heat, a rapid and irregular pulse, tremors, fatigue, profuse sweating, increased appetite, a feeling of anxiety, and/or bulging eyes.

The red light warning signals of an underactive thyroid are: cold intolerance, feeling cold all of the time, loss of memory, generalized body swelling (especially of the face), irregular and slow pulse, and/or a high cholesterol level.

The thyroid gland is located in the center of the base of the neck (see Figure 14). It serves as the body's thermostat, regulating the metabolic functions—that is to say, how quickly or

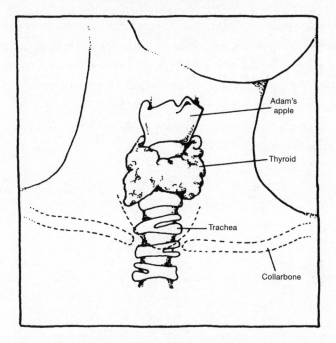

Figure 14. Thyroid Gland.

slowly you burn up calories. An overactive thyroid promotes a rapid metabolic rate, while an underactive one slows it down.

The size of your thyroid gland has nothing to do with whether it is overactive or underactive. If the gland has not changed in size but is functioning abnormally, you may not know to seek treatment since the symptoms may have developed gradually.

An overactive thyroid gland, producing excess thyroid hormone, causes the symptoms listed above, and may even cause heart failure.

An underactive thyroid produces an insufficient amount of thyroid hormone. Besides the general symptoms listed above, you may experience marked weakness, confusion, and/or paleness or a yellowish appearance.

Both conditions are frequently associated with fatigue and

double vision. An overactive thyroid can cause dangerous heart rhythm abnormalities, while an underactive thyroid can result in a high cholesterol level. These and many other complications are a good reason to seek medical care as soon as possible when the symptoms creep up on you.

(Also, see Appendix C, page 371, for information on thyroid screenings.)

WEAKNESS

TIP 186

> In women, senior citizens, and diabetics a general sense of weakness and/or shortness of breath without any chest pain may be the only warning sign of a heart attack.

The pain of a heart attack usually occurs in the center of the chest, under the breastbone or in the front-left breast area. The pain is most often a sensation of pressure, like a heavy weight on the chest or a squeezing tightness. Profound weakness often accompanies the pain. A cold and clammy sweat may be present, with nausea and vomiting. In some cases, however, a heart attack may occur in an entirely atypical manner.

If you are a woman, senior citizen, or diabetic, be aware that shortness of breath and/or profound weakness may be the only signs of a "silent" heart attack. Consult your physician immediately for an evaluation, which includes an EKG, blood tests of certain heart chemicals, and special X-rays of the heart, to determine if you are having a heart attack. Life-saving treatments may be necessary.

(See Appendix C, page 392, about heart disease screening.)

TIP 187

Severe constipation, dehydration, muscle weakness, bone pain, loss of memory, confusion, depression, psychosis (loss of contact with reality), anxiety, heart rhythm abnormalities, and kidney stones are all symptoms that may indicate an overactive parathyroid gland (hyperparathyroidism). There may also be other general symptoms such as increased thirst and urination, nausea, vomiting, loss of appetite, and/or abdominal pain (gastric ulcers).

The parathyroid glands (there are usually four) are located in the front base of the neck, near the thyroid gland. These small glands produce a hormone that controls the amount of calcium in your blood. If one of the glands develops a growth, or gets larger than normal, the hormonal output is increased, causing the amount of calcium (stored primarily in the bones) to increase in the bloodstream.

A high level of calcium in the blood increases the risk of developing the above symptoms and ailments. In addition to these, it can cause a loss of calcium from the bones that will result in softening of the bones, and thus bone pain. The life-threatening consequences of high calcium include abnormal heart rhythms and severe dehydration.

Tumors or growths of the parathyroid glands are rarely large enough to be felt by examining the neck, so you have to rely on appropriate blood studies to provide evidence that they are present.

Surgical removal of a diseased parathyroid gland is usually curative. Preservation of the remaining glands is important since without them and the hormone they produce, the blood calcium level would drop too low, causing seizures and muscle spasms. This condition could even be life-threatening.

The symptoms of an overactive parathyroid gland can be subtle and slowly creep up on you. If you notice these symptoms, notify your doctor for an evaluation as soon as possible.

WEIGHT LOSS

TIP 188

If you have unexplained weight loss and/or loss of appetite, you may have a serious underlying medical illness.

How much weight loss is significant? If your body weight rarely changes, losing as little as five pounds could be significant. If your body weight varies eight to ten pounds from one season to another, you may be fine. But never ignore an unexplained weight loss of more than seven percent of your total body weight. The more rapid the weight loss, the more likely it stems from a disease.

Body weight is determined by many different factors, including genetics, caloric intake, and physical activity. Caloric intake is the most important factor. Your body burns a certain number of calories per day, regardless of what you do. This is known as your basal metabolic rate (BMR). If you eat more calories than you burn, then you will gain weight, and if you eat fewer calories than you burn, you will lose weight.

Diseases cause weight loss in numerous ways:

- If you are depressed, you may lose your appetite.
- If you have a disease of the stomach or colon, you may

limit your food intake due to the pain associated with eating.

- If you have dementia, you may simply forget to eat.
- Cancer releases substances into the system that can cause the wasting of body tissues and/or loss of appetite.
- Diabetes results in an increase of sugar in the urine and therefore a loss in calories and dehydration.
- An overactive thyroid gland increases the metabolic rate, and therefore causes you to burn more calories. If you have this condition, you will often lose weight despite eating more.

If you have a significant unexplained weight loss, you need medical evaluation as soon as possible.

Sometimes you may lose weight even though your belly size increases. Liver and heart disease as well as cancer of the ovaries can cause fluid to accumulate in the belly cavity, thereby creating this effect. (However, in extreme cases fluid accumulation could even cause you to gain weight.) Watch out for symptoms like bloating, indigestion, heartburn, and changes in bowel habits, as these may also occur with ailments such as ovarian, pancreatic, stomach, or liver cancer. Therefore, if you lose weight, but your waistline increases, it is important for you to seek medical evaluation as soon as possible.

PART THREE

Pregnancy and Postpregnancy

INTRODUCTION:
Preventive Measures
to Increase the Chances
of Delivering a Healthy Baby

A pregnant woman can take many preventive measures to increase the chances that she will deliver a healthy baby, including the following:

- She should avoid certain medications, because the side effects may endanger the fetus.
- It is important to be aware of past and existing illnesses as well as possible exposure to various diseases during preganancy. For example:
  - If she is exposed to hepatitis B or whooping cough (pertussis) and she has not been previously immunized, she and her baby can benefit from vaccinations to reduce the risk of developing these life-threatening ailments.
  - If she is pregnant during the flu season (between October and May), it is recommended that she get a flu vaccination.
  - She should be seen routinely by her doctor for early

detection of infections with subtle or no symptoms. These include periodontal (gum) disease, urinary tract infections, etc. These conditions increase the risk of preterm labor.

○ If she has papillomas (growths) in the vagina, she may need a cesarean (C-section) delivery so that the baby doesn't get these growths in her throat when she is born.

○ If she has had high risk sexual behavior, chlamydia screening is recommended during the first and third trimester. Treatment during pregnancy can prevent passing the infection to the newborn baby.

• A pregnant woman should be aware that though some degree of nausea and vomiting is very frequently the result of "morning sickness" during a normal pregnancy, severe nausea and vomiting associated with weight loss may indicate a more severe condition that may lead to dehydration, acidosis, and, rarely, premature labor. The inability to tolerate food, along with severe nausea and vomiting, should prompt an immediate evaluation by your physician.

• Vaginal spotting is very common during all stages of pregnancy. It may follow intercourse or be due to a minor condition like a cervical varix (a small fragile vein in the cervix that leaks a little blood). Vaginal spotting warrants a phone call to the physician, but bleeding as much as or more than a period warrants an immediate evaluation by your ob/gyn doctor or family physician, and may represent an impending miscarriage. If it is accompanied by any amount of pain, it is even more urgent.

• Any pregnant woman who has experienced trauma of any sort should consider getting evaluated by a doctor. There are multiple potential risks to the mother and fetus for which early intervention is important.

- Some degree of shortness of breath during pregnancy is normal, but in the postpartum period it may indicate a more serious condition that requires medical evaluation, such as a blood clot in the lung. Symptoms of a blood clot may also include chest pain and/or an impending sense of doom.

Unfortunately this book cannot address all the preventive measures that can increase the chances of delivering a healthy baby. We recommend that pregnant women be monitored closely by their health-care provider and that they seek out educational programs and literature addressing these issues. It is proven that early prenatal care reduces death rates for both mothers and infants.

TIP 189

If you are pregnant and you notice tenderness in the upper-right or upper-middle part of your belly (under the breastbone) and/or are experiencing a headache, blurred vision, double vision, dizziness, nosebleeds, swelling, and/or sudden weight gain, immediate medical evaluation is necessary. You may have preeclampsia, a dangerous condition associated with very high blood pressure.

Preeclampsia can cause severe high blood pressure, which can in turn lead to seizures (eclampsia) and coma. This condition usually appears during the last four months of pregnancy or during the postpartum period.

The exact cause of preeclampsia is unknown. It begins with changes in the body's blood pressure control mechanisms that cause the blood vessels to constrict. The high blood pressure affects the kidneys, leading to significant weight gain and swelling. As the blood pressure rises to very high levels, you may also develop swelling in the brain and liver, leading to seizures and coma. This cascade of events is usually preventable when early treatment is instituted. The condition of preeclampsia may require delivering the baby early. If you develop the symptoms of preeclampsia, contact your doctor immediately.

TIP 190

If you are pregnant and have any of the following symptoms, seek immediate medical care:
- Severe belly pain
- Leaking or breaking water
- Decreased or absent fetal movements

There are many potential causes of these symptoms. The more serious ones may put you and your unborn baby at serious health risks.

An emergency medical evaluation is needed for:
- **Severe belly pressure or pain.** In some of the most serious cases, this type of pain can be associated with internal bleeding in the uterus or rupture of the uterus at the site of the scar of a previous cesarean section. Other causes may include (depending on gestational age) tubal pregnancy, miscarriage, preterm labor, or infections.
- **Premature leaking or breaking of your water.** This can cause a serious infection in both you and the fetus. Also, in certain circumstances your water breaking early may compromise the blood and oxygen supply (via the umbilical cord) to the fetus.
- **Absence of fetal movement.** If you do not feel the fetus move or you feel a substantial change or decrease in fetal movement, you must be evaluated immediately by your ob/gyn.

TIP 191

Certain infections during pregnancy cause pre-mature delivery. Thus if you experience either burning on urination or a foul-smelling vaginal discharge, contact your doctor immediately.

To avoid premature delivery, contact your doctor immediately for:

- **Bladder infections.** Such infections cause frequent urination, pain, and/or burning on urination. They can lead to a serious kidney infection, which can precipitate a premature delivery of the baby and make the mother very ill.
- **A foul- or fishy-smelling vaginal discharge due to bacteria.** This discharge may need to be treated to avoid premature delivery of the baby.

TIP 192

If you are in the first four months of pregnancy and you have noted the reappearance of vaginal bleeding and/or cramping, it is important to check with your doctor immediately.

This bleeding and/or cramping could be the first sign of an inevitable miscarriage, or a pregnancy that is failing. In this case, the embryo is likely to pass from the uterus (womb) through the vagina. You may have severe bleeding during a miscarriage, and surgery may be required in order to stop this bleeding.

Another life-threatening cause could be an ectopic pregnancy. In this condition the pregnancy is in your fallopian tube. A pregnancy test will come back positive. An egg fertilized in the fallopian tube normally moves to the uterus and implants in the uterine wall, where it continues to grow. But if the embryo does not make it to the uterus, it will continue to grow in the fallopian tube, and the tube may rupture. This can lead to a severe life-threatening hemorrhage into the belly. You will not see the bleeding, although you may experience symptoms such as belly pain, weakness, a rapid pulse, dizziness, and a dark bloody vaginal discharge. (Also see Tip 7 for more information about emergency internal bleeding.) Sometimes you can feel when the tube ruptures; the sharp pain you may have been experiencing suddenly diminishes.

Both of these conditions require immediate evaluation by a doctor. Vaginal bleeding and/or cramping in these circumstances are the warning signs of a potentially life-threatening condition.

Alternatively, the symptoms may result from other causes, including certain hormonal imbalances.

TIP 193

Any bleeding, with or without belly cramps or uterine contractions, demands immediate medical evaluation if it is on or after the fifth month of pregnancy. It may be a warning sign of a life-threatening hemorrhage.

The life-threatening causes of bleeding during the later stages of pregnancy are related to the location of the placenta or "afterbirth." Usually a fertilized egg situates itself inside the upper wall of the uterus. As the embryo grows, it is connected by the umbilical cord to the placenta (which is attached to the uterine wall). The placenta is like a pancake, filled with many small blood vessels growing on the inside wall of the uterus.

If part of the placenta grows on the lower wall of the

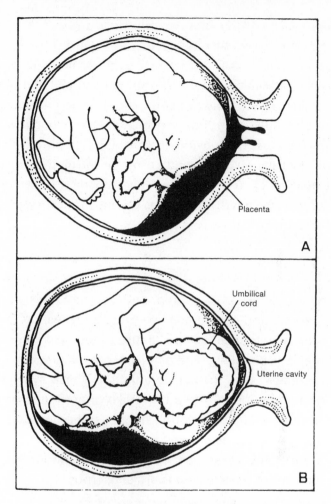

Figure 15. Vaginal Bleeding After the
Fifth Month of Pregnancy.
A. Placenta previa
B. Abruptio placentae

uterus, over the opening of the birth canal (the cervix), it is
more likely to cause painless bleeding and may hinder the fetus' growth, as blood supply to the fetus is compromised (see
Figure 15-A). With a complete placenta previa (when the placenta completely covers the opening of the cervix), a C-section

delivery is needed. This is usually performed prior to the thirty-seventh week of pregnancy.

In a condition called abruptio placentae, a normally placed placenta partially separates from the uterine wall and bleeds (see Figure 15-B). This condition is usually accompanied by severe abdominal pain and/or strong uterine contractions.

In either case the baby can lose its blood supply, which deprives the baby of oxygen and nutrition, endangering its life. The mother's life is also threatened because there is the potential of massive internal bleeding. Urgent medical evaluation and treatment are necessary.

TIP 194

If you think you are pregnant (you have missed periods and have a positive pregnancy test), and you experience severe nausea and vomiting, vaginal bleeding, and/or discharge of grapelike particles, seek medical evaluation. These symptoms may be due to a tumorlike growth in your womb, which puts you in danger of hemorrhaging. An early evaluation and therapeutic extraction of the mass can be life-saving. About six percent of these growths are cancerous.

A hydatidiform mole is a tumorlike mass that can grow in your womb such that you seem to be pregnant. This condition, which occurs in about one out of 1,200 pregnancies, is caused by an abnormal egg implanting in the wall of the womb. The fetal parts (tissue) may or may not be present, but the placenta (the pancakelike attachment that normally provides nourishment for the baby) grows rapidly and produces the hormones of pregnancy. Fingerlike projections of the placenta invade the wall of the womb, acting like a cancerous growth. They swell and degenerate, causing you to bleed from the vagina. The projections themselves look like grapes when they pass with the bloody discharge. This condition is known as a molar pregnancy.

If you think you are pregnant but have signs and symptoms suggesting a molar pregnancy, it is important that you seek emergency medical care to have the mass removed from your womb. Not only are you in danger of a life-threatening hemorrhage, but the fingerlike projections of the placenta can also turn cancerous and spread throughout your body.

TIP 195

> If you have a fever and belly discomfort soon after you have given birth to a baby, it may indicate that you have a serious infection of the womb, which could spread rapidly. Heavy bleeding is also a possible warning signal of a life-threatening hemorrhage.

You may already be home after delivering your baby when you develop a fever and belly pains. These symptoms may indicate an infection in your uterus (womb). This is dangerous; even a mild infection in this location can become major and spread rapidly throughout your body, because after delivery the internal lining of the uterus has many small blood vessels. Immediate medical evaluation and treatment can be life-saving.

If you are soaking blood through more than one pad (sanitary napkin) each hour, you are at risk of having a serious hemorrhage. Contact your health-care provider immediately.

PART FOUR

Pediatrics: Body Part–Specific Conditions

by Joy Lawn, M.D.

*Revised with the assistance
of a team of pediatricians*

INTRODUCTION:
Childhood Conditions

Children are not just small adults, and this must be accounted for in the diagnostic process. While some conditions occur more commonly in children than in adults, there are other conditions that are entirely specific to children. Also, it can be much more difficult to assess what is wrong with a child, particularly a younger child who cannot communicate clearly about his or her symptoms or cooperate fully with a doctor's examination.

Parents often fall into two groups: those who constantly worry about their child's health, and those who never seem nervous about anything. Unfortunately a parent may worry and consult the doctor frequently and still be worrying about the wrong things. This guide is intended to inform you about which of your child's symptoms you *do* need to worry about.

This information is not intended to make you more nervous, but is instead meant to direct you in situations in which you need medical help fast. If anything, this guide should *reduce* your anxiety! It is not intended as an exhaustive course on general pediatric conditions or as a first-aid guide. The conditions included have been chosen because they are either a significant cause of childhood disability and/or death, or be-cause—though they may be rare—they are only treatable if diagnosed early.

Our overview starts by listing the main red light signals that indicate that your newborn or child is dangerously ill, and then moves on to a more specific head-to-toe guide to your child's symptoms.

How Do You Know When to Consult a Doctor Quickly?

Many parents with a sick child struggle with the decision of whether to contact a doctor. Some see their child's doctor so often that the doctor's office feels like their own living room! Yet even these overattentive parents may not act quickly enough when faced with a critical condition. In many in-stances, it may be important to get the child to the ER with-out delay. If you are in serious doubt about the severity of the problem, however, another valuable resource is the local nurse advice line, a service offered by many children's hospitals. Many of the nurses keep abreast of new medical advances and can answer specific questions relating to your child's condi-tion.

The following guidelines provide you with significant signs and symptoms that you need to watch out for. However, every child is different, and there are always extenuating circum-stances, so never hesitate to call your doctor's office or a chil-dren's hospital hotline about a symptom. Note: If your baby was premature, this is a special case and you should speak with your pediatrician for additional important instructions on when to bring your baby in for a checkup.

Is Your Newborn (up to 2 months of age) Really Ill?

An infant under the age of two months should be evaluated immediately by a physician if he or she has any of the following symptoms:

- If his/her skin is yellow and keeps getting more yellow, he/she may have jaundice. Note: During the first three days after discharge from the hospital, slight changes in color may not be a problem. Check with your baby's doctor.
- Forceful or yellow vomiting, as opposed to spit-up (which dribbles out of the mouth and/or nose without any wrenching or body contracting)
- A rectal temperature of 100.4 degrees Fahrenheit (38 degrees Celsius) or greater, or a significantly reduced temperature—lower than 97 degrees Fahrenheit (36.1 degrees Celsius)
- A "spell" or frightening event. For example, if the newborn stops breathing for a moment—fifteen seconds or more—or is making unusual movements, turns blue, etc. *(Call 911 for an ambulance and watch your baby. Stimulation such as flicking his/her toes may help.)*

Is Your Baby or Child Really Ill?

There are many signs to indicate whether your child is really ill. These include an abnormal temperature, the sudden onset of feeding difficulties, a change in responsiveness, signs of underlying long-term ailments, and a host of other specific symptoms that require emergency evaluation. Your child needs medical evaluation if he or she has any of the symptoms described in this section.

ABNORMAL TEMPERATURE

Any child with a nonserious viral illness may be feverish and sleepy but should improve when the fever comes down. Do not overbundle a child with a fever. Dressing them in light clothing and/or wrapping them in a light blanket is generally the best way to avoid overheating or causing a chill. Also, if you bathe a feverish child to cool them down, you have to be very careful because you can overdo it and the child can get chilled. The water should not be too hot or too cold (a lukewarm temperature) and you should not bathe them for too long a period of time. If the child is unable or unwilling to orally take a dose of fever-reducing medicine (for example, they may be having a seizure or vomiting), you may use a suppository fever-reducer such as FeverAll, which is inserted in the rectum and works equally well as medicines taken orally, such as Tylenol. Medicines are slower acting than bathing. However, using medicine is usually adequate unless the fever is very high.

Your child may be ill if he or she has a fever along with other symptoms, such as acting lethargic and irritable, looking tired, coughing, wheezing, and/or developing a bad rash. These cases should be promptly evaluated by a physician. Also, a high fever alone—as outlined below—warrants a prompt evaluation. Always take your child's temperature at the first sign of concern.

Get the child to his/her doctor or an emergency room immediately in the following "fever" situations:

Note: The ages listed below are specifically relating to full-term babies. If your child was premature, it is very important to discuss the appropriate age cutoffs with the doctor prior to leaving the hospital after delivery. You will have to be more rigorous in the follow-up of your child than outlined in the guidelines for a full-term child listed below.

- The child is under eight weeks of age with a temperature over 100.3 degrees Fahrenheit (37.94 degrees Celsius).
- The child is between two and six months of age with a temperature of 102.2 degrees Fahrenheit (39 degrees Celsius) or greater.
- The child's temperature is over 103 degrees Fahrenheit

(39.4 degrees Celsius), he or she doesn't have any symptoms of a cold, and one of the following is true:

- ○ The child is female, between one and two years of age, and her fever lasts for more than twenty-four hours.
- ○ The child is female and under one year of age.
- ○ The child is male, under one year of age, and uncircumcised.
- ○ The child has had a temperature for five days.
- A child of any age has a return of malaise (feeling badly) after twelve to twenty-four hours of improvement.
- The child has a reduced temperature (less than 97 degrees Fahrenheit/36.1 degrees Celsius).

Note: To convert Fahrenheit to Celsius, subtract 32 and divide by 1.8. To convert Celsius to Fahrenheit, multiply by 1.8 and add 32.

Many doctors feel that taking a rectal temperature is best for a child under two years of age, and especially for a child younger than six months. A rectal temperature is the most accurate measurement for a child too young to use an oral thermometer. In a young child, a fever can indicate a life-threatening condition, so missing an elevated temperature can result in a delay in very important treatment. Every parent of a child under two years of age should ideally own a rectal thermometer and know how to use it SAFELY (see Appendix D, page 393, for tips on taking a child's temperature and the proper use of a rectal thermometer).

On the other hand, some doctors feel that other methods of taking a temperature are simpler and potentially less traumatic for both the parents and the baby. These include taking an underarm (axillary) temperature or the use of the special types of thermometers that take the child's temperature from his or her ear or temporal artery (forehead). An underarm temperature is considered less accurate than a rectal or oral temperature, and is generally slightly lower than the actual core temperature.

Most digital thermometers can be used to take either a rectal, oral, or underarm (axillary) temperature, and these can be found at an inexpensive price at any pharmacy. The ear thermometer and the temporal artery (forehead) thermometer can be more expensive to purchase, and there is debate about how accurate they are when taking temperatures in certain situations (see Appendix D, page 393). Although an oral temperature is very accurate, all doctors agree that a temperature should be taken orally only when the child is old enough to cooperate (usually over four years of age). Digital thermometers register a temperature more quickly than glass thermometers, and are generally considered easier and safer to use.

SUDDEN ONSET OF FEEDING DIFFICULTIES

Take note if your child refuses to eat or drink, or if they substantially decrease their consumption (in infants, this will be manifested in a decrease in sucking and the intake of a lower-than-normal amount of formula or breast milk).

CHANGE IN RESPONSIVENESS

One of the first and most important things to look for, regardless of any other signs or symptoms, is how your baby or child is acting. Every child should have a period of acting normal (or close to normal) and playful every few hours. If this is not the case, it is a red flag and should prompt immediate medical evaluation.

More specifically, you should watch out for:

- Persistent drowsiness (in an infant this can manifest as poor eye contact, poor suck, weak cry, etc.), sleepiness (i.e., being difficult to rouse), or sleeping much more than what is normal for them

- Persistent and/or extreme irritability (being difficult to calm or, in an infant, crying inconsolably at the slightest stimulus)
- Behavior that suggests the brain is not functioning properly, such as a failure to recognize people, seeing things that are not present, fighting off attempts to help, uncontrollable jerking movements, or limbs that appear floppy and have decreased muscle tone
- Paradoxical crying: The baby cries when he/she is picked up, and is quiet when left alone.

Rare but Potentially Correctable Life-Threatening Metabolic Disorders

Occasionally, rare conditions that interfere with chemical processes within the body (known as metabolic disorders) occur, and detection and early treatment may be life-saving. For example, a lack of the substance carnitine is an infrequent cause of a life-threatening condition seen in young children in the emergency room. Once the more common causes of life-threatening conditions have been ruled out, the rare disorders should be considered. It is very important to inform your doctor of any clues of an underlying long-term ailment, such as poor weight gain, muscle weakness, recurrent infections, or developmental delays.

General Signs and Symptoms

If your child exhibits any of the following serious signs and symptoms, it may be an emergency. Make sure to seek medical evaluation.

- Severe headache or recurrent headaches (see advice on headaches, page 269)

- Convulsions (seizures)
- Severe diarrhea or blood in the stools (particularly if there are more than streaks of blood in the stools)
- Severe belly pain that occurs on the right side, worsens with movement, occurs in regular intervals, or is accompanied by diarrhea
- Signs of dehydration, such as no tears, lethargy, dry mouth, and/or markedly reduced urine production (in an infant, you may notice a dry diaper for six to eight hours)
- Persistent vomiting that lasts more than twelve to eighteen hours, vomiting bile (green), or repeated vomiting without the presence of diarrhea or fever
- Waking up in the morning with vomiting or a headache
- Breathing takes increased work (the chest contracts—skin between the ribs gets sucked in when inhaling, nostrils flare with each breath, the child grunts while breathing, etc.). Count the ribs with each breath. If two or more ribs can be counted, the child is having difficulty breathing. If four to six ribs can be counted because the skin between the ribs is being sucked in, he/she is in substantial respiratory distress.
- Slow, irregular breathing
- Jaundice; yellow eyes and skin (This condition should be monitored by the child's pediatrician if it occurs during the newborn period. Beyond the newborn period, eating large amounts of yellow/orange vegetables can also give the skin a yellow hue, especially in toddlers. However, yellow eyes always warrant prompt evaluation.)
- Cyanosis (blue color of the mouth and lips)
- Weakness in one part of the body
- A change in vision or appearance of pupils
- Unexplained bruising

- Rapidly enlarging belly
- Sudden difficulties walking

Preventing Life-Threatening Conditions
In addition to being aware of these red light warning signals, it is important that you practice prevention. The death toll of children worldwide could be cut dramatically if parents adhered to these recommendations:

- Keep children away from windows that are only protected by screens.
- Keep children in the house when visitors leave in their cars.
- Breast-feed all babies for at least six months (although it is recommended that you breast-feed for at least one year if possible).
- Immunize all children (bring them to get shots).
- Follow child safety regulations, and use car seats, bicycle helmets, etc.
- Lock swimming pool gates and keep toddlers out of the pool area.
- Keep toddlers away from any container of water (particularly those over eight inches deep).
- Don't leave a child unattended in an open area.
- Block access to stairs.
- Keep small objects out of reach.

Body Part–Specific Health Problems (Pediatric): Listed from Head to Toe

In addition to the preceding general safety and precautionary measures, there are also a number of specific childhood afflictions that parents should be aware of. The following are a series of symptom-specific tips for parents from specialists and generalists in pediatrics. The outcome for many ailments is directly related to how early the doctor can evaluate and treat a problem. Obviously, it is impractical to contact a doctor for every symptom. Though it is also impossible to list in a book every critical symptom ever reported, many of the important ones to watch out for are discussed in the following pages, listed in order from head to toe.

HEAD

Headache

A Special Note on Assessment

Headache is a common childhood complaint and has many simple causes. Yet it can also be an early warning signal of several very serious but less common conditions. If your child has any of the specific symptoms listed below, call your doctor immediately. Even if you have a family history of migraines and you suspect your child is having a migraine, you should leave this diagnosis to a physician so that more serious diagnoses are not missed.

If the headache has any of the following characteristics, go to an emergency room:

- It is the worst headache the child has ever had and it does not respond to treatment.
- It is associated with any of the following:
  - a stiff neck
  - persistent vomiting
  - drowsiness or confusion
  - body weakness
  - unusual eye or limb movements
  - personality change
  - loss of previous skills such as walking

A headache that has any of the following characteristics requires a prompt visit to the doctor:

- It wakes the child from sleep or occurs early in the morning.
- It lasts over twenty-four hours consistently, especially if worsening, or not responding to home treatment.

TIP 196

A child with a headache, a stiff and/or painful neck, and fever should always be seen by a doctor immediately to rule out meningitis. Early diagnosis and treatment are critical. Children with meningitis often refuse to eat and want to be left alone.

Meningitis is an infection of the membranes covering the brain. It is most common in infants, who usually do not show specific signs (see Tip 232 for additional important information on meningitis in infants). Bacterial meningitis is more serious than the viral type, and early diagnosis can dramatically reduce the chances of deafness, cognitive impairment, and death.

If your child has the above symptoms, especially if they are accompanied by photophobia (sensitivity to light), he or she must be seen on an emergency basis by a doctor. In the early stages of meningitis, the child may not have a stiff neck.

Early treatment with intravenous antibiotics has a high cure rate (see Tip 3 for additional information on meningitis).

TIP 197

Headaches in young children, especially when associated with vomiting or visual disturbances, should be taken very seriously and investigated by a physician.

Brain tumors are the most common type of childhood tumor. The early diagnosis of certain tumors can have a major impact on the child's survival.

If the cause of your child's headache is a brain tumor, then the increasing pressure on the brain will cause headaches, usually in the morning, and these may be accompanied by vomiting and visual disturbances, most often double vision. Other symptoms may include unsteadiness during walking, slow growth in height, early puberty, seizures, or a personality change. Headaches can be caused by many nonserious conditions too, but it is important to have your child assessed and thoroughly evaluated as soon as possible.

TIP 198

Adolescents or young adults who experience headaches that get progressively more severe over a few days or longer, along with visual changes, may have a rare but treatable condition in which the pressure on the brain is increased. While not usually life-threatening, it can cause serious complications such as the permanent loss of vision.

This condition, known as benign intracranial hypertension or pseudotumor cerebri, is most common in adolescent girls. Usually the cause is unknown, but it may occasionally be the result of factors such as a hormonal imbalance, a drug side effect (for example, it could be caused by tetracycline and/or other medicines used for adolescent skin conditions), high doses of vitamin A, or obesity. Frequently no specific origin can be found.

The first step toward diagnosis is a brain scan, as this will help exclude other causes of increased pressure of the fluid around the brain, such as a tumor. If the scan is negative, a spinal tap can be used to detect when there is very high pressure of the fluid on the brain. This condition is important to diagnose because it may cause symptoms similar to a brain tumor but has a much better outcome. See your doctor as soon as possible for assessment and possible referral to a neurologist (brain specialist).

TIP 199

Carbon monoxide gas is odorless and tasteless, and inhaling it can be fatal. If your child is in an enclosed area and starts developing headaches, possibly with nausea and vomiting, and especially if others in the area begin experiencing simmilar symptoms, it may be due to carbon monoxide poisoning. Symptoms are often subtle and may include weakness and/or drowsiness, which can cause one to fall asleep rather than evacuating the contaminated area. A more distinctive sign is that your lips and gums may turn cherry red. If you are experiencing any of these symptoms, you must evacuate the area and seek urgent medical treatment. Children and pets will usually be affected first.

Sources such as a leaking gas furnace, pipe, or water heater may result in carbon monoxide poisoning. Using a charcoal grill, camp stove, or kerosene heater without proper ventilation, leaving a car running in an enclosed area, or inhaling fumes from a boat motor are other common causes of carbon monoxide poisoning.

Sometimes the sources are not immediately apparent. Inexpensive carbon monoxide monitors are sold in most hardware or department stores and will alert you to dangerous gas levels. Consider installing one on each level of your home or boat. Have your home heating system (including chimneys) checked and cleaned by a professional each year, and if you use any kind of boat with a motor, the engine and exhaust system should be checked regularly as well. If you develop any of the symptoms of carbon monoxide poisoning while in your car, get the exhaust system checked and make sure there are no holes in the floorboard.

Though any children in the area will probably come down with symptoms first, carbon monoxide poisoning can kill both children and adults quickly. If several people in the household develop headaches simultaneously and/or become drowsy, everyone should leave the house immediately. Call the gas company, and get emergency medical attention.

TIP 200

If your child experiences a head injury, is initially fine, and then becomes abnormally drowsy, vomits, or develops other symptoms within hours or sometimes even days following an injury, he or she may be experiencing bleeding inside the head. This is an emergency! Any loss of consciousness, even for a short period of time, requires immediate medical evaluation.

After a significant injury to the head, slow bleeding may start inside the skull, and the child may gradually get drowsy due to the increasing pressure within his or her head. If your child injures his/her head and initially seems fine, observe him/her closely for at least the next two or three days. This includes waking the child every hour for the first six hours following the injury to make sure he/she has not lost consciousness, and then every four hours for the next eighteen hours. Go to the hospital emergency room or call an ambulance (911 in most locations) if your child gets more drowsy, experiences weakness or jerking on one side of the body, and/or develops double vision, personality changes, speech problems, loss of sensation, seizures, dizziness, a headache, or any other major changes (see Tip 10 for more information on head injuries). If your child has lost consciousness, even for a short period of time, have him or her evaluated immediately.

TIP 201

> If your child has a fever and starts convulsing (having seizures), it is important for you to know how to react. The convulsions may affect only one side of the body and/or the child may possibly turn blue. Regardless of how long the convulsions last, you should follow the safety steps described below and call an ambulance. The child will need to be evaluated by a physician.

Children between the ages of six months and six years with a high fever are at risk of convulsing. This condition is known as a febrile seizure. It is more common in children with a family history of febrile seizures. This type of seizure will usually occur early in an illness, during the first spike of fever. It might even be the first sign that the child has a fever. If the temperature rises quickly, febrile seizures are more likely to occur. They can last anywhere from a few seconds to over fifteen minutes.

It is upsetting to see your child convulsing. Try to be calm and do the following:

- Lay your child on his/her side with his/her face tilted toward the floor to prevent him/her from choking on any food or fluids in the mouth. Do not try to restrain him or her.

- Do not try to insert your fingers or a spoon into the mouth. It will do more harm than good: You may block his/her airway or lose a finger! A bulb syringe can be used to clear the nose.
- FeverAll is a fever-reducing medicine like Tylenol, which is inserted in the rectum instead of given orally. It is equally as effective as Tylenol, and can be used in a child who is convulsing.
- Call an ambulance (911 in most locations). If it is the first episode and the child is under eighteen months, medical evaluation is necessary to rule out possible causes such as meningitis. In all cases, you should notify your child's doctor about the seizure.
- Remove the child's outer clothes immediately after the seizure if they are bundled up in a lot of clothing. If the child gets too warm, the temperature may rise again. On the other hand, avoid letting the child get chilled, since this can also make the temperature go back up. Many doctors warn against giving the child a bath, as this may cause the child to get chilled. Other doctors say that it's okay, as long as the bath is short and the water is not too hot or cold (i.e., lukewarm), especially if the fever is 104°F (40°C) or higher. If the child shivers, cover him/her with a light blanket or light layer of clothing.
- Do not give the child anything to eat or drink immediately after the seizure until he or she is able to respond to you. Then, if you haven't given the child FeverAll during the seizure, give him/her a fever-reducing medicine other than aspirin (ibuprofen or an acetaminophen, such as Tylenol). Never give a child aspirin unless it has been specifically recommended by the child's pediatrician.

If your child has had a febrile convulsion, he or she has about a 30 percent chance of having another seizure associated with the onset of a fever. Speak to your child's doctor about special precautions to prevent future febrile seizures. These include the use of medicines to keep the temperature down or to stop the seizures. The risk continues to decrease over time. Less than 2 percent of children with simple febrile seizures will go on to develop epilepsy. For a child with a simple febrile convulsion, there is no association with learning difficulties later in life. All febrile seizures warrant medical evaluation.

TIP 202

> Convulsions in a baby can be very subtle. If your baby has unusual rhythmic movements, especially in the face, eyes, or limbs, call a doctor.

In adults the most common type of convulsion is a generalized one, where the whole body shakes violently and the person becomes unaware of his or her surroundings. In babies, especially in the first month of life, seizures are less obvious. Watch for the repetitive "cycling" of one leg which lasts for around a minute, smacking movements of the lips, eyes or head deviating to one side, or eye twitching. These may be the only signs of a convulsion in an infant.

Let your doctor know as soon as possible if your baby exhibits these kinds of repeated unusual rhythmic movements, especially in the context of other problems such as feeding difficulties or a complicated delivery. Keep a record and description of these episodes, so that he or she can make the appropriate diagnosis.

PSYCHOLOGICAL PROBLEMS

TIP 203

> If you suspect that your child or adolescent is depressed, immediately seek appropriate help. Suicide is one of the most common causes of death among teenagers.

Depression can happen in even the most loving of homes. Whether or not it is precipitated by a personal crisis, it is usually caused by a chemical imbalance and/or a family predisposition. Children and teenagers with depression are often labeled "difficult" or "moody" rather than given appropriate help. The stigma of depression can also cause people to avoid seeking help—a delay that can have tragic results.

Clinical depression is a prolonged, persistent disturbance of mood, often with associated physical symptoms. The warning signs may include:

- Persistent sadness and complaints, with a negative self-image
- Lack of interest in favorite activities and food
- Withdrawal from family and friends (at times with hostility)

- Worsening school performance
- Anxiety about simple tasks and events
- Sleep disturbances, either insomnia or hypersomnia (long periods of sleep)
- Appetite changes: loss of appetite or overeating
- Multiple physical complaints: aches and pains everywhere
- Hinting at suicide or giving away prized possessions
- Irritability
- Apparent personality change in a teenager/extreme teenage rebelliousness

There is a greater risk that your depressed child might commit suicide if the following risk factors apply to him/her:
- Male sex (although more girls attempt suicide, more boys actually succeed)
- Alcohol or drug abuse
- A gun in the house (firearms are used the most to commit suicide in America)
- A previous suicide attempt
- A recent suicide in your area
- A bereavement experience: a death, a divorce, a failed exam, rejection by friends, and the like

If your child exhibits symptoms of depression and/or is at risk of committing suicide, get them assessed and treated before they can injure themselves seriously. With counseling and medication (if appropriate), he or she can go on to live a full and normal life. (See Tip 12 for more on depression.)

TIP 204

> Anorexia and bulimia are dangerous, life-threatening conditions that require expert treatment as soon as possible. Overeating and obesity can also be serious health hazards.

Anorexia is common in preadolescent and adolescent girls and is sometimes even seen in boys. The affected individual has an overpowering fear of being fat, accompanied by behavior intended to result in weight loss, such as not eating, excessive exercise, etc. Bulimia tends to occur in older adolescents or adults and is associated with binge eating and purging (self-induced vomiting or use of laxatives). Bulimia can be more difficult to recognize in an individual, since body weight and shape may appear normal. However, frequent vomiting can cause wear of the enamel on the back teeth, which may be picked up during a routine dental checkup.

An affected teenager may:

- Be preoccupied with their weight and body size
- Avoid eating with the family and eat very little
- Use laxatives and diuretics, and induce vomiting
- Exercise excessively
- Wear shapeless clothes
- Have irregular menstrual periods or a persistent absence of periods
- Develop fine, downy hairs on the face and trunk

There are many medical complications associated with anorexia and bulimia, which may include kidney and heart complications, damage to the esophagus and/or stomach, and aspiration pneumonia. Self-induced vomiting and purging with laxatives can also cause dangerous imbalances of electrolytes (minerals) in the blood. There is a 10 percent mortality rate among those who have anorexia.

The earlier a diagnosis is made and professional help is obtained, the better chance that your daughter or son will have a normal adult life. Lead her/him by your positive example and good eating habits!

EYES

TIP 205

Three red light warning signals that may indicate a tumor in the back of the eye are:

- "Unparallel" eyes—one eye looks straight ahead and the other looks in a different direction (this may be normal for infants under four months of age, but you should still consult your pediatrician).
- One pupil appears white or consistently different from the other pupil.
- There is a change in the color of one iris.

If your child has any of these signs, it is important to have him or her assessed by an ophthalmologist (eye specialist).

Tumors of the retina (in the back of the eye) usually occur in the first two years of life and are more common in children with a family history of this condition. There is usually no pain associated with this type of tumor, which is known as a retinoblastoma.

Over 90 percent of children can be cured when there is an early diagnosis; rapid diagnosis and treatment increase the chances of preserving sight in the affected eye and saving the child's life. Genetic evaluation of the child and family is advised, because some of these cases are hereditary.

(Also, see Appendix C, page 387, about pediatric eye screening.)

THROAT

TIP 206

Chronic or persistent hoarseness, often with difficulty breathing, may be caused by papilloma (viral induced growths) on the vocal cords. Chronic
hoarseness and/or pain when swallowing may be
the first signs of gastric reflux. A child with any of
these symptoms should be evaluated. If the
growths (warts) become large, they can obstruct
breathing. Also, they can progress farther down
the airway and become impossible to treat.

Children are often hoarse for a short period of time after a
cold—or too much shouting! However, if your child (especially a child under five) is hoarse repeatedly or has hoarseness
that persists for about a month or more, he/she may need assessment by a pediatric ENT (ear, nose, and throat) doctor
who will look in the throat with a scope. Then the doctor will
institute proper treatment.

Note: There is a vaccine that may have value in preventing
the growth of these papillomas. (See Appendix C, page 376,
about the HPV vaccine, Pap smear, and pelvic exam.)

TIP 207

If your child has become suddenly ill and is drooling, is unable to open his or her mouth wide, has any decrease in the range of motion in his or her neck, cannot swallow liquids (including his/her own saliva), and/or is having difficulty talking or breathing, take your child to the emergency room immediately. Swelling, possibly caused by an infection, could be blocking the child's throat. Another sign that this is the case is if the child refuses to assume any position besides sitting up and forward. Try to keep the child upright.

Children may not want to eat or drink when sick. But when given a pain or fever reducer, they can usually be convinced to swallow small amounts of cool liquids. If your child refuses to take any liquids, even after being given the correct dose of an over-the-counter pain medicine and especially if they exhibit the above symptoms, you should take them to the emergency room immediately.

ARMS, HANDS, FINGERS, AND NAILS

TIP 208

An infant with swollen, tender fingers or toes may be showing the first signs of sickle cell disease. The early diagnosis of this disease and the treatment and/or prevention of accompanying infections (including additional immunizations) will reduce the child's risk of dying very young.

Sickle cell disease is an inherited disorder common in Africans and African Americans, affecting one in five hundred. It can also be found in people with Asian, Mediterranean, and/or South American origins. The condition affects the shape of red blood cells and causes anemia (a low red blood cell count). The abnormal red blood cells block the blood vessels, resulting in pain and a high risk of infection, particularly from certain bacteria. Some children with this condition die before they reach the age of five, yet with appropriate treatment and education, many patients with sickle cell will survive to their fifties or older.

The typical first signs in an infant, as mentioned, are swollen, tender, red, and/or shiny fingers or toes. These signs may last for several days. The fingers and toes will be very painful, and the infant may seem distressed. An older, school-age child or adult will tend to have pain in the arms, legs, chest, and belly instead.

The sickle cell diagnosis can be made from a simple blood test. Seek medical advice on how to deal with the various problems relating to this ailment. If younger children with sickle cell disease take certain antibiotics regularly, the risk of developing life-threatening infections will be reduced. Fortunately, these severe infections are now very rare in the United States, since hospitals screen for sickle cell disease at birth.

BACK

TIP 209

If your teenager's back and ribs appear asymmetrical (especially when bending over to touch his/her toes), he/she may be developing a curved spine. It can get worse rapidly, causing serious problems.

Progressive curvature of the spine occurs more commonly in adolescent girls. Rapid worsening of the curvature can result in a severe deformity and breathing difficulties. Early treatment may prevent progression—surgery is occasionally needed.

If you suspect this condition, look at your child's back

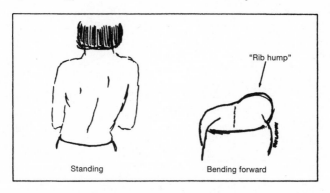

Figure 16. Girl with Scoliosis.

from behind while they are touching their toes. Note if the ribs on one side (in 80 percent it will be the right side) form a hump (see Figure 16), or if the shoulder blade appears to protrude on that same side. If you suspect your child has this condition, seek medical evaluation and treatment early. (See Appendix C, page 388, for information about scoliosis screening.)

CHEST

TIP 210

A child who suddenly develops a harsh noisy sound when breathing in (called stridor) that does not go away when he or she is at rest should be seen immediately in the emergency room. However, if the stridor is from an inhaled object, it requires emergency first aid (see Appendix A, page 350). Croup (a "seal-like" barking cough) also requires an emergency room visit.

Sudden onset of stridor is usually associated with difficulty breathing. The most serious cause used to be an infection of the epiglottis (the "hinged" flap over the windpipe that stops food from entering the lungs when you swallow). This is very rare now thanks to Hib immunization, which protects children from the germ responsible for this problem. In the case of a sudden onset of stridor, do not administer first aid for choking because this could make the condition worse. Do not put your fingers in his or her mouth. The first thing to do is to walk outside with your child if it is cool out, or open the freezer door and sit in the cool air. Even if his or her condition does improve with cool air, go to the emergency room.

Frequently, the stridor will get better when the child calms down, but he or she should still be seen by a physician as soon as possible. Croup and inhaled objects are the remaining most common causes of stridor. If you suspect that an infant has inhaled an object (such as a coin, peanut, little toy, hard candy, piece of popcorn, carrot, or battery) and if he/she has a sudden onset of difficulty breathing, immediately administer emergency first aid. (See Appendix A, page 343, for basic instructions.)

Croup is a viral infection around the voice box that typically causes a seal-like, barking kind of cough that gradually worsens. It is important to notify the child's pediatrician if he or she develops this type of cough. However, if a younger child with this ailment develops noisy breathing that does not get better when the child quiets down, it may be life-threatening. Keep the child as calm as possible (agitation worsens the condition), and get him or her to an emergency room immediately. Do not administer first aid for choking because this could make the condition worse.

While stridor is caused by the swelling—and thus narrowing—of the airway, croup is caused by an irritation of the airway. Croup can turn into stridor in certain cases.

TIP 211

If your child has recurrent wheezing, especially when he or she gets a cold, or a recurrent nighttime cough, he/she may have asthma and should be assessed and started on appropriate treatment.

Note: In rare cases, the wheezing may be caused by a foreign object lodged in the airway, which requires urgent medical evaluation. If the

child cannot speak and is clearly choking, you
need to attempt to get the object out. (See
Appendix A, page 343, for instruction.)

Asthma is an allergic or inflammatory condition. Certain triggers cause the small "air pipes" in the lungs to become inflamed and narrowed, making breathing more difficult and causing the individual to wheeze, cough, and, if severe, even struggle for breath. Some common triggers are sudden exposure to cold air, secondhand smoke, cats, dogs, dust mites, cockroaches, and exercise. Days with high ozone levels are also unhealthy for asthmatics; outdoor time should be limited when the air quality is bad. The morning news (both on television and radio) often gives reports on air quality. The daily Air Quality Index can also be found online and on the Weather Channel.

Asthma is increasingly common, with many cases occurring in families with no previous history of it. Sometimes the child's only symptom is a recurrent nighttime cough, and the diagnosis of asthma may be delayed, which could have serious consequences. Do not use over-the-counter cough syrups or over-the-counter bronchodilators (like Primatene Mist) if your child has asthma, unless prescribed by his or her pediatrician. In children with asthma, coughing is usually related to early wheezing.

Asthma is a variable condition, and most children have mild disorders that are easily treatable, usually with inhaled medicine. Many will "grow out of it." Some children, however, will experience severe life-threatening attacks. So get your child assessed by a doctor as soon as possible for appropriate treatment, and learn to avoid the specific "triggers" of his or her asthma attack (see Tips 57 and 212 for more information on asthma attacks). If your child has asthma and is over five years of age, ask his/her doctor about having your child's breathing tested on a breathing machine called a spirometer, which measures respiratory gases. Also, do not allow anyone to smoke around your child.

TIP 212

When your child has an asthma attack, you need to recognize the symptoms and know how to react immediately. The key to treating asthma is to prevent an attack from becoming severe (symptoms of a severe attack include struggling to breathe, difficulty speaking, possibly turning blue, etc.). You can do this by responding appropriately to the first symptoms, which will be more innocuous and will include coughing, wheezing, etc. You also need to learn what triggers severe attacks of asthma for your child and try to specifically avoid these triggers. For many children with severe or persistent asthma symptoms, being placed on daily inhaled steroids can significantly improve quality of life with minimal to no side effects.

Nine million children in the United States have been diagnosed with asthma. A severe attack can rapidly become life-threatening in a child, whereas a mild attack may be managed carefully with home treatment using inhaled medication. The treatment at home should be conducted in consultation with the child's physician. This involves using a nebulizer or metered dose inhaler that contains a bronchodilator to open up the airway and an inhaled steroid that reduces inflammation of the airway. The metered dose inhaler is most effective when used with a spacer.

You need to be able to recognize a severe attack immediately. The child will struggle to breathe, will be unable to speak easily or walk across the room, and will possibly even turn blue. The loudness of the wheeze is irrelevant, and in fact a "silent chest" is even more serious. Call an ambulance (911 in most locations), and while you are waiting, start your child on their emergency medication (such as albuterol), if you have it. (See Tips 57 and 211 for more information on asthma attacks.)

Be sure that the child's medicine is constantly with them, even when you are not. Get a refill as soon as you start running low on the medication; do not wait until the next asthma attack.

BELLY

TIP 213

If you have a child between the ages of two and six, and you notice a firm mass in his or her belly, seek medical evaluation. You may only notice that the child's belly is getting bigger and bigger, or is more firm than normal. Early diagnosis and treatment of a mass observed or felt in the belly will increase the chances of survival if he or she has kidney cancer.

Wilms' tumor of the kidney occurs mainly in the two-to-six-year age group, with a peak at the age of three. At the time of diagnosis, most children seem well and are simply found to have a large mass in the belly area, often discovered by a parent while bathing the child. The mass can often become surprisingly large before its presence is even noticed. There may also be a variety of nonspecific signs or symptoms, including constipation, nausea, vomiting, weight loss, and high blood pressure. Twenty-five percent of children with Wilms' tumor will also have a small amount of blood in the urine, which can only be detected when the urine is tested.

Children with any of the following characteristics are at an increased risk of Wilms' tumor:

- Abnormal kidney shape or structure (like a horseshoe kidney) from birth
- Genital abnormalities (like hypospadias)
- A family history of Wilms' tumor
- Certain syndromes, especially if one side of the child's body is bigger than the other (hemihypertrophy)
- No iris in the eye
- Abnormalities of chromosome II (detected with a blood test)

Children with any of these risk factors should be checked regularly by a doctor to exclude a kidney tumor. An early diagnosis will result in around a 90 percent cure rate.

URINE

TIP 214

Though it is rare, a child can develop acute kidney failure with a low blood count (anemia) following diarrhea or a respiratory infection. Symptoms of kidney failure include reduced urine output, red or brown urine, drowsiness, irritability, paleness, and tiny "needlepoint" red spots on the skin. Immediate medical management (ideally by a pediatric kidney specialist or nephrologist) is necessary to save the child's life in a case of acute kidney failure.

Sometimes after bloody diarrhea (particularly when caused by the bacteria *E. coli*), or more rarely after a respiratory infection, a child may suddenly develop temporary kidney failure and severe anemia. This is called hemolytic uremic syndrome and is more common in children under the age of three. Emergency medical therapy improves the chance for survival and lowers the risk of long-term kidney problems.

TIP 215

If your child is experiencing an unexplained fever and/or frequent, sometimes painful urination, he or she may have a urinary tract infection. The child may wet his/her pants or bed, even if he or she is potty-trained. The urine may also have a dark color and/or strong smell. The signs and symptoms in a child are subtle, so it is important to be aware of them and take this condition seriously. Recurrent, untreated urinary tract infections in young children are one of the most common causes of kidney failure.

Urinary tract infections (UTIs) in infants and young children can be extremely difficult to recognize because the signs and symptoms are usually nonspecific: mild fever, frequent urination (sometimes with pain), and/or urine that smells particularly strong. It can also be difficult to get a clean sample of urine from a small child.

If your child has a persistent fever with no other obvious cause (such as a cold or ear infection), you should have his or her urine checked by a doctor as soon as possible. If your preschool child has had a proven UTI, he or she should be thoroughly checked, in order to exclude a condition where the urine refluxes up into the kidney from the bladder. A child who has this problem is at a higher risk of damaging his or her kidneys and needs to be carefully supervised and treated. A delay in diagnosis and treatment can result in permanent kidney damage and high blood pressure later in life. (See also Tip 130.)

TIP 216

> If your child is drinking much more than normal, passing a lot of urine, and/or losing weight, you should get him or her tested to exclude diabetes mellitus. Early diagnosis and treatment can improve his or her overall long-term health.

Many children with diabetes mellitus are not diagnosed until they go into a coma and develop a life-threatening condition called ketoacidosis. In retrospect most parents of newly diagnosed diabetics realize that their child has not been "right" for weeks or even months, often displaying symptoms of weight loss, low energy, and excessive thirst.

Parents who notice these symptoms in their child should take the child for a checkup as soon as possible, especially if there is a family history of diabetes. Any child who has previously been dry at night but then starts bed-wetting should have his or her urine checked for diabetes. If the diagnosis is diabetes, the careful control of the child's blood sugar (with diet and insulin injections) can decrease the risk that he or she will develop the complications of diabetes.

(Also, see Appendix C, page 383, for information on diabetes screening.)

BOWEL MOVEMENT

TIP 217

Constipation is a very common symptom in babies, and is often associated with dietary issues. Also, the bowel habits of babies are different from those of adults—babies can often go longer without a bowel movement. However, if your baby has suffered from chronic severe constipation since birth, which may have included problems with passing meconium (the dark sticky stools) at birth, he or she may have an abnormality in his/her nerve supply to the large bowel. This condition requires surgery to prevent bowel obstruction and life-threatening inflammation or perforation of the bowel. There are also other problems that may cause severe constipation, including a defective anus.

Hirschsprung's disease is a condition in which the nerve supply to the large bowel is abnormal. Boys are affected about five times more commonly than girls, and the disease is more frequent in children with Down's syndrome. The symptoms depend on the length of bowel affected, which varies from a few centimeters near the anus to the entire length of the large bowel.

If only a short segment of the bowel is involved, diagnosis may be delayed. Any baby who does not pass a stool in the first twenty-four hours of his or her life and does not have another obvious bowel problem or an anal abnormality should be investigated for this condition. Children who have been constipated since birth should also be investigated. If a diagnosis is not made quickly, the bowel may become blocked, inflamed, and could even burst (perforate). Note: It is common for a healthy toddler who has previously had normal bowel movements to experience constipation while potty-training.

TIP 218

If your infant is crying abnormally as if having labor pains, pulling up his or her knees, and/or passing bright red or maroon-colored stools, he or she needs to be brought to the emergency room immediately.

Babies may get a condition in their bowels (called intussusception) wherein one portion of the bowel telescopes into the next and gets stuck. This blocks the bowel and cuts off the blood supply to that portion of bowel. If the condition is not reversed rapidly, the bowel will die, and the infant will become very ill.

It may be difficult to differentiate a baby with colic (spasmodic pain in the abdomen) from one with intussusception. A baby with intussusception may spontaneously cry in regular intervals when he or she is apparently content. This pattern can be likened to the pattern of labor pains. A sausage-shaped lump may be felt in the belly, and in rare cases the baby may pass jellylike stools. If intussusception is diagnosed early, it can often be cured by a special enema, avoiding the need for surgery. This should always be done by an experienced doctor.

This condition is an emergency. Get your child to an emergency room immediately.

TIP 219

If a child or infant has more than a small amount of blood in his or her stools repeatedly and/or severe cramping during an episode of diarrhea, it increases the chance that the illness is a serious one and will require immediate medical attention.

Older children may flush the toilet without observing the nature of a diarrhea stool. They should be asked to look at the stool and show it to an adult if it is abnormal. With the emergence of *E. coli* as a potentially very dangerous germ, it has become important that parents watch diarrhea carefully (see Tip 220 for more emergency information on diarrhea in babies and children). Large numbers of stools, severe cramping with diarrhea, and blood in the stools should cause parents to seek medical attention.

Remember, when observing the stool, that if the child drinks red liquids or eats beets, the stool may have a red color.

TIP 220

Dehydration or other complications due to excessive loss of fluid needs to be avoided in a baby or child who has diarrhea and/or vomiting. It can be life-threatening.

Diarrhea and vomiting are both common problems in babies and infants. Dehydration can occur rapidly, especially if the infant also has a fever.

If your child has diarrhea and/or vomiting and any of the following symptoms, you should get him or her to the emergency room.

- Frequent vomiting if the baby is under three months of age. Some doctors suggest that "frequent" means more than three times in four hours, but it could be less often, depending on the severity of the vomiting.
- Signs of dehydration:
  - excessive drowsiness or irritability, or limpness
  - sunken eyes and sunken fontanel (soft spot on the head)
  - loose, dry skin
  - dry mouth and tongue
  - very little, dark-colored urine (less than three wet diapers in twenty-four hours)
- Persistent belly pain
- Very forceful, recurrent vomiting (projectile), in a baby; green or bloody vomit
- Blood in the stools (small streaks without any other signs or symptoms are not an emergency, but warrant contacting the child's doctor)

In children over six months, dehydration may be prevented by giving oral solutions such as Pedialyte. Consult with the child's physician before giving these solutions to babies younger than six months of age, since they do not have the important nourishment that a baby needs. You may be able to continue giving breast milk or formula. They are best when given in small volumes at frequent intervals, and they can be very effective. If your child is still vomiting occasionally, you may have to give him/her as little as a teaspoon at a time.

Solutions that contain a high sodium content, such as Rehydralyte, should only be given to a child (of any age) on the advice of a physician.

Viruses are the most common cause of diarrhea in children. Babies who are exclusively breast-fed until they are six months of age very rarely get significant diarrhea. Eating undercooked ground beef and unwashed vegetables increases the risk for dangerous *E. coli* diarrhea.

If your child has vomiting or diarrhea, ask a physician how much regular food and how much of these rehydration solutions are appropriate for him or her.

GENITALIA

TIP 221

If your child develops signs of puberty too early, he or she should be evaluated. Signs of puberty may include rapid growth, hair growth (pubic and armpit), acne, and adult body odor, as well as breast enlargement and the onset of menstruation in girls or increasing genitalia size, a deepening voice, and growth of facial hair in boys. These signs can be due to an infection, a hormone problem, a tumor, a brain abnormality, or a brain injury.

Signs of puberty are considered abnormal when developed under the age of eight years in girls and nine in boys. Precocious or early puberty has many nonserious causes, and in certain cases there's no known cause. However, it is important to rule out infections, tumors, brain abnormalities, brain injuries, or hormonal problems. Take your child to the doctor for assessment and possible investigation. Early diagnosis may be life-saving.

LEGS

TIP 222

> If your son learned to walk late, falls frequently, and/or has difficulty walking, standing up from a sitting position, or going up stairs, you must take him to a doctor to make sure that he does not have a muscular dystrophy such as Duchenne's.

The most common muscular dystrophy occurs only in boys (about one in every 2,500 male births). Many cases are in families with no previous history of this condition.

The afflicted boy is usually slow at learning to walk (over eighteen months old) and has difficulty climbing stairs or getting into the car. He may get up from sitting on the floor by climbing up his legs (e.g., holding onto his legs to pull himself up). He may waddle as he walks and tend to fall a lot. His tongue and calf muscles may look bigger than normal. This condition may also have associated learning difficulties. Treatment is supportive rather than curative, and thus the most important measures will be to improve quality of life. Early diagnosis also allows for genetic counseling about future pregnancies.

TIP 223

> If your child starts complaining of significant, persistent pain in the bones, he/she should be evaluated by a doctor to exclude cancer of the blood or bone. The pain often first appears in the arms and legs, and gets worse over a period of a few days or weeks. Any refusal to bear weight (either standing up to bear one's own weight or carrying things) also warrants evaluation.

Acute lymphoblastic leukemia is a cancer of the blood and is the most common childhood cancer, occurring especially in two- to six-year-olds. Two-thirds of children with this cancer first complain of bone pain, particularly around the knee. A preverbal child may simply cry a lot and want to be carried much more frequently. Sometimes the diagnosis of this disease is delayed because doctors fail to consider cancer as a cause of these signs. This cancer has a 90 percent cure rate, especially if it is diagnosed early.

The most common childhood bone tumors occur in boys around the time of puberty. Early diagnosis is important because once the cancer has spread elsewhere in the body, the prognosis is much worse.

Obviously there are many simple causes for leg pains in active children that are not worth worrying about. Bone pains that occur during the night after a vigorous day of activity in a child who is otherwise normal are generally not serious (e.g., growing pains). But if the pain is severe and constant, you should take your child to the doctor to rule out serious causes.

SKIN AND HAIR

TIP 224

A child who has a fever (usually over 101 degrees), flu-like symptoms, possibly a stiff neck, and a rash that does not disappear when pressure is applied to it could have a serious bacterial infection (meningococcosis). He or she should be brought to the emergency room immediately. Note: The rash may appear faint and pink, or it may be flat, blotchy, and red or purple. It could also look like blood spattering or tiny pinpricks.

Fever and rash in a child can have many causes. The majority of them are viral, and in an otherwise healthy child they are not usually life-threatening. However, if your child suddenly develops a fever along with the type of rash mentioned above, especially if he/she is acting abnormally in any way, emergency evaluation is needed. Even a *one-hour delay* could affect your child's chances of survival. Get him or her to an emergency room immediately.

One cause is a bacterium called meningococcus (most common in children under two years old or between fifteen and twenty-four years of age), which produces a serious contagious infection in the blood that progresses rapidly. It often responds well to early treatment with intravenous antibiotics. Current recommendations are for adolescents to be immunized against meningococcosis between the ages of eleven and eighteen. However, the vaccines do not protect against all of the strains of this bacterium, and it may only offer protection for five to eight years.

A fever, flu-like symptoms, and a quickly developing rash can also be caused by other medical conditions, including inflammation of the blood vessels after a viral infection. Also, a similar-looking rash that usually develops more slowly and without a fever or other symptoms could be due to a reduced number of platelets in the blood. The child is at risk of severe bleeding, for instance a brain hemorrhage. (See Appendix D, page 393, for tips on using a thermometer.)

TIP 225

> A red, flat birthmark (which may look like a wine stain) covering approximately one third of a child's face on one side may be associated with serious underlying brain abnormalities. The child should be thoroughly evaluated by a physician.

Children with Sturge-Weber syndrome have a red, flat birthmark covering one third of their face. There is an underlying abnormality, usually in the back area of the brain, on the same side. It may result in epilepsy, mental retardation, and/or a stroke (which will affect the opposite side of the body). Expert neurological (nerve) and ophthalmological (eye) assessment and care are needed to prevent or treat possible complications associated with this disorder. The condition is not known to be inherited.

TIP 226

> If your child has (or at one time had) freckling
> and increased coloration of the skin around the
> mouth or anus, they may have a condition called
> Peutz-Jeghers syndrome. This condition leads to
> multiple polyps (fingerlike growths) throughout
> the bowel, which may bleed, causing anemia (a
> low blood count) or bowel blockage.

Peutz-Jeghers syndrome, a genetic condition, has a 50 percent chance of inheritance. The affected person has increased pigmentation and freckling around the mouth and often around the anus. This pigmentation can be a telltale signal of the presence of polyps in the wall of the gut. The polyps often bleed, resulting in anemia, and may also cause intussusception (where one part of the gut telescopes into the next). These polyps usually do not turn cancerous, but the child needs to be assessed thoroughly by a gastroenterologist (stomach/intestine specialist). (See Tip 157 for more information on this disorder.)

TIP 227

> Does your child have five or more flat light brown
> birthmarks (each more than three quarters of an
> inch or 1.5 centimeters in diameter)? If so, they
> should be examined by an expert to exclude neu-
> rofibromatosis, an inheritable condition that may
> be associated with learning disabilities, epilepsy,
> and a high risk of malignant tumors.

Neurofibromatosis is an inherited condition that occurs in 1 child per 2,500. It is very variable in its manifestations. A child who has one or more of the following should be assessed by an expert:

- Five or more "café au lait" spots (light brown, flat moles) on the skin (each measuring over 1.5 centimeters or three quarters of an inch in diameter). They are most commonly found on the trunk of the body, and are usually not present at birth but appear in the first two decades of life.
- Freckling in the armpits and/or groin
- Plexiform neurofibroma, a lumpy overgrowth of parts of peripheral nerves, most common on the jaw and eyelids
- Fibromas, or small, pink, nonpainful lumpy growths on the skin that do not occur until puberty
- Speckling on the iris of the eyes
- Scoliosis or bowing of the legs

Adults may have neurofibromatosis but be unaware of it. Affected children may experience neurological problems during infancy, such as epilepsy, attention deficit disorder, and mental retardation. Those affected are at a high risk of developing tumors of the optic nerve (the nerve to the eye), the main nerve to the ear, and the brain. A precise diagnosis is especially important, since the family should seek genetic consulting.

TIP 228

A combination of signs may be associated with Kawasaki's disease in a young, very irritable child. These include fever, red eyes, a redder-than-normal mouth, a rash, and/or enlarged neck glands. Signs may also include swelling and red and/or peeling skin on the hands and feet. Early diagnosis and appropriate treatment are essential to prevent life-threatening heart problems.

Your child may have Kawasaki's if he or she is under five and has a high fever (over 104 degrees Fahrenheit) that lasts for several days, accompanied by the following symptoms (doctors expect to observe at least four of these):

- Light sensitivity and red eyes
- Mouth and lips that are redder than normal (the surface of the tongue may look like a strawberry)
- Changes in the hands and feet (initially swollen, then red and peeling)
- Rash
- Swollen glands in the neck

Kawasaki's disease may initially resemble many other childhood illnesses, but it is important to make the diagnosis and treat this condition as early as possible. Expert assessment is needed. Treatment for Kawasaki's usually includes gamma-globulin and low-dose aspirin to prevent the formation of aneurysms (outpouchings) in the arteries supplying blood to the heart muscle, which may cause a "heart attack" in young children.

See your doctor as soon as possible. Early treatment, including intravenous gamma-globulin and low-dose aspirin, can decrease the risk of life-threatening heart damage.

TIP 229

If your baby is jaundiced (has a yellow hue to the skin and/or eyes) during the first week of life, you need to talk to his/her doctor as soon as possible in order to determine if there is risk of life-threatening complications from high levels of the substance bilirubin.

Jaundice in the first week of life is often benign (not dangerous), but there are certain cases where it may be very serious.

If the bilirubin (the substance that causes the jaundice) reaches high levels, it can cross into the brain, causing brain damage or even death. Mild jaundice is very common, affecting 80 percent of premature babies and 60 percent of regular-term babies, and is not serious. But certain causes of jaundice can result in a dangerously high level of bilirubin.

A common cause of severe jaundice is an incompatibility between the mother's blood type and the baby's blood type. An inherited red blood cell disorder, including G6PD deficiency and sickle cell disease, can also cause severe jaundice. In these cases red blood cells are destroyed, and bilirubin is released into the bloodstream, causing the yellow coloring. Both of these conditions occur much more commonly in Asians and African Americans than in Caucasians. Since a yellow hue is harder to detect in these babies due to their skin coloring, their jaundice can be more easily detected by examining the color of their gums and the whites of the eyes. During the first weeks of life, babies have their eyes closed most of the time, so parents have to make a conscious effort to look carefully every day for the first week. Gently open your baby's eyes and mouth to check for signs of yellowing. You may want to try darkening the room and using a flashlight. Babies open their eyes in the dark.

Be aware that jaundice during the first weeks of life may also be caused by an extremely serious bacterial infection in the blood or a urinary tract infection.

If there is no underlying illness, mild jaundice requires no treatment. Moderate jaundice can be treated easily by putting the baby under a special blue light, thus preventing the jaundice from becoming more serious. Severe jaundice may require an exchange blood transfusion, which is a major procedure.

If your baby has these red light warning signals, see your doctor as soon as possible.

TIP 230

There is an inherited disorder that is associated with the following signs: sparse hair, fragile nails, dry skin, and abnormal development of teeth (pointed teeth, missing teeth, etc.). This disorder is also associated with a condition whereby the body is unable to maintain the correct temperature. A child with this condition is in danger of dying from extreme heat within his/her body (i.e., an extremely high temperature).

Several conditions, collectively called ectodermal dysplasias, involve the above abnormalities.

Since the ability to sweat may be impaired, the child may be unable to regulate his or her temperature and become dangerously hot (hyperthermic). Even a mild illness may cause extremely high fevers. You must take specific measures to keep your child from overheating. Children with these conditions are also more susceptible to getting nasal and lung infections.

A child with the above symptoms should be assessed by a skin specialist (dermatologist) as soon as possible.

ALLERGIC REACTIONS

TIP 231

In susceptible individuals, a severe allergic reaction affecting the entire body, called anaphylactic shock, may follow an insect sting or the ingestion of certain medications or foods. The red light warning signals include sudden swelling of the eyes, lips, and tongue; difficulty breathing; and weakness, a feeling of faintness, or fainting. Immediate emergency care is required to prevent death.

Individuals who are more prone to allergies or who have a family member who has had a life-threatening reaction to an allergen are more likely to go into anaphylactic shock when they come into contact with certain substances.

The most common causes are:
• Insect bites
• Medications, especially in the penicillin family
• Foods such as peanuts, shellfish, and strawberries

The individual may have a flushed or pale appearance. They may first experience a burning of the lips followed within minutes by a puffy face and neck, as well as breathing difficulties. They may complain of itching or belly pain, begin to vomit, and/or develop a blotchy, raised red rash or hives. Call an ambulance immediately (911 in most locations).

If you or your child has had a reaction like this one before, always carry an epinephrine injection kit (i.e., an EpiPen) with you, and know how to use it. If your child is old enough, teach him or her how to self-administer the injection. Get him or her an identity bracelet, clearly showing the medical details of his/her allergies and the necessary treatment. An allergist should also be consulted, as he or she may be able to reduce the severity of your child's reactions with appropriate treatment, often including a series of shots. (See Tip 169 for more information on allergies.)

FEVER

TIP 232

The vast majority of fevers in children have benign causes (that is, they are not life-threatening). However, if, along with a fever, your child is also irritable, not drinking, and/or difficult to awaken, it may be a serious life-threatening illness such as meningitis.

A temperature taken rectally is thought by many doctors to give the most accurate measurement. Many doctors recommend taking a rectal temperature if the child is under two years of age, and especially if the child is under six months old. Missing an elevated temperature in a baby can have life-threatening consequences. Ideally, every parent should own a thermometer that can be used rectally and know how to use it *safely* (see Appendix D, page 393, for instructions on taking a rectal temperature and discussion of other types of thermometers).

If your infant has the preceding symptoms, see a doctor immediately. (See the introduction to the pediatric section under Abnormal Temperature, page 261, to determine which levels of fever require immediate attention at various age groups.) Do not overwrap your baby, as this may raise his or her temperature further.

One important potential cause of a high fever in babies is meningitis, which is an infection of the membranes covering the brain. The fever may actually be an important first clue of the disease. Though babies get meningitis more commonly than older kids or adults, the disease is harder to detect in them, because they are unable to communicate about their symptoms (such as a headache). Also, before the soft spot on top of your baby's head is closed, they are less likely to show the classic physical signs of a stiff neck, although the soft spot on their head may bulge out. This is why it is crucial to watch out for the infant's behavior; if he or she is not in a happy, playful state at least every few hours, and/or he or she exhibits the other symptoms listed above, it is very important to get your baby to the emergency room immediately. The doctor needs to determine whether the child has a life-threatening condition. Urgent treatment is essential.

It is important to note, though, that babies without a fever can still have meningitis. Teenagers and young adults are also prone to getting meningitis.

MISCELLANEOUS

TIP 233

The loss of basic skills, such as walking and talking clearly, or the regression to behavior such as thumb-sucking, "baby talk," bed-wetting, or wetting themselves is known as developmental regression. It has a number of serious causes, and the affected child should be thoroughly evaluated.

Occasionally when a child has been ill or has had a major emotional upset—such as the arrival of a new brother or sister—he or she may temporarily lose recently acquired skills, such as potty-training. But a child who loses several skills progressively, especially if there is no obvious reason, should be evaluated by a physician. There are many possible causes, including brain disorders, a tumor, HIV infection, child abuse, a mental or learning disability, or autism.

TIP 234

If you have a family history of crib death [also known as SIDS (sudden infant death syndrome)],

or an infant who has had "near-miss crib death,"
you can take some simple measures to dramatically reduce the risk of a recurrence.

In developed countries, SIDS (sudden infant death syndrome)
or crib death is still the most common cause of death in babies
age one month to one year. Most cases occur in babies under
six months of age. The incidence has decreased dramatically
since the public education campaigns of the early 1990s on the
sleeping positions of babies.

The following babies are especially at risk:

- Premature and low-birth-weight babies
- Twins, triplets, etc. (multiple pregnancies)
- Babies from a lower socioeconomic status
- Babies in households where anyone smokes, especially
  the mother. This risk increases with the number of cigarettes smoked; for every additional ten cigarettes per day,
  the risk of crib death increases threefold.

In order to reduce your baby's risk of crib death:

- Do not smoke during pregnancy, or permit anyone to
  smoke in your household after the birth of your baby.
- Put your baby to sleep on his or her back. If the baby has
  reflux (a spitting baby), tilt the baby on his or her left
  side to prevent fluid from regurgitating into his or her
  lungs (aspiration). Once your baby is old enough to roll
  over, this is irrelevant.
- Do not overdress your baby or use too much bedding,
  especially if the baby is already warm. Use only one thin
  blanket if needed. Tuck it in so it cannot cover the baby's
  head. A blanket sleeper or warm sleeping garment is an
  alternative in a cold environment.
- Never put your baby on a water bed, sheepskins, or very
  soft bedding material.

- Select a crib that conforms to Consumer Product Safety Commission recommendations and has a firm and snug-fitting mattress.
- Never leave stuffed animals in the crib while your baby is sleeping.
- Breast-feed your baby for at least six months if possible (of course, there are other advantages of breast-feeding for six months or more).
- If you think your baby is sick, contact your doctor.
- Learn simple cardiopulmonary resuscitation (CPR) methods. (See Appendix A, page 350.)

A baby is generally diagnosed as having died of SIDS if no specific cause of death is found.

TIP 235

Babies and young children can easily swallow a harmful medicine or a dangerous household item like bleach, batteries, etc. If your child does not talk yet, look for signs that they have been poisoned with a toxic substance. If you are in doubt, call your regional poison control center or the American Association of Poison Control Centers (1-800-222-1222) for advice.

If your child has swallowed a potentially dangerous substance, it may be obvious—he or she may tell you, or you may see him/her with the container. But your child could have swallowed a toxic substance unobserved. The following are some of the symptoms resulting from poisoning:
- Difficulty breathing
- Severe throat pain
- Burns on the lips or mouth

- Convulsions
- Unconsciousness
- Sudden unusual behavior, dizziness, weakness, or illness
- Abdominal pain, nausea, or vomiting
- Blurred vision, a change in pupil size
- Loss of bowel or bladder control

If you suspect that your child has swallowed a toxic substance, do the following:

- Stabilize your child. Check his or her breathing, and then resuscitate him/her if necessary (see Appendix A, page 350, for information about CPR). Place him/her in the recovery position (lying on the side with the mouth aimed toward the ground so that if your child vomits he or she will not choke). If the child is ill or not fully awake, call an ambulance (911 in most locations).
- Identify the substance and the amount that was swallowed. Search carefully for any suspect containers, and bring anything you find with you to the ER. If the swallowed substance was vitamin tablets with iron, for example, try to estimate the number missing from the container. If there are toxic chemicals on your child's skin or eyes, remove the contaminated clothes and place them in a plastic bag so that you can bring them with you to the ER without further contaminating anyone. Wash the child thoroughly with plain water and get him or her to an emergency room right away.
- If your child is stable, or even has no symptoms, but you know that he or she has ingested a potentially poisonous substance, you should still call your local poison control center (the number should be listed in your phone directory under emergency numbers) or the American Association of Poison Control Centers at 1-800-222-1222.

- Do not induce vomiting. Induction of vomiting is no longer suggested in the management of accidental poisoning, because it can cause complications in the esophagus (the tube leading from the mouth to the stomach) or lungs.

If you happen to witness your child swallowing a potentially harmful substance, do not wait for him or her to become ill. Seek advice immediately. Delay can be fatal! Remember, the best way to save your child's life from poisoning is to not let him or her get near any toxic compounds. Store all your medicines and dangerous household items in a safe place.

TIP 236

Teenagers, in particular, are more likely to abuse substances (alcohol, tobacco, marijuana, inhalants, Ecstasy, methamphetamine, GHB, crystal meth, etc.). Inhaled substances such as adhesives, aerosols, solvents, and cleaning agents are especially dangerous, as they can cause brain, liver, and kidney damage, and sometimes even sudden death.

Substance abuse is more common in adolescent boys than girls. Tobacco is addictive and often causes death in later years, while alcohol is a major killer of both teenagers and adults. Inhalant use is prevalent among younger teens, and even in prepubescent kids. Inhalant abuse may be harder to detect in your child, because the "high" is only momentary and inhaled substances are found in every setting (homes, schools, stores, the workplace, etc.). The excessive use of household or office products that come in a spray can may be a tip-off that someone has an inhalant abuse problem. These might include products such as glues, spray paint, air fresheners, lighter fluid, oven cleaner, Dust-Off, or even dessert topping sprays. This is serious; even experimenting with inhalants can result in serious long-term physical or psychological problems, or even death.

Watch out for changes in personality, mood, sleeping patterns, and/or appetite. Attempt to verify the facts, and contact self-help groups for advice. If you are unsure of whether your child is taking drugs, get professional help quickly. Lead your children by positive example, and spend time with them so that they will trust you and know that you accept them. A comprehensive resource is the National Institute on Drug Abuse website: www.drugabuse.gov.

PART FIVE

Prevention of Errors in the Hospital

INTRODUCTION

Do you need to worry about medical errors when you're sick in the hospital? The Institute of Medicine, a group of medical authorities monitoring quality of health care, says that you do. In 1999 this organization released a report revealing that 48,000 to 98,000 patients die each year from medical errors occurring in the nation's hospitals. This announcement shocked health-care providers and patients, prompting a much closer look at the health-care delivery system. Patients, insurance companies, the government, and other groups demanded changes to decrease these errors.

Additional investigation determined that the infrastructure of the health-care delivery system has not kept up with rapidly advancing medical technology. While the wonders of modern medicine have indeed reduced suffering and death, these same advances have made treatments more complex. Indeed, medical advancements have resulted in a dramatic increase in the variety and volume of interventions, such that there are greater odds for hospital staff to make mistakes. For example, if five physicians in the hospital are doing a procedure or treating an illness differently, the hospital staff must learn and remember how to do a task five different ways.

Fortunately, death rates from errors in hospitals are declining because of innovative efforts by hospitals, nonprofit organizations, and government agencies to improve quality control. However, there is more work to be done. A major positive step is to improve patient education. An informed patient can take a more active role in maintaining the quality of his or her health care. Be pleasant, but don't be shy about expressing your concerns.

The following tips are provided to empower patients and help them protect themselves from errors that commonly occur in hospitals. These tips are based on recommendations from the National Patient Safety Goals advocated by the Institute of Medicine, the Institute for Healthcare Improvement, and the Joint Commission on Accreditation of Healthcare Organizations. If you are a patient in the hospital or are helping a friend or relative in the hospital, you will benefit from reviewing these tips.

HOSPITAL POLICY

TIP 237

> If you don't feel safe, say so. Your instincts might be right.

If for any reason you don't feel safe, report this to the nursing supervisor. If you still do not feel safe, request a visit from the case management team, the patient advocate, and/or the compliance officer of the hospital. Do not remain silent. Voice your fears and concerns so that they can be properly addressed.

TIP 238

> Make sure help is available: Rapid physician response to a sudden change in a patient's condition can save lives.

There are teams of doctors and nurses specifically assigned to respond to any change in a patient's condition long before he/she experiences cardiac arrest and a "code" is called. However, a significant change in a patient's condition may be missed by the nursing staff. Inquire about the availability of rapid response teams and how they can be accessed if the family identifies a problem. If a rapid response program does not exist at your hospital, suggest that they implement one.

TIP 239

> If you observe anything that is occurring that isn't right or appears questionable, "stop the line."

Every hospital should have a "stop the line" policy that clearly states that when anyone observes an event involving the care of a patient that is, or appears to be, in error, they should immediately notify the floor nurse, who should "stop the line." This means that every activity involving that patient should stop until whatever is in question is resolved. Ask and make sure that this is a hospital policy. You and/or your advocates should use it when it's necessary. For example, if a nurse brings in a medicine for you that appears to be different from what you have been taking, you should question the change. If the nurse then discovers a mistake has been made, he or she should "stop the line" to find out why. Maybe there is someone with the same name or a similar name on the hospital floor. In this case, the error could happen again if the necessary precautions are not taken. Make certain that if there is an actual error, its cause has been resolved. If possible, this should be done before care measures are resumed. In such a case, special identifiers should be put in place. For example, a note might be placed on the front of the chart and/or on the door of the room.

Note: Sometimes the same generic medicine is manufactured as pills that look different.

SANITIZATION

TIP 240

Hand hygiene is important. If the people who are treating you have not properly sanitized their hands, you could be exposed to many different germs. Make sure your caretakers do not make this mistake.

Reduce your chance of getting infected while in the hospital by observing the hand hygiene practiced by the hospital personnel and physicians. If they are not using hand sanitizers prior to performing their services, ask them why. When appropriate, request they do so.

TIP 241

Improper removal of hair before surgery can increase the likelihood of a postoperation wound infection.

For over a century it was the custom to shave a body area prior to surgery at that site. A recent study found that this method of hair removal actually increases the incidence of wound infection. So what now?

The proper way to prepare a site for surgery is to clip the hair instead of shaving it. So, if someone comes at you with a razor, ask them to use clippers instead. This may seem like a small point, but it is important. One-hundred-year-old customs do not die easily.

MISTAKEN IDENTITY
AND
COMMUNICATION ERRORS

TIP 242

Name confusion seems like a silly and unlikely error, but it happens more than you might think. Don't take chances.

When two patients in the hospital have the same name, or even names that look similar, there is a greater chance of error. You are especially at risk if there is another patient with the same name or a similar name in the treatment area (hospital floor) where you are located.

How do you find out if this is the case during your hospital stay? Simply ask the nurse who is caring for you. If the answer is yes, then ask if the hospital has a system for alerting staff members to the coincidence of two patients having similar names. If they don't, then request special identifiers such as name alerts (which are often either stickers on written charts or red labels on electronic files). In certain cases, it might even be wise to ask to be moved to another area of the hospital. If the nursing staff refuses to cooperate, notify the CEO's office. There are strict patient privacy rules, but you don't need to know the identity of the other person to prevent a situation of name confusion. All you need to do is request that the increased risk be addressed.

TIP 243

> Correct identity is essential; make sure you are accurately identified before any treatment is initiated.

Check your armband to be certain that it's your name printed on it. You should also look for your correct birthdate printed on the armband. It is required that every health-care provider obtain two sources of identification prior to treating you, usually by checking your armband and by asking you your name. Make certain they do this and ask for an explanation if they do not.

TIP 244

> Make sure that all of your health-care providers know the facts of your case.

Miscommunication among physicians, nurses, and hospital personnel is a major cause of medical errors. Ask your doctor what his/her schedule is and which doctor covers for him/her on off hours. Make sure that all of the doctors who are caring for you know why you are in the hospital, as well as what your diagnostic and treatment plans are, particularly during the next twenty-four hours.

When you are taken from your hospital room, make sure to ask where you're being taken and why. When you arrive at another location, ask what is to be done. Make sure all the answers from the different practitioners are consistent. Also, upon any visit to the ER, make sure that your own medical specialist(s) is contacted and advised or consulted with if you have a past medical history relating to your current condition.

TIP 245

Believe it or not, wrong site surgery happens. This could be deadly; don't take a chance.

Make sure that your surgeon marks the appropriate surgery site on your body before you are taken to the operating room. Make certain that the area is marked while you are awake and cognizant of what he or she is doing. You know what needs to be done; make certain everybody else does.

MEDICATION

TIP 246

> The most common errors occur when medications are given. This can lead to fatalities. Don't let it happen to you.

Ask the nurse who is administering your medication to identify each medicine you are being given. Remember the appearance of each one, even if you have to write it down. If you are offered something that looks different from what you have previously been given, ask what it is. Bear in mind that there are some situations with generic medications where the same medicine comes in a different shape or color. If your prescriptions have been changed, ask why. Learn about all of your medications, why you are taking them, what drugs or foods they should not be taken with, when they should be taken (with or without meals), and what the potential side effects are. Errors relating to medication are the most frequent mistakes made in the hospital. The consequences of taking the wrong medicine can be very serious. Note: Be sure that everyone treating you knows about any allergies you have to medications (see Tips 169, 170, and 171).

TIP 247

Obtain a list of the medications that you are supposed to take after being discharged from the
hospital.

Confusion relating to which medications you should take following your discharge from the hospital is a major source of
error, especially when multiple doctors have treated you during your hospital stay. Request that your doctor review all the
medications you were taking prior to coming to the hospital
as well as those you were taking during your hospital stay. You
should be given a written list of what you are supposed to take
after discharge. Don't settle for verbal instructions.

SECONDARY CONDITIONS
That You Can Develop in the Hospital and How to Avoid Them

TIP 248

> Pneumonia and flu can be contracted from other patients while you are in the hospital. This is particularly dangerous (and there is a higher risk of a resulting fatality) if you are elderly.

Reduce the risk of developing pneumonia and influenza. Particularly if you are elderly, make sure that you are up-to-date on all your vaccinations, and that you are not placed in a room with anyone who is infectious. Many doctors recommend that hospitalized patients take a few deep breaths and cough to clear their airway every hour or so. Some doctors even prescribe the use of a spirometer to facilitate deep breathing. It is felt that these measures decrease the risk of developing infections in the lungs. (See Tip 72 for more on pneumonia.)

Note: It may be helpful to remind yourself to breathe deeply at set times, for example during commercial breaks if you are watching TV.

TIP 249

If you have ever had a blood clot, you are at an increased risk of having another, no matter why you are in the hospital. Discuss this with your physician immediately upon being admitted to the hospital, since you may need anticoagulation (blood thinning) to prevent a recurrence. This treatment is called deep venous thrombosis (DVT) prophylaxis. Note: There are a few rare situations in which active bleeding could prohibit this strategy.

A previous blood clot is not the only reason that you might need a blood thinner while you are in the hospital. An immobilizing illness and prolonged bed confinement both increase your risks of getting a blood clot, whether you have had one before or not. Therefore, if your condition is serious and you are bound to your hospital bed, it might be a good idea for you to start prophylactic anticoagulation (blood-thinning medication). Another reason you might want this preventative therapy is if you are massively obese. Since massively obese people have poor circulation, they are more likely to develop blood clots.

The use of prophylactic anticoagulation is also extremely important after certain surgical procedures. Orthopedic procedures are at the top of this list. Almost any operation on a major bone, such as hip replacement or knee replacement, warrants anticoagulation. Discuss this with your doctor before and after your admission to the hospital, as well as before and after your operation.

The mortality from blood clots is quite high, so it is well worth your effort to take every possible step to prevent them. There are a number of simple measures for reducing the risk of developing blood clots, which include getting out of bed and walking around intermittently, if tolerated. There are also intermittent compression devices that your doctor may prescribe if appropriate. These are placed around the legs to squeeze and massage the calves, and thus improve circulation. (For more on blood clots, see Tips 64 and 81.)

TIP 250

> If you have coronary heart disease and need surgery, taking the medication referred to as a "beta-blocker" before, during, and after your operation may reduce the risk of cardiovascular complications from the surgery.

This tip applies to surgery performed anywhere on a person with coronary heart disease, not just operations on the heart or blood vessels.

There are a few contraindications concerning the use of these medications, especially for patients with certain heart or lung conditions, but the majority of patients who need them are able to take them. Mention beta-blockers to your surgeon just to make sure that the possibility of using them has not been overlooked. Multiple assistants may be involved in your care, and somebody on the team may have forgotten to prescribe this medication.

TIP 251

> In certain surgical cases, taking the right antibiotic within one hour before your skin is surgically cut will reduce your likelihood of getting an infection.

This very important discovery was made by investigators reviewing two million cases in the Veterans Administration Healthcare System. It is so important that it has become the standard of care in all American hospitals. Make sure that the proper antibiotic is given if you are having one of certain surgical procedures performed, including:

- Blood vessel surgery
- Colon/large intestine surgery
- Hip joint replacement surgery
- Hysterectomy
- Knee joint replacement surgery

The proper use of preoperative antibiotics involves two steps. Number one: selecting the appropriate antibiotic for the anticipated surgical procedure, taking into account the patient's history of medication allergies. Number two: making absolutely sure that it is given within one hour of the actual surgical incision. Sometimes the antibiotic is given in the operating room. If it is given too early or after the skin is cut, its effectiveness is lost.

This seems simple enough. You would expect it to happen 100 percent of the time or at least nearly 100 percent. Not so. The compliance to this required safety measure is often as low as 60 percent in some hospitals.

Discuss the use of antibiotics with your surgeon before you go to the hospital, and consider insisting that the surgery not be performed without it. If it comes time to cut and the appropriate prophylactic antibiotic has not been given to you an hour earlier, it may be necessary to reschedule the surgery, unless delaying it could cause serious health problems.

This preemptive step of using a prophylactic antibiotic can prevent devastating infections that could cause prolonged hospitalization, deformities, disfigurations, and even death. It is a giant step forward in patient safety.

ACCIDENTS

TIP 252

Falls are a danger. Reduce the risk of falls by being aware of the side effects of your medication.

Make sure that you know if you are being given any medication that may increase your risk of falling. If additional medication is added to your treatment plan, ask again whether these additional medications might make you dizzy or lightheaded when taken in combination with your current medications. If you begin to feel unsteady, call for help before moving about. Ask whether your medications can be altered to decrease these side effects.

APPENDIX A

EMERGENCY MEDICAL TREATMENT

Courses on how to respond to the following emergencies are available through the American Red Cross, American Heart Association, or local hospitals. It is advisable to take these courses for in-depth training so that you can be better prepared for emergency situations. Also, remember to ask someone to call for emergency help (911, etc.) while you are attempting to administer care.

Choking

Choking often happens because something is obstructing the airway. The choking person may have a sudden onset of coughing and redness, or he or she may suddenly turn blue in color and be unable to cough or speak.

Partial Airway Obstruction
If the choking person is still able to cough and/or speak, stay with them and encourage them to continue coughing. Pay close attention and be prepared to act when needed.

Full Airway Obstruction

If the choking person is unable to cough or speak, you need to act rapidly before they become limp and pale.

How to Help If the Person Is Above the Age of One and Conscious—Abdominal Thrusts, i.e., the Heimlich Maneuver

- **Position:** Kneel or stand behind the child or adult with your arms joined firmly against his or her upper abdomen in the center, between the belly button and the bottom of the rib cage (see Figure 17). If the person is alert and conscious, explain gently what you are about to do.
- **Action:** Give up to five rapid, firm, upward thrusts until the object dislodges and the individual begins to breathe. Try to avoid pulling on the ribs.
- **If no success:** If the victim is still conscious, repeat the maneuver. If he or she becomes unconscious, begin CPR. (See the following guidelines for CPR.)

IN THE CASE OF PREGNANCY OR OBESITY

In pregnant or obese persons, you may need to place your hands or arms at the location of the chest, that is, the center of the breastbone, instead of below the rib cage. If you are unable to get your arms around the person from behind, you can have them put their back against a wall, and you can provide the thrusts directly to the front of the chest. Give up to five rapid, firm chest thrusts—either from behind or from the front.

IF YOU ARE ALONE AND CHOKING

Find a hard, blunt edge (for example, the back of a chair or the edge of a countertop), and drop yourself onto it, so that the edge strikes you between the belly button and the bottom of the rib cage. Repeat the action until the object is dislodged.

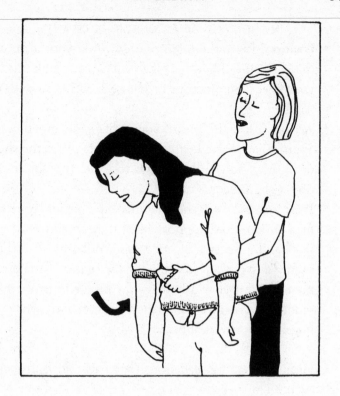

Figure 17. Heimlich Maneuver.

Pick up a telephone (if available) and dial 911. A regular landline telephone is better than a cell phone; in most cases, emergency services will be able to track your location from the call, even if you are unable to speak. If you must use a cell phone, be sure to give them your exact location immediately if you are still able to speak.

How to Help an Infant Under the Age of One:

Note: If it is a child with croup, suspected epiglottitis, or asthma (see Tips 210 and 211), do not undertake these procedures unless he/she cannot utter a sound and is clearly choking.

IN THE CASE OF A CONSCIOUS INFANT

- **Position:** Place the infant facedown on your arm, with the child's head and neck below his/her trunk (e.g., on your knee). Support his or her neck and head with one hand.
- **Action:** Using the heel of your other hand, give him/her approximately five firm, quick blows between the shoulder blades, forcefully enough to expel the object. The object should come out.
- **If no success:** Turn the infant faceup on your lap or on a firm surface, and support his/her head and neck with one hand. Use two fingers of your other hand to thrust inward and upward five times in the center of the breastbone, one finger-width below the nipple line. Watch the mouth, and remove the offending object with your pinky finger as soon as it appears.

Continue the above maneuvers (five back blows, five chest thrusts) until one of two things happens: the object is expelled and the infant begins to cry, or the infant becomes unconscious or unresponsive.

IN THE CASE OF AN UNCONSCIOUS INFANT

- **If still no success:** Call an ambulance (911 in most locations).
- **Position:** Turn the infant faceup on a hard surface (tabletop, counter, or floor).
- **Action:** Look in the mouth for any object on which the infant could be choking. If you see anything, use your pinky finger to remove the object. Do not blindly sweep fingers into the infant's mouth.
- If you are unable to see anything, open the airway by tilting the head back very slightly (if at all), put your mouth over the baby's nose and mouth, and give 2 gentle breaths

(puffs of air, using only the amount of air you can hold in your cheeks).

- Watch to see if the chest rises and falls.
    - If the chest does not rise and fall, the airway may still be blocked. Immediately begin CPR: thirty compressions followed by two attempted breaths. (See the following guidelines on CPR.) Check the mouth for the object each time you are about to provide a breath. Do not reach into the infant's mouth unless you see an object to remove.
    - If the chest does rise and fall, stop and reassess whether the infant has begun breathing. Keep the infant's airway open with a slight tilt and look toward the chest for chest rise, feel for breath on your cheek, and listen for sounds of breathing. If the infant is not breathing on his or her own, immediately begin CPR: thirty compressions followed by two breaths. (See the following CPR guidelines.)

*Special note: Remember when alone with a child or infant it is always best to initiate two minutes of care before calling 911. If there are any bystanders, have them contact 911 while you begin care.

Choking Prevention in Children

The best way to save a child from choking is to avoid it altogether. In general, children under three years old are the most at risk. Within this age range, children between nine months and two years are particularly prone to choking. At this stage, they are increasingly mobile and very likely to put items in their mouth, but are not yet responsive to your commands. Supervise your child well, and keep small items out of reach. Check under furniture and between cushions for small items (such as pen/marker caps, thumbtacks, etc.) that children could find and put in their mouths. Also supervise the actions of older children (such as siblings) who may give a younger child an object that poses a choking threat.

When choosing playthings for small children, be sure to follow the age recommendations on the toy packages. Also, think carefully before giving your child certain foods, and supervise infants and young children at mealtime. Do not allow them to run, play, or lie down with food in their mouths.

Toys and Household Objects with Particular Risks

- **Balloons:** Balloons are the most common cause of fatalities from choking. Always supervise children under the age of six when playing with balloons. Use Mylar, not latex, balloons, and make sure to dispose of broken pieces of balloons immediately. Note: Balloons pose a choking risk to children of any age.
- **Small items:** Avoid giving a child any item that can fit entirely into his or her mouth or with small (under two inches) parts. This includes coins, small balls, marbles, beads, medicine syringes, and toy food. If it can fit through the opening of a toilet paper roll, it is too small for a young child.
- **Small batteries:** These are especially dangerous, as sometimes the acid can seriously damage the stomach lining.

Foods with Particular Risks

- **Nuts, seeds, or popcorn:** These are the most commonly inhaled foods. Do not give these to an infant or young child.
- **Firm fruits or vegetables:** Prepare carrots, grapes, apples, pears, and celery appropriately: Peel them, chop them finely, or cook them until soft.
- **Sausages:** It's safest not to give sausages to children under six years old.

- **Hot dogs:** It's safest not to give hot dogs to children under six years old.
- **Chunks of meat, cheese, or peanut butter:** Shred or grate any firm cheeses. Spread soft cheese or peanut butter on a cracker or piece of bread. Grind, crumble, or shred meat into small bits before serving to an infant or young child.
- **Raisins, prunes, or apricots:** Boil any dried fruits so they become soft and easily chewed. Prunes and apricots need to also be cut into smaller pieces.
- **Hard, gooey, or sticky candy:** Do not give hard candy to children under the age of three.
- **Chewing gum:** Avoid giving gum to young children.
- **Marshmallows:** Do not let children play any games where they try to fit as many large marshmallows in their mouth as possible. When a marshmallow is pulled into the airway, it becomes moist and sticky, and then expands.

Cardiopulmonary Resuscitation (CPR) and the Use of Automated External Defibrillators (AEDs)

Quick Emergency CPR Reference Guide:
If you don't try, the person's going to die . . .

> Only use this quick guide if it's a crisis situation. For every minute without CPR, the chances of survival for the victim decrease by about 10 percent. When there is time, it is preferable to review the entire table in the following pages, since it's much more comprehensive.
> If another person is around, he or she might review the entire table while you are starting CPR.

Step 1: Get somebody to call 911.
> If alone: For an adult, call 911, then begin CPR.
> For a child or infant, perform 2 minutes or about 5 cycles of CPR, then call 911.

Step 2: There are two choices:
> Choice 1: Give 2 rescue breaths (in about 2 seconds).
> Then give cycles of 30 compressions (in about 15 seconds): 2 breaths (in about 2 seconds).
> Continue to alternate between compressions and breaths.
> Choice 2: Give compressions only (100 per minute).
> If you don't feel comfortable giving breaths, compressions alone could still save somebody's life.
> Note: Breaths along with compressions are much more important for children and infants.

Step 3: If there is an AED (automated external defibrillator) available, attach it as soon as possible and follow the automated directions.
> Note: AEDs are not recommended for infants.

Remember: **Time is of the essence.** Never delay or pause more than 10 seconds when giving CPR. The ideal is to continue CPR until you revive the person or someone of equal or higher training takes over.

THE SPECIFICS

Breaths:
a) Place the heel of one hand on the forehead, and two fingers of the other hand under the chin. For an adult, tilt the head back as far as it goes. For children and infants, do not bend the neck too far. Remove anything you see in the mouth. Check for breathing.

b) For adults and children, pinch their nose and place your mouth over their mouth to give breaths. For infants, place your mouth over their mouth and nose to give breaths.

Chest Compressions:
a) For adults and children, place your hands one on top of the other on the center of the chest at the nipple line. For infants place the tips of two fingers in the center of the chest, one finger-width below the nipple line.

b) Give fast hard compressions at a rate of 100 per minute. For adults, push 2 inches deep. For children and infants, push ⅓ to ½ inch deep.

AED (Automated External Defibrillator):
a) For adults, place one AED pad on the right side of the chest and the other on the back at the same level, or place one pad high on the right side of the chest and the other low on the left over the ribs. For children, place one pad on the chest and the other on the back.

b) Turn on the AED and follow the visual and/or voice prompts.

Overview

Any infant, child, or adult whose breathing or heartbeat stops will rapidly experience damage to his or her vital organs, especially the brain. Cardiopulmonary resuscitation (CPR) allows oxygen to reach the vital organs until expert help can be given in a hospital. This is a critical skill for you to learn. In this section, we provide you with general CPR guidelines. Of course, attending a CPR training course is the best way to learn; a written summary can give you only an outline.

However, even if you have not had CPR training, do not let this prevent you from acting in an emergency situation. If you don't try, the person's going to die. In fact, the American Heart Association is now encouraging a "Hands-Only" approach for untrained lay people who have any hesitation about performing CPR. In the past, many people who needed CPR have died as a result of bystanders not stepping in to help for fear of acting incorrectly or because they hesitated to breathe into the mouth of a stranger. While many doctors think that the very best option is to do compressions in combination with breaths, doing compressions alone is much better than doing nothing. If you don't feel comfortable giving breaths for any reason, then just do compressions. However, it is always very important, if at all possible, to give breaths along with compressions to children and infants.

CPR training now includes instruction relating to the use of an AED (automated external defibrillator). This is a laptop-size device that analyzes the rhythm of the heart for abnormalities and gives an electrical shock, if necessary, to the victim. Though often considered inaccessible, AEDs can be found in a surprising number of public places, such as airports, parks and recreation facilities, government and corporate facilities, and schools. Start asking people, start looking for them, so that you'll be able to find one in an emergency situation. Using an AED is easy even for laypeople with no prior training.

There are many reasons a person can end up in a situation where he or she is unconscious, unresponsive, and not breathing, but regardless of the cause, they need CPR. Whether someone is drowning, choking, struck by lightning, having a stroke or heart attack, or suffering sudden cardiac arrest, if he or she ends up unconscious, unresponsive, and not breathing, then time is of the essence. Call 911 and begin CPR immediately. Also use an AED if readily available, or ideally get the help of a bystander to assist with the AED.

Important Facts to Consider:
- For every minute that care is not given, the chance of survival decreases by about 10 percent.
- After someone goes five to seven minutes without oxygen, brain damage usually occurs.
- After ten to twelve minutes without oxygen, there is usually irreversible brain damage.
- Even compressions alone are better than doing nothing, and may help the victim if you are unable or unwilling to provide breaths.
- Most studies we reviewed suggested that the chest compressions are the most important part of CPR. However, breaths in combination with compressions are very important for children and infants.
- Try to do your best to follow the recommended CPR guidelines. However, the most important thing is to dive in and start CPR, even if you are unsure. If you don't try, the person's going to die.

Remember: **Time is of the essence.** Never delay or pause more than ten seconds when giving CPR. The ideal is to continue CPR until you revive the person or someone of equal or higher training takes over.

UNIVERSAL CPR GUIDELINES

Assess the situation:	Are they moving? Are they conscious? Is he/she breathing? Tap them. Shout, "Are you okay?" Do they seem to have any serious or life-threatening injuries? Also, is the scene safe for you as the rescuer?
Alert:	Call 911. Send someone to get an automated external defibrillator (AED). Shout for help.
Attend:	Attend to the victim. Begin Emergency Action Steps (see ABCs below).
Preparing for CPR	• Do not move the person unless necessary, especially if you suspect a neck or spinal injury. If you must move the person and they are unresponsive, position them on their back, ideally on a hard, flat surface. Turn the victim's entire body at once—head, shoulders, back, hips, and legs—in the same direction (log roll them) to protect the neck and prevent possible additional injuries. Avoid twisting the back. (Note: This is more easily done with two people.)

A = Airway	HEAD TILT–CHIN LIFT Place a hand on the forehead and two fingers on the chin. Open the airway by tilting the head and lifting the chin (in order to extend the neck). Make sure there are no objects in the mouth, but clear the mouth only if you see something. For children and infants: You still need to open the airway, but do not bend the neck too far—because this will actually close the airway.
B = Breathing	Check for breathing by leaning down and placing your ear and cheek just above the victim's mouth. **Look** toward the victim's chest, **listen** and **feel** for breaths (5–10 seconds). If the victim is not breathing, prepare to begin breathing for them, following the guidelines below. *Note: Blowing too hard or too long into any age victim can force air into the stomach and cause vomiting. However, vomiting is a reflex; it does not mean that the victim is breathing or has a heartbeat. If vomiting occurs, roll the victim onto their side, help clear out the mouth, roll them back over, and continue providing CPR.* 1. Check to make sure that there are no objects in the mouth. Clear the mouth only if you see an object. 2. Position your mouth to give breaths to the victim. The proper positioning of your mouth when

giving breaths to adults, children, and infants are as follows:

- **Adults** (> 8 yrs of age): Pinch the victim's nose with your fingers and make a seal around their mouth with your mouth.
- **Children** (1–8 yrs of age or < 55 pounds): Pinch the victim's nose with your fingers and make a seal around their mouth with your mouth.
- **Infants** (<1 year of age): Make a seal with your mouth around both the mouth *and* the nose of the infant.
- Give **two** slow and steady breaths, for about one second each, lifting your mouth from the victim's after each breath to let them exhale. Watch to be certain that the chest visibly rises when you provide each breath.
- If the chest does not visibly rise, continue trying to give the victim breaths until the chest does rise (retilting the head to open the airway before each try).
- If the victim does not begin breathing on their own after two successful breaths, prepare to follow with chest compressions.

C = Compressions	Compress the chest 30 times, HARD and FAST at a rate of 100 beats/

minute, following the guidelines below for adults, children, and infants:

- **Adults** (>8 yrs old or >55 lbs): Place the heel of one hand on top of the other with your fingers pointing along the direction of the ribs. Use two hands to push firmly two inches deep on the center of the chest (the sternum) at the nipple line. Allow the chest to recoil between each compression.

- **Children** (1–8 yrs of age): Positioning is the same as an adult, but depending on your size and the size of the child, you may not need the extra force of the second hand over the first. With one or two hands, push on the center of the chest at the nipple line $\frac{1}{3}$ to $\frac{1}{2}$ inch deep. Allow the chest to recoil between each compression.

- **Infants** (<1 year of age): Since an infant is much smaller than an adult, your actions will be adjusted accordingly. Place the tips of your two fingers in the middle of the breastbone, one finger-width below the nipple line. With two fingers, push on the chest $\frac{1}{3}$ to $\frac{1}{2}$ inch deep. Allow the chest to recoil between each compression.

If the victim does not begin to breathe on their own after 30 compressions,

	then **continue to repeat the CPR cycle,** alternating between 30 compressions and 2 breaths.
	*Do not be surprised if you feel popping or cracking under your hands when you are providing good, hard, and fast compressions to someone's chest. This is normal and they will heal from this in the hospital. Continue providing the good, hard, and fast compressions; they are crucial to keep moving the blood and oxygen around the body to keep the victim's vital organs oxygenated.
	*Some experts in CPR training suggest that the rate of compressions is approximately the beat of the Bee Gees song "Stayin' Alive." Humming this melody to yourself may help make it easier to do compressions at the proper rate.
D = Defibrillation	AEDs are to be used on adults and children over 1 year of age. The AED should not be used on an infant younger than 1 year of age. Note: If an AED is put on someone who does not need to be shocked, then it will not shock.
	You cannot hurt someone with an AED! • The purpose of an AED is to analyze the heartbeat of the victim and shock the heart if needed. • All AEDs look different; they come in different shapes, sizes, and colors, but as long as you can get your hands on the AED and turn it on,

you will be able to figure it out. All AEDs have some type of voice or visual prompts.

- Once the AED arrives, bare the chest of the victim and turn the machine on. Do not stop providing CPR until the AED is in position and turned on.
- Follow the voice and/or visual prompts to attach the pads and begin analysis.

Positioning of AED pads:

For adults, place one pad high on the right side of the chest and the other on the back at the same level. If unable to move the victim, place one pad on the right side of the chest and the other low on the left over the ribs. For children, one pad should be placed on the front of the chest, and the other on the back. The purpose of each of these positionings is to sandwich the heart in between the pads.

The following are directions for special circumstances when placing the AED pads:

- Hairy chest—Use the razor in the pouch attached to the AED to shave the area, and then apply the pads.
- Water—If the victim is lying in water, move them out of the water.

Use a towel or whatever you have available to quickly dry the chest, then apply the pads.

- Implanted device—A lump will be under the skin on the left or right side of the chest. If the device is on the right side (which is where one of the pads should be placed), place the pad one inch from the device and not directly on top of the device.
- Medication patches—If there is a patch on the victim's chest, remove it and wipe the area quickly before you place the pads on the chest.

The AED will make one of two decisions once it is attached:

Shock advised: In this case, stand clear to allow the machine to provide a shock. Once the shock is provided, the machine will prompt when it is safe to touch the victim. Do not turn off the machine or remove the pads. Look, listen, and feel for breathing. If there's no breath, open the airway (by lifting the chin and tilting the head back) and proceed with two minutes of CPR (5 cycles of 30 compressions: 2 breaths). Always begin with compressions.

Shock not advised: The machine will prompt you to return to the victim. Do not turn off the machine or remove the pads. Immediately open the airway (by lifting the chin and tilting the head back), and proceed with two minutes of CPR (5 cycles of 30 compressions: 2 breaths). Always begin with compressions.

After two minutes, the AED will analyze and decide again whether it should shock or not. Usually when an AED is used, a normal heartbeat may restart after the first or second shock, but sometimes more shocks may be required.

The AED will continue cycling through analyzing, shocking—if needed—and then allowing two minutes to provide CPR. Continue to follow the prompts until emergency medical professionals arrive.

Order of Emergency Action	When you are alone with a person who stops breathing and they are in need of CPR and an AED, there are a few things to consider:

When alone with a(n) . . .
- **Adult:** Immediately CALL 911 and get the AED if it is readily available. Give 2 initial rescue breaths, then begin to provide CPR (alternating between 30 compressions: 2 breaths) and use the AED.
  Remember: The chance of survival decreases by 10 percent for every minute you delay starting CPR.

	• **Child:** Immediately give 2 initial rescue breaths, then begin CPR. Provide TWO MINUTES of CPR (about 5 cycles of 30 compressions: 2 breaths). If the child is not responding to the CPR, call 911 and get the AED (if readily available). Then continue CPR, and use the AED. **Remember: The chance of survival decreases the longer there is a lapse in giving CPR.*
	• **Infant:** Immediately give 2 initial rescue breaths, then begin CPR. Provide TWO MINUTES of CPR (about 5 cycles of 30 compressions: 2 breaths). If the infant is not responding to the CPR, call 911. Then continue CPR. **Remember: The chance of survival decreases the longer there is a lapse in giving CPR.*
When Do I Stop CPR?	• The victim begins breathing on his/her own. • A person of equal or higher training arrives to help. • Emergency medical professionals arrive to take over. • You, the rescuer, are physically exhausted and can no longer continue. • The scene becomes dangerous and you, the rescuer, are now in danger.

Good Samaritan Laws	In the United States of America, in most cases the Good Samaritan law covers any individual who attempts to help a person in need. There are four main points to keep in mind when you step in to help: • You must be reasonably careful and not purposely try to hurt someone. • Act in "good faith." You cannot be paid or rewarded for your service. • Do not try to provide care beyond your skill level. • Once you have begun to help, you are expected to stay with the victim and continue providing aid until someone of equal or higher training takes over, unless the scene or situation becomes dangerous for you.

Always Remember Your ABCs!

The following steps are involved with CPR: A-A-B-C-D

Assess: Assess the situation and call 911 for help.

Airway: Open the airway.

Breathing: Rescue breaths (2)

Compression: Chest compressions (30)

Defibrillation: If an AED is available

APPENDIX B

SELF-EXAMINATIONS

Breast Exam

Many doctors recommend that you perform a self-examination on your breasts in the same way at least once a month. The best time to perform a breast self-exam is about seven to ten days after your period, when your breasts are not swollen and tender. After menopause, check your breasts on the first day of every month. Regular self-examinations will familiarize you with what your breasts feel like normally so that you will be able to detect any changes. *However, it is important to remember that this should not take the place of a mammogram, which can pick up curable breast masses you can't feel.* Ask your doctor to review your self-exam technique when you go in for a routine health exam. The early detection and treatment of cancer increases the chance of a cure.

The following are the current guidelines for examining your breasts:

- Lie down flat on your back with a pillow under your right shoulder.
- Place your right arm behind your head (see Figure 18).
- Press the pads of the three middle fingers of your left hand firmly on your right breast. (A ridge in the lower curve of each breast is normal.)

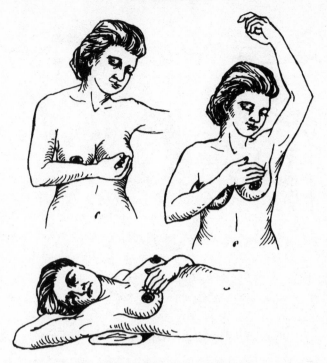

Figure 18. Breast Self-Exam, Palpation.

- Move your fingers around all parts of the breast, using a sequence of three different motions. Make sure you check the entire breast area between your ribs and your collarbone (clavicle):
  - First, use an overlapping, dime-size, circular motion.
  - Second, use an in-and-out motion with three different levels of pressure—light, medium, and firm—so that you can feel the tissue closest to the skin, the tissue that's a little deeper, and the tissue closest to the chest and ribs. Use each level of pressure before moving your hand to the next spot. You may want to talk to your doctor or nurse about how hard to press.
  - Third, a vertical up-and-down pattern, starting at the underarm and moving across the breast to the middle of your torso or sternum (breastbone).

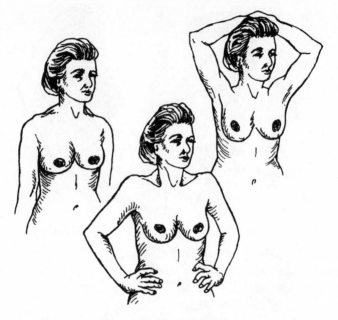

Figure 19. Breast Self-Exam, Observation.

- Examine your breasts while taking a shower. Soapy hands over wet skin make it easy to check for lumps. Use a similar technique to the one noted earlier.
- Put the pillow under your left shoulder, and repeat the above steps, this time with your left breast.
- Stand in front of a mirror with your hands pressed firmly on your hips, and note any changes in the way your breasts look, such as dimpling of the skin, changes in the nipple, changes in the texture of the skin (so that it resembles an orange peel), redness, or swelling (see Figure 19).
- Examine each underarm from a sitting or standing position with your arm slightly raised so the underarm skin is not stretched tight.

If you find any changes, see your doctor as soon as possible.

Testicular Exam

Many doctors recommend examining your testicles at least once a month beginning at puberty (see Figure 20). Performing regular testicular exams will help you become familiar with what is normal, and may help you detect a mass early. This should be in addition to, not as a replacement for, the testicular exam performed by your doctor as part of your routine cancer-related checkup (especially between the ages of fourteen to thirty-five). The doctor may discover an abnormality you might miss. Early detection and treatment of cancer may lead to a cure.

The following are the current guidelines for examining your testicles:

- During or after a warm bath or shower is the best time to perform the self-exam.
- Separately examine each testicle, holding the penis out of the way.
- Holding the testicle between your thumb and two fingers,

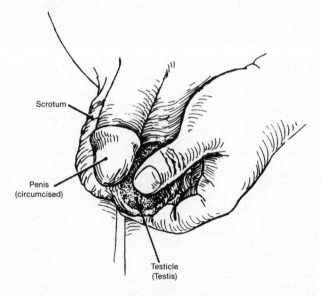

Figure 20. Testicular Self-Exam.

roll it gently between your fingers. A normal testicle is smooth and round and feels like a hard-boiled egg. Each should move freely in your scrotal sac.

• Feel for hard lumps, nodules (smooth, rounded masses), irregularities, or a change in the size, shape, or consistency of the testes. If you experience pain or a dragging sensation, contact your doctor immediately. All of these are possible signs of a tumor. You may feel a small crest of equal size and consistency in the back or edge of both testicles. This is the sign of a normal epididymis (the tubes carrying sperm from the testicles). Normal testicles should be symmetrical and of equal size. You should not feel any differences.

• Check your inguinal area (the area where your thighs meet your body). This is a common area for lymph nodes, which, if enlarged, can signal the presence of cancer.

If you detect anything that you have doubts about, consult your doctor.

APPENDIX C

VALUABLE PREVENTIVE SCREENINGS
(LISTED FROM HEAD TO TOE)

by Zoe Haugo

There are many medical screening tests that can detect risks of illnesses or actual illnesses early, thus providing the possibility of preventing or curing a disease. The following are a few of the common screening procedures, though it is not all-inclusive. An extensive list of screening tests is available at the United States Preventive Services Task Force website at http://www.ahrq.gov/clinic/uspstfix.htm. Talk with your primary care doctor about making long-term plans for medical screenings for all of the members of your family. Remember that recommendations for screenings change as new tests and new treatments are discovered, and that health organizations and doctors don't always agree on which tests are useful and how often they should be administered.

Feel free to discuss the pros and cons of these guidelines with your doctor. It's also a good idea to check the most current recommendations on the websites and in the literature of respected organizations. Some examples of reputable organizations are WebMD, the American Heart Association, the American Cancer Society, the Centers for Disease Control and

Prevention, the American Academy of Family Physicians, and the American Academy of Pediatrics.

Important note: There are certain situations when one experiences very common signs or symptoms, and a simple and inexpensive screening test might help identify a rare but serious problem. Subsequently, the serious illness can then be treated early enough to save the person's life. An example of this is somebody who is experiencing fatigue, lingering infections, excessive bruising or bleeding, and/or swollen gums. A simple blood test, the CBC (complete blood count), identifies the specific kinds of white blood cells and the red blood cell count. An abnormal result from this simple test in a person with any of the above symptoms might trigger an extensive evaluation resulting in an early diagnosis of leukemia. Unfortunately, people with this disorder are frequently diagnosed too late to receive effective treatment when it will have the greatest benefit.

Eyes

Vision

Consider going to an eye doctor for an eye exam at least twice between the ages of thirty and forty, or any time you think your vision may be declining. People who use glasses, contacts, or other vision correctors should get their vision retested every year. Also, if you are taking any medications or have a chronic disease such as diabetes or hypertension, you should ask your primary care doctor how often you should see an ophthalmologist.

Note: An ophthalmologist is not the same as an optometrist. An optometrist fits people for glasses and contact lenses, as well as tests for vision and performs many other evaluations of the eye. He or she is also well trained in many other activities relating to eye care. An ophthalmologist is a medical doctor who has extensive training in surgery of the eye, and the medical evaluation and treatment of eye diseases.

Glaucoma

Many eye doctors recommend that everyone, even if they have no risk factors, be screened once a year after the age of fifty for glaucoma (a condition of increased pressure in the eyes). Risk factors for glaucoma include nearsightedness, a family history of glaucoma, African-American ethnicity, and/or a history of trauma to an eye. Note: Although glaucoma is far more prevalent in older people, it can even appear in kids. The testing can be done easily and painlessly by an optometrist or ophthalmologist.

Teeth

Dental Screening

Regular dental checkups and cleanings are recommended at ALL ages every six months.

Neck

Thyroid Screening

A timely diagnosis of thyroid cancer is very important, since it can be cured if detected early. The screening for thyroid cancer involves clinical evaluation by a doctor, who observes and feels the thyroid gland for abnormalities. This is done at the time of a routine physical examination. If irregularities are found, an ultrasound may be requested to further define abnormalities. Various conditions in a person's history may increase the risk of thyroid cancer, including excess exposure to X-rays. Diagnosing other thyroid diseases such as goiter (an enlarged thyroid), hypothyroidism (an underactive thyroid), and hyperthyroidism (an overactive thyroid) may require blood tests and/or biopsies.

The risk of hypothyroidism increases with age. The American Thyroid Association recommends that all women over thirty-five years of age should be screened for hypothyroidism every five years. Also, women who are pregnant or planning to get pregnant should get tested; a mother's thyroid problems can affect the fetus.

Chest

Breast Cancer Screening

The key to beating breast cancer is early detection. Knowing what is normal for you may help you identify a lump, so many physicians feel that monthly breast self-exams are valuable. *However, they should not take the place of mammography so that very small curable cancers are not missed.* Routine breast exams by a physician are also important. Contact your doctor immediately if you detect a lump in your breast.

The following are guidelines for early detection:

- Every woman should know what her breasts normally feel like, and report any breast changes promptly to her physician. Starting in their twenties, women may choose to perform breast self-exams. (See Appendix B, page 364, for instruction on how to perform a breast self-exam.)
- A clinical breast exam performed by the doctor should be part of a woman's routine health exam. This should happen about every three years for women in their twenties and thirties and every year for women forty years of age or older.

Many doctors recommend that all women should have a mammogram every year, beginning at the age of forty, especially those with a family history of breast cancer. Some health groups recommend getting a baseline mammogram at age thirty-five. Obviously, screenings for breast cancer may not be appropriate if a woman has a short life expectancy because of other medical problems or because she is elderly and frail. In general, survivors of breast cancer should continue to have a mammogram every year, regardless of age.

Women at increased risk should start screenings earlier and discuss with their doctor the pros and cons of having additional tests such as an MRI or ultrasound. Women with a family history of breast cancer or ovarian cancer should be checked for BRCA1 and BRCA2, which are genetic mutations linked to these diseases.

Risk factors for breast cancer include:

- a previous history of breast cancer
- a family history of breast cancer (if your mother, sisters, or daughters have had breast cancer, you are at a two to three times greater risk)
- increasing age (85 percent of breast cancers occur after the age of 40 and half of all breast cancers occur in women over 65). Note: Younger women can also get breast cancer.
- exposure to radiation
- not having children
- pregnancy at a late age (usually after 30)
- early menstruation (before the age of 12)
- going through menopause at a later age than normal (usually after 55)
- long-term use of hormone replacement therapy with progesterone as a component
- genetic predisposition (certain mutations of BRCA1 or BRCA2 genes)
- the use of oral contraceptives
- the regular consumption of alcohol

However, it's important to remember that the NUMBER I RISK FACTOR FOR BREAST CANCER IS BEING A WOMAN. All women need to be conscientious about taking measures for early detection.

Lung Disease Screening
During routine physical checkups your doctor will listen to your lungs with a stethoscope and take a health history that includes questions about smoking. If you have symptoms of shortness of breath and respiratory problems, your doctor may suggest pulmonary function testing to help diagnose asthma and other lung ailments. This involves breathing in and out of a machine to measure the volume of air that you inhale and exhale.

If you are a smoker, have been exposed to a lot of asbestos or other toxic airborne substances, or the doctor suspects that you have pneumonia or fluid in your lungs, he/she may recommend that you get a chest X-ray or chest CT scan. There is no uniform opinion concerning how often to get these screening tests or whether it's valuable to get them at all. There are cases in which these tests—especially the CT scan—have picked up the disease early, allowing for a cure. However, there are also cases where an abnormality is discovered, resulting in invasive diagnostic interventions (with the associated complications from these procedures) that fail to uncover a medical problem.

Colorectal

Early Detection of Cancer in the GI Tract
Whether you have risk factors or not, routine colorectal screenings are generally recommended starting at a minimum of age fifty. Both men and women without any risk factors should be examined with a colonoscope (colonoscopy) every

ten years. Various health committees have recommended other options for screening, such as sigmoidoscopy and barium enemas, but many experts of the GI tract (gastroenterologists) feel that colonoscopies are more likely to identify any cancer.

At a minimum, you should get a special test called a fecal occult blood test every year. This is a test that is performed at home at three different times to detect whether there is blood in your stools. It is much less accurate than a colonoscopy, but is also less costly and intrusive. If blood is detected, additional tests are needed. Of course, any test may miss curable cancers, so the decision about which test to use (colonoscopy, sigmoidoscopy, etc.) as a screen for colon cancer should be made with your personal risk factors in mind. Your doctor can help you decide which test is most appropriate for you.

You should talk to your doctor about when to start and how often to undergo screening if you have risk factors including:

- A personal history of colorectal cancer or polyps
- A relative with a history of colorectal cancer or polyps
- A personal history of ulcerative colitis or Crohn's disease
- A polyp or early cancer discovered on a prior colonoscopy
- A family history (mother, father, brother, or sister) of a hereditary colorectal cancer syndrome (one of several disorders that usually lead to cancer; namely FAP—Familial Adenomatous Polyposis—which is a condition identified with lots of polyps and can appear in a person as young as five years of age, or HNPCC—Hereditary Nonpolyposis Colon Cancer—which can also start at a relatively young age, but causes few polyps)

Following a routine screening schedule could save your life. Early detection, before you have any warning signs, can improve your chances of being cured of the cancer. This disease is not rare!

Screening for Kidney Disease

A simple urine dipstick (a strip of paper that turns different colors depending on the contents of the urine) is dipped in a urine sample to detect early kidney disease, particularly in diabetics. A positive result can indicate that you need to go on medication to prevent diabetes-related kidney failure.

Reproductive System

Pap Smear/Pelvic Exam

It is important to see a physician (a gynecologist, familiy physician, or internist) for a thorough pelvic examination on a regular basis in case changes suggestive of cancer occur. The Pap smear is the test used to check for abnormalities of the cervix (the lower opening of the uterus, or womb). It should first be performed the same year that a woman begins to have vaginal intercourse, but no later then when she turns twenty-one years of age. After the initial screening, she should get a Pap smear done every year with the regular Pap test and a pelvic exam.

There is now a vaccine for HPV (human papilloma virus), which many medical groups recommend, in general, for females between eleven and twenty-six years of age. However, there are other considerations that should be discussed with the doctor. Also, all women should continue to be screened for cervical cancer regardless of whether they get the HPV vaccination.

Starting at age thirty, any woman who has had three normal Pap test results and negative HPV (human papilloma virus) tests in a row may choose to be screened every two to three years instead of annually. However, women should continue to be screened every year if they have certain risk factors such as exposure before birth to DES (diethylstilbestrol, a specific type of estrogen), an HIV infection, or a weakened immune system (which could be due to organ transplant therapy, chemotherapy, or chronic steroid use). If a woman has no risk factors, is over the age of seventy, and has had three normal Pap test results in a row along with ten consecutive years without an abnormal Pap test, she may choose to discontinue cervical cancer screenings. Also, a woman of any age who has no risk factors and has had a total hysterectomy (unless it was done as a treatment for cervical cancer or precancer) may want to discuss with her doctor the option of discontinuing her routine Pap smears. However, these women should continue to have their doctor perform a routine exam of the pelvic area.

Pelvic Exam/Ovarian Cancer Screening

Ovarian cancer can sometimes be found during a pelvic exam, but it would be much more valuable to pick it up before it is advanced enough to be detected by the doctor in this way. At the time of the writing of this book, it appears that there is not enough data to come up with an absolute policy of routine ovarian cancer screening. If you are at risk, it may be recommended that you get a more thorough evalation than the routine pelvic exam. You can assess your risk factors by going to www.wcn.org for a confidential questionnaire. If you are at moderate risk, your doctor may recommend a test known as CA125 radioimmunoassay, and possibly a transvaginal ultrasound. If you are at high risk, you should consider seeing a genetic counselor who is an expert in this area. He/she will likely recommend further testing.

Sexually Transmitted Diseases
(Chlamydia, Gonorrhea, and Syphilis)

One of the most important STDs to test for is chlamydia. It doesn't always cause symptoms, however it's important to diagnose and treat it because it can—if left untreated—lead to infertility. All sexually active women are at risk and should be screened for it. Additional factors that put women at an even greater risk include sexual activity under the age of twenty-five and high-risk sexual behaviors at any age. High-risk sexual behaviors include multiple partners (or a partner with multiple sexual partners), intercourse without a condom with more than one partner, and shared sex toys. Victimization by sexual assault also increases the risk. Women with pelvic inflammatory disease (PID) and/or with symptoms of a cervical infection (cervicitis) found during a pelvic exam should be screened for chlamydia as well. Additionally, chlamydia screening is recommended during the first and third trimesters of pregnancy if the woman has had high-risk sexual behavior. Treatment during pregnancy can prevent passing the infection to the newborn.

Chlamydia, gonorrhea, and syphilis are all becoming more common. Therefore, it is more important than ever for you to regularly get screened for all of these sexually transmitted diseases if you are a sexually active man or woman, especially if you are under the age of thirty-five.

Another reason in particular to screen for syphilis is that the symptoms may disappear on their own without treatment, allowing the disease to remain dormant in the body for many years. The reproductive organs may be seriously compromised by syphilis if it is left untreated on a long-term basis. Also, life-threatening complications may appear later in life in those not treated.

Note: Of course, all people who have high-risk sexual behaviors should also be screened for HIV/AIDS.

Early Detection of Testicular Cancer

A testicular exam should be part of every man's routine checkup. Often, testicular cancer can be picked up early by finding a lump. Testicular cancer is most common between the ages of fourteen and thirty-four, but can also occur later in life. Many doctors believe that self-examination of your testicles for lumps once or twice a month beginning at age fourteen may contribute to the early detection of cancer (see Appendix B for instructions on how to perform a self-exam). However, self-examination should not take the place of examination by your doctor as part of your routine physical exam. Men whose testicles did not descend naturally and were surgically placed in their scrotum as babies are at a higher risk of developing testicular cancer. They should let their doctor know so they can be closely monitored. Other risk factors for developing testicular cancer include a family history of this type of cancer or a previous germ cell tumor in one testicle.

Early Detection of Prostate Cancer
African-American men and also men who have first-degree relatives who have had prostate cancer should consider having a PSA (prostate-specific antigen) blood test and digital rectal exam annually beginning at age forty. All other men should begin screening at age fifty. However, there is an ongoing debate among doctors about the advantages of routine PSA screenings. You can have a normal PSA level and have life-threatening prostate cancer. You can also have an elevated PSA level and not have cancer.

Prostate cancer is much more common in men over sixty years of age. However, when older men get prostate cancer, the cancer will often (but not always) act "old" as well, in that it is slow growing. It is usually less aggressive and less likely to spread and become fatal than in a younger man. Therefore, the younger you are, the more important it is to diagnose it early. (The main reason there are not routine screenings recommended before age fifty is that the cancer is relatively rare in younger men.)

African-American men are at higher risk and should consider

starting their annual screenings at age forty. Men who have a father, brother, or son who was diagnosed with prostate cancer at an early age (younger than sixty-five years old) are at a higher risk and should consider starting screening at age forty or forty-five. Being overweight and eating a high-fat diet are also risk factors.

Skin

Melanoma Skin Cancer Screening

If you have a family history of abnormal moles or melanoma, you should have an annual total body skin exam. Other risk factors include fair skin that easily burns, blond or red hair, and/or lots of moles. People with these characteristics should also get annual skin exams. Any time you notice a mole that is changing, appears different, or is very dark, you should have it examined by a dermatologist as soon as possible, since melanomas can spread quickly. (Also, see Tip 155 for further information on the detection of malignant melanomas.) Patients with melanoma skin cancer can be cured if it is caught early enough. Note: In general, the risk of developing skin cancer increases with exposure to the sun, especially under the age of 18.

General

Blood Pressure Screening

High blood pressure puts you at a greater risk of developing health problems, including heart disease, kidney disease, and stroke. Your blood pressure is typically checked by your doctor at every checkup. All healthy individuals over twenty-one years of age should be screened regularly—at least every two years—for high blood pressure. However, with childhood obesity on the rise, it is never too early to begin blood pressure screenings. Normal blood pressure is less than 120 systolic and 80 diastolic. If you are an adult with blood pressure that is 120/80 mm Hg or higher, you may need to see a doctor more frequently for blood pressure management and monitoring. If it is only slightly higher than normal (120 to 139 systolic or 80 to 89 diastolic), you have prehypertension, which your doctor will likely try to manage with diet and exercise. And if your blood pressure continues to rise, your doctor may prescribe medications for hypertension. He or she may suggest starting medications sooner if you have preexisting conditions, such as diabetes or kidney disease.

Both adults and children can have high blood pressure, but it's most common in people over thirty-five years old. Risk factors for high blood pressure include race (African Americans are more at risk), age (men often develop it in their thirties, and women after menopause), a close family history of high blood pressure, obesity (a body mass index of 30 or higher), eating too much salt (the recommended salt intake for adults is 2,300 grams or one teaspoon per day), heavy drinking of alcoholic beverages, not getting enough physical activity, and stress. Also people with diabetes, gout, or kidney disease, as well as women who are pregnant, postmenopausal, or taking birth control pills, have a greater chance of having high blood pressure. Anyone at high risk should consider getting screened more often.

If you have been diagnosed with high blood pressure, you need to talk to your doctor about how often to have it monitored. Many public places such as shopping malls, drugstores, and fire stations have arm blood pressure machines that are fairly accurate. You can also purchase a blood pressure cuff for home use. Neither of these options should replace routine blood pressure monitoring by your doctor, but they can alert you to an unhealthy spike in blood pressure that may merit more rigorous evaluation and/or treatment. Owning your own blood pressure cuff also allows you to get a series of blood pressure measurements throughout the day. Providing this information to your doctor may be helpful in determining your medical regimen. To ensure accuracy, have your physician check your monitor for you when he/she sees you.

Cholesterol Screening

Healthy men younger than age forty-five and healthy women younger than fifty should be screened for high cholesterol every five years. After the age of forty-five for men and fifty for women, cholesterol levels should be checked every two years. Ideally, this should be done by getting a fasting blood test called a lipoprotein profile (which requires fasting for nine to twelve hours beforehand). This tests for your current levels of total cholesterol, LDL (low-density lipoprotein), HDL (high-density lipoprotein), and triglycerides (other blood fats). A high level of LDL, which is the bad or "lousy" cholesterol, can lead to serious medical problems such as a heart attack, stroke, or kidney failure. A low HDL, which is the good or "happy" cholesterol, could also contribute to these problems.

A family history of high cholesterol and/or a diet high in the bad cholesterol (for example, if you eat too many high-fat animal foods) puts you at a high risk for cholesterol problems. Under these circumstances, you should be screened for high cholesterol more often and eat more foods that help elevate your good cholesterol, such as unsalted nuts and certain kinds of fish (for example, salmon and trout).

If you are taking medications for high cholesterol and/or are on a special low-fat diet, and if you have other risk factors for heart disease, your doctor will recommend more frequent cholesterol testing (for example, every six to twelve months). The more risk factors you have, the more likely you will have heart disease. A personal or family history of heart attacks, coronary stents, or bypass surgery are risk factors for heart disease. Other important risk factors include diabetes, physical inactivity, cigarette smoking, alcohol consumption, stress, high blood pressure (140/90 mm Hg and above, or you are on blood pressure medications), increasing age (forty-five or older for men, fifty or older for women), and/or a combination of risk factors called the metabolic syndrome (most common in middle-aged men with abdominal obesity).

Any child who has a close relative with heart disease (for example, a mother, father, or sibling) might benefit from a cholesterol screening at the age of two, and many doctors recommend at least one blood cholesterol screening at age twenty.

Type 2 Diabetes Screening

Anyone at a high risk for developing type 2 diabetes should get screened every three years starting at an early age. Many doctors feel that everybody (even without risk factors) should be routinely tested, starting at least at the age of forty. The doctor orders a fasting glucose test or glucose tolerance test to see if your blood sugar levels are higher than normal. If these levels are high, your treatment plan may include diet, exercise, and/or medications. Detecting diabetes early is important, since it can damage your heart, kidneys, eyes, nerves, or blood vessels if it is not treated. Any result over 100 merits physician follow-up at a minimum. Early treatment of this potentially prediabetic state is beneficial. The current definition of diabetes is a fasting blood sugar equal to or above 126 mg per dl or two random blood sugars equal to or above 200 mg per dl. Risk factors for type 2 diabetes include a family history of diabetes (type 1 or 2), a personal history of gestational diabetes, high blood pressure, obesity, inactivity, giving birth to a baby heavier than nine pounds, or certain ethnic backgrounds (African, Hispanic, Native American, Asian, or Pacific Islander).

Other Blood Test Screenings

Some doctors recommend getting a panel of blood tests every five years starting at age fifty. This panel should include tests for blood chemistries as well as for white and red blood counts. There are many ailments that can be picked up with these tests.

Obtaining blood in order to check your red blood count to find out if you are anemic simply involves a finger stick. If your red blood count is low, you are anemic. Causes include chronic diseases, poor nutrition, various cancers, or internal bleeding at different locations in the body. While routine testing for anemia is recommended for pregnant patients, a regular schedule for testing the blood count in the general population has not been established. One recommendation is to test your blood count at a minimum of every few years at the time of a physical exam.

Bone Density Screening

Every woman over age sixty (particularly Asian and petite Caucasian women) should be tested for osteoporosis every two years with a bone density test, which consists of a simple low-dose X-ray. Consider beginning routine screenings earlier if you have risk factors for osteoporosis, including a family history of osteoporosis, a low body weight/small body frame, or tobacco use. Also, any woman who has been on steroids or other medications that affect the bones may need to be screened earlier, with more frequent follow-up screenings. There are also many other risk factors for the development of osteoporosis. You should consult your doctor to determine whether preventive treatment is appropriate. Routine screenings are currently only recommended for women, but it's important to be aware that this disease can also occur in men.

Immunizations

The following are some general recommendations for adult vaccinations. These guidelines may vary, depending on your previous immunization history. There is a seperate regimen of immunizations for children, which may be recommended by your doctor if you have missed your childhood vaccinations or do not have any record of having received them. A complete listing of the current vaccination schedules for all ages can be found at www.cdc.gov/vaccines. Always check this website because recommendations change. Note: Always let your health provider know of any anaphylactic (life-threatening) allergic reactions to anything before you receive a shot.

- All adults need a booster for tetanus and diphtheria every ten years. It's also recommended to get a TDAP vaccination (for tetanus, diphtheria, and pertussis/whooping cough) once between the ages of eleven and sixty-four years old.

- There is now a vaccine for HPV (human papilloma virus), which is recommended in general by many medical groups for females between eleven and twenty-six years of age. However, there are other considerations that should be discussed with the doctor.

- College students are required to be assessed for a number of vaccinations such as tetanus, MMR (measles, mumps, and rubella), varicella (chicken pox), and hepatitis B. These assessments are based on age, living situation, and—in special cases—their major. For example, a dorm-living freshman is often required to get a meningococcal vaccination, and veterinarian students are required to get vaccinated for rabies.

- There are many medical organizations that recommend that you get a flu shot every year if you suffer from a chronic disease, or if you are fifty years of age or older. Women who are over three months pregnant during flu season, as well as people with babies in the home or caregivers of children, should also consider getting the flu shot. College students may benefit from a flu shot, especially if they live in a dorm. Also, people who spend a lot of time around the sick and elderly (such as caregivers and health-care workers) should get the flu vaccine.

• Every older adult should talk to his or her doctor about getting pneumococcal and Herpes Zoster immunizations.

Body-Mass Index
Height and weight should be checked as part of every regular physical examination in order to screen for obesity.

PEDIATRIC HEALTH SCREENINGS

Starting at birth, it's important for every child to be taken to his or her pediatrician or family physician for regular checkups. At their physical checkups, all kids should have their vital signs checked. They should also get their immunizations and have their growth and development tracked. Besides these routine health checks, there are a number of very important standard screenings every child should have. These include the following:

Eyes
Children younger than three years of age should have their eyes screened at each checkup with their primary care physician, using the red reflex test. Another important screening test is where the doctor alternately covers and uncovers each eye. These tests can identify serious eye problems that are treatable when caught early. Starting at three years of age, vision should be checked once a year using standard picture or letter optotypes. At any age: If one or both eyes constantly cross or the red reflex looks different between the eyes in photos, the child should have a complete eye exam by an ophthalmologist.

Ears
At ages four and five, hearing should be checked. For a hearing screening, an odeometer is used to play sounds at different frequencies. The child is usually asked to wear headphones and raise his/her hand on whichever side he or she hears a beep.

There are also a variety of tests you can do at home to monitor your child's hearing. If the child is under two years old, you can test their "startle response" by slapping your hand on a table when they aren't looking. Watch to see if they jump at the noise. If the child is between two and four years old, turn on one of their toys that makes noise and keep it hidden from their view. Watch to see if they look in that direction. If the child is between four and six years old, monitor whether the child responds when asked questions.

Dental Exams

The American Academy of Pediatric Dentistry recommends taking your child for his or her first dental checkup when his/her first tooth appears or when he or she turns one year old. The dentist will examine the child's mouth to make sure the gums and teeth are healthy, as well as give the parents guidance about helping the child develop good dental hygiene habits. This initial visit also begins to familiarize the child with being in the dental chair. Speak to the dentist about appropriate follow-up visits.

Scoliosis

Around the age of puberty (eleven to thirteen), all children should be screened for scoliosis. This involves having the child stand in different positions and postures to measure the curvature of the spine. Most schools now provide scoliosis screenings for all students around the age of puberty.

Immunizations

The National Immunization Program (part of the CDC) provides the best resource for current immunization schedules as well as other important issues relating to vaccinations at www.cdc.gov/vaccines/.

Blood Tests

- At ages one and two all children should have their hematocrit checked (to screen for anemia: a low blood count). The hematocrit test measures the proportion of red blood cells in the individual's total blood content.
- If there's a family history of high cholesterol and/or

heart disease, consider having your child's blood choles-terol level checked at age two. Many doctors recommend that every child get screened before he or she reaches adolescence, or at least once at age twenty.

• Consider having your child's blood tested for lead con-tent, especially if you live in an older home. Lead poi-soning can contribute to growth problems, learning disabilities, and anemia in children. Most lead poisoning in children results from ingesting paint chips or dirt contaminated with lead, which was an ingredient used in house paint prior to 1977.

Type 2 Diabetes
Considering the growing diabetes epidemic and how diabetes is becoming more common in children, many public health ex-perts are suggesting that children with weight problems be closely monitored for this disease. Risk factors include obe-sity, having a close relative with type 2 diabetes, ethnicity (Native American, African American, Hispanic American, or Asian/South Pacific Island ancestry), and existing conditions that may indicate insulin resistance (acanthosis nigricans, dys-lipidemia, hypertension, polycystic ovarian syndrome, etc.). Parents can lower a child's risk of developing diabetes by en-couraging healthy eating habits and activity choices.

Alcohol and Drug Use
Between the ages of eleven and twenty-one, juveniles should be assessed for the risk of developing alcohol and drug abuse patterns.

Depression and Thoughts of Suicide
Screening teenagers for their mental health should be a routine part of the adolescent history and physical exam. Suicide is the third most common cause of death among teenagers. Early

identification and treatment of depression is thought to be the most effective way to prevent this tragedy. Between the ages of eleven and thirteen, children should spend quality time with their doctor, developing a safe environment to ask questions and seek help. The physician can screen for drug, alcohol, sexual, and mental factors.

SCREENINGS FOR OLDER ADULTS

- All older adults should be screened regularly for thyroid function, vitamin B12 deficiencies, vitamin D deficiencies, anemia, obesity, unintentional weight loss, alcoholism, vision and hearing deficits, osteoporosis, incontinence, and pain.
- Some doctors suggest that older adults be screened for dementia (including Alzheimer's) and depression.
- Screening for increased risk of falls can be valuable for the elderly population. This involves taking the patient's history in addition to observing him or her while he/she performs simple actions like sitting down, rising from a seated position, and walking.
- At each medical checkup, older adults should make sure that the doctor reviews all the drugs being prescribed by their treating physicians. They should bring all their pill bottles with them to all their doctors' visits.
- Every older adult should get an annual influenza vaccination, as well as the pneumococcal vaccine every five years, and a tetanus booster every ten years. The CDC has also recommended that seniors get immunized for Herpes Zoster.
- Routine visits to the dentist continue to be important with increasing age.
- Some doctors recommend that all men who have ever smoked should be scanned once between the ages of sixty-five and seventy-five for an abdominal aortic aneurysm.

OPTIONAL SCREENINGS

You may want to ask your doctor about the following optional screenings, with the knowledge that certain tests are not without risks themselves. Obviously, you must also factor in the cost of any test.

Aneurysm Screening
- An ultrasound of the aorta (a picture taken with sound waves of the aorta in the abdomen) screens for aneurysms. Aneurysms are more commonly found in those who have high blood pressure, have smoked cigarettes for five years (or longer), or have family members who have had aneurysms.

Heart Disease Screening
- An exercise stress test (EKG) can detect serious heart disease.
- A nuclear stress test is very accurate at detecting heart disease, but is one of the more expensive tests.
- A "quick echo" (sound wave study) of the heart may be helpful for the early detection of serious heart disease in athletes.
- Calcium scoring of the coronary arteries with a special type of CT scan may pick up early heart disease.

Stroke Prevention
- An ultrasound of the carotid arteries may help to screen for blood vessel blockages that may cause a stroke. However, many doctors only recommend these tests for patients with symptoms that suggest a risk of stroke, such as transient ischemic attacks (TIAs).

APPENDIX D

TAKING A CHILD'S TEMPERATURE

Tips for Taking a Child's Temperature

- Take your child's temperature when he/she is calm and quiet.
- The amount of activity or emotional stress, as well as the amount of clothing and the temperature of a child's environment, can influence his/her body temperature.
- When reporting a fever to the doctor, always tell him/her where on the body the temperature was taken, and the exact number of the reading.
- To convert Fahrenheit to Celsius, subtract 32 and divide by 1.8. To convert Celsius to Fahrenheit, multiply by 1.8 and add 32.

What Kind of Thermometer to Use

Most standard digital thermometers can be used either orally, rectally, or under the arm (for an axillary temperature). There are also digital thermometers that are designed for taking temperatures in other specific locations, such as the ear or the forehead. However, these specialized thermometers may not be as widely available and may cost more than a standard digital thermometer.

Digital thermometers are easier to read and take a much shorter time to register a temperature than glass thermometers. They are also generally considered safer to use than glass thermometers. If a glass thermometer breaks, there is the danger of broken glass as well as the possible danger of mercury poisoning. However, if you do plan on taking a rectal temperature with a glass thermometer, make sure that the thermometer is one designed specifically for taking a rectal temperature—it should have a round bulb at the tip so that it won't be sharp against the walls of the rectum. The bulb on the glass oral thermometer is long and thin. Either one of these types of glass thermometers can also be used for an axillary (under the arm) temperature.

Rectal

Most emergency room doctors recommend taking a rectal temperature in a young child, especially under six months of age, and ideally up to two years of age, because it gives the most accurate measurement. Taking an axillary temperature might be easier for some parents and children, but it is definitely less accurate. Using a thermometer rectally should almost always be safe and reliable when done correctly (see instructions on the following pages for the proper use of a rectal thermometer). A digital thermometer usually registers a rectal temperature within a minute, while a glass rectal thermometer takes two to three minutes to register the temperature.

Axillary (Under the Arm)

For babies and children up to four years of age, an axillary temperature can be taken as an alternative to a rectal temperature. Most standard digital thermometers will work for this, although thermometers specifically designed for the armpit are available. It typically takes under a minute to register an axillary temperature with a digital thermometer. If you are using a glass thermometer, either a rectal or oral thermometer will work. It normally takes three to four minutes to register an axillary temperature with a glass thermometer.

Make sure to hold the thermometer snugly in the armpit with the bulb completely covered between the child's arm and side. Keep in mind that an axillary reading is not as accurate as a rectal or oral temperature, and is often lower than the actual core temperature.

Ear or Forehead (Temporal Artery)

Either of these kinds of thermometers is an alternative to the rectal or axillary thermometer. There is no uniform consensus about how much more or less accurate than an axillary temperature they are. If you decide to use an ear or forehead thermometer, always be sure to read the instructions to be sure you are using it properly. It may be wise to also ask your child's physician or nurse to show you how to properly position it to ensure that you get as consistent and accurate a reading as possible.

When using an ear thermometer, it is important to place it in the right location in the ear and at the proper angle. Remember also that the outside temperature may influence the reading (for example, a child's ears may be cold from being outside in cool air). When using the forehead thermometer, keep in mind that there are some situations where the forehead is cool, even though the core body temperature is elevated. This can be due to narrowing of the blood vessels that supply the forehead with blood.

Oral

When the child is cooperative and at least four years old, taking an oral temperature is recommended. Make sure that the child keeps his/her mouth closed with the thermometer held underneath the tongue. A digital thermometer usually takes less than a minute to register an oral temperature. With a glass thermometer, it takes two to three minutes to register.

A Summary of the Accuracy Issue

A temperature properly taken either orally or rectally is considered to be the most accurate. When taking an oral temperature, the child must keep his/her mouth closed and the thermometer under his/her tongue. Most children cannot do this until they are at least four years of age. Accuracy is very important in identifying an elevated temperature in children under two years of age, and especially in children under six months old. Elevations in temperature can be missed with less accurate axillary (under the arm) measurements. Missing an elevated temperature can have life-threatening consequences in a young child, particularly in an infant.

An axillary temperature is generally considered to be lower than the actual core temperature. There is no consensus about the accuracy of other methods, such as the use of the ear or forehead thermometer. Some doctors suggest the use of the ear thermometer as an alternative to taking a rectal or axillary temperature, while others feel it is often inaccurate—the readings can vary greatly depending on the angle at which the thermometer is held within the ear, variations in ear anatomy, and the temperature of the child's environment (i.e., the ear, itself, may be cold). Some doctors suggest that the forehead (temporal artery) thermometer is a good alternative to taking a rectal or axillary temperature, but others question the accuracy since, in certain circumstances, the forehead may be cooler than the core body temperature. When in doubt—for example, if any of these alternative methods do not register an elevated temperature and you still believe the child has a fever—it may be wise to take a rectal temperature.

How to Take a Rectal Temperature

- If using a digital thermometer, begin by pressing the power button and wait until the display appears. Follow the instructions.
- If you are using a glass thermometer, shake it until it reads below the 97 degrees Fahrenheit mark (36.1 degrees Celsius). Hold the thermometer by the tip and snap your wrist and hand sharply, keeping it over a couch or bed so it won't break if it slips from your hand.
- Apply a lubricant like Vaseline or K-Y Jelly to the tip of the thermometer that will be inserted.
- Lay the child on his/her stomach.
- Spread the buttocks with one hand and lay the same arm on the child's back to limit struggling.
- Insert the thermometer gently and slowly about an inch into the rectum. NEVER force the thermometer; it should slide in easily.
- Hold the buttocks together to help keep the thermometer in place. Do not leave the child unattended while waiting for a temperature reading.
- If using a digital thermometer, wait until the display indicates the child's temperature.
- If using a glass thermometer, wait three minutes before reading the temperature. Slowly turn the thermometer until you see the line of mercury. Each long line represents one full degree and each short line represents 0.2 degrees.
- Wash the thermometer with warm water and soap after each use and store in a safe place.

About the Authors

Neil Shulman, M.D., is associate professor in the Department of Internal Medicine at Emory University School of Medicine in Atlanta, Georgia. He has been on the medical school faculty since 1972, teaching, seeing patients, and conducting medical research with over $10 million in funding. He is also author or coauthor of over one hundred scientific papers and author or coauthor of over thirty books, including fiction, nonfiction, and children's books. One book was made into the movie *Doc Hollywood*, starring Michael J. Fox. He lectures internationally on serious medical topics and performs as a comedian. He is president of Patch Adams' organization, the Gesundheit! Institute. For more on Neil Shulman and contact information, visit his website at www.neilshulman.com.

Jack Birge, M.D., has served for 50 years as the medical director for performance improvement for Tanner Medical Center in Carrollton, Georgia. He is also clinical assistant professor of community medicine at Mercer University School of Medicine in Macon, Georgia. Dr. Birge has been practicing primary care medicine since 1959 and has had over 200,000 encounters with patients from all walks of life, from delivery to nursing-home care.

Joon Ahn, M.D., is a practicing cardiologist in Gainesville, Georgia. He did additional training at Washington University in St. Louis, Missouri, after graduating from Emory University School of Medicine.

The pediatric section was written by **Joy Lawn, M.D.** Dr. Lawn received an undergraduate medical degree with distinction from Nottingham University, England. She is a member of the Royal College of Pediatricians and has been a lecturer in child health at Kumasi Medical School, Ghana. She has had over 60,000 pediatric visits.

INDEX